THE NIGHT MASTER

THE NIGHT MASTER

by
Robert Sampson

1982
PULP PRESS
Chicago

Second Printing 1982

Library of Congress Card No: 81-82237
ISBN Number: 0-934498-08-3

To Walter B. Gibson, who created that most difficult of literary forms —— an enduring figure.

TABLE OF CONTENTS

Cover and Interior Artwork by Frank Hamilton

ACKNOWLEDGEMENTS

I want to thank all of you who have been so free with the loan of books and manuscripts and the donation of your own time. To you all, not for the first time, I am much indebted.

Particular thanks are due the copyright holders, as indicated, for their permission to quote from published materials. Particular thanks are due to:

Conde Nast Publications, Inc., and Paul H. Bonner, Jr., for permission to quote from various Jimmie Date adventures in 1914 and 1916 PEOPLE'S MAGAZINE, and from those Shadow novels identified in the text, and to reproduce SHADOW MAGAZINE covers and selections from the magazine's interior art.

Penelope Wallace for permission to quote from Edgar Wallace's *The Terrible People.*

Edward T. LeBlanc, in whose publication, the *Dime Novel Roundup*, part of the "Preface" has appeared.

Bill Blackbeard, whose long essay, "Foreshadowings," has opened that region of literary history, so far hardly explored, where the themes and character types of the pulp magazines were formulated.

Frank Eisgruber, whose book on The Shadow, *Gangland's Doom*, is filled with interesting interpretations and packed with information.

J. Randolph Cox, whose article, "Sinister Sleuth," provided the first impulse toward this book.

Fred Cook for permission to quote from *Bronze Shadows #10* (1967), and Dick Myers, whose article, "The Case of the Elusive Author," drove the cost of the February 1929 FAME AND FORTUNE MAGAZINE beyond hope of acquisition.

Wooda Nicholas Carr for his constant support and encouragement and permission to quote, *ad lib, from the vast body of his articles on the pulp magazines.*

Nils Hardin, whose publication, **Xenophile**, has provided a major forum for the discussion of popular magazine literature, and who, for years, has served as the conscience for us all.

John Nanovic, former editor of THE SHADOW MAGAZINE, whose information about the early days of that publication was of great assistance in clearing out entrenched error.

7

Mary Tinsley for permission to quote from the letters of her late husband, Theodore A. Tinsley.

Theodore A. Tinsley for a wealth of information and for the astringent tonic of his scorn for sliced baloney.

Anthony Tollin for the information contained in *The Shadow Scrapbook*, which helped greatly.

Robert and Phyllis Weinberg for permission to quote from *Pulp*, as cited herein, and for a decade of friendship and support, regardless of my peculiar letters.

And, finally, to the godfather of this piece, Will Murray, for permission to quote from *Duende* 1 and 2, and *The History of The Shadow Magazine*, that definitive work; and for the endless hours of assistance that he cheerfully gave, sharing information available no place else, and ploughing thru the endless pages of this work, while somehow remaining enthusiastic, astute, and full of incisive advice.

TO THE CURIOUS READER. . .

"The Night Master" is the first in a series of volumes about influential characters of the 1930's pulp magazines—adventurers, detectives, fiends, jungle men, secret avengers.

Through these volumes, we will follow numerous series characters across the decades. We will sort out who they were, how they changed, and how each, in his own way, contributed to tne literary tradition of his time, during this time of heroes.

The Shadow, The Night Master, was a figure of his times. Although in many ways unique, he also embodied characteristics that had evolved and entered popular fiction over a period of roughly fifty years. The Shadow represented one specialized fictional line—that of the justice figure—which includes such earlier figures as The Avenging Twins, Zorro, and The Just Men.

By the 1930's, the magazines brimmed with other, equally specialized series characters. Of these, many could be traced back to the dime novels and story papers of the late 1800's. Still others took form in the early popular magazine fiction of England, France, and America. The creation of the general-fiction pulp magazine in the early 1900's, and the fecund proliferation of these magazines during the 1920's, provided a medium in which series characters could seek their audiences and grow, in rich, repetitive clusters, to a diversity of types.

History breeds history. The Twenties, those interesting times, drew upon themes and character types already well established. The Thirties would do the same, for each decade builds upon the masonry of the past.

Since myriads of characters swarm through the pulps, it would be quixotic to attempt enumeration of them all. As far as possible to fallible man, the emphasis will be on the great originals and their immediate successors.

But it is acknowledged that, for every character recognized, fifty less prominent are slighted, even though each was once popular enough to hold a share of audience. By care and luck, some of these lost may be recovered. But the main fact of their survival depends on chance—whether their stories can be located and read.

There are difficulties.

Many magazines are unavailable or sealed so well into private collections that they might as well not exist. Many more languish, undetected, in unrummaged attics. Others lie buried in publishers' warehouses or the basement of The Library of Congress. Many are, plainly, gone forever, existing only as a flicker in memory.

Even if issues are available, certain characters appear only fleetingly. And so, too often, reference to them has been limited or omitted entirely.

For these omissions, and for the crime of not mentioning your favorite character as this series progresses, the reader's kind understanding is solicited. In any case, you will find many familiar faces in these volumes. And perhaps, in reading, you may renew some of that excitement that sweetened your days, back when the world was made of pearl.

Bob Sampson

Huntsville, Alabama
1979

LIST OF TABLES

PREFACE—
ABOUT FORMER GLORIES

1.

Across the 1930's news stands, the pulp magazines, like gaudy flowers, spread row on row on row.

Their vivid covers blazed yellow and orange and scarlet. They pictured flaming pistols, masked gunmen, fiery skulls. From the covers burnt intense words—*Hell! Doom! Murder! Terror!*—nouns that burnt like a fiend's eyes beside safe stacks of GOOD HOUSEKEEPING and SATURDAY EVENING POST.

You paid ten cents a copy. Or fifteen cents. Or twenty. You received a 128—page magazine slightly larger than a book, about 6 x 9 inches. Back covers and inner pages flaunted advertising. Inside, amid a wonderous scramble, you found a novel, serials, short stories, departments, a letter column for readers heated to correspondence. The fiction was violent. It shouted. It was all agog. It featured gangsters, cowboys, people in costumes, crazy ideas. All printed double column on paper about the same texture as fried mush.

A pulp magazine was published on any subject that might catch a coin. Adventure stories, wild west action, air combat, love fiction, spicy experiences, detective action—each category boiled up dozens of titles. Sports fiction and science fiction crammed the shelves, intermixed with magazines devoted to avengers, costumed and deadly, who blazed away at the underworld.

Pulp magazines piled everywhere. Millions were published and millions sold, and readers were legion. Yet they enjoyed no high status. By some curious twist, they were widely regarded as trashy productions, read by the vulgar and the unwashed. Mothers, teachers, and other guardians of the hearth viewed the pulps with relentless disdain, convinced they warped the youthful mind. And, from literary summits, the guardians of national taste dismissed them as sub-literature, crass, warped by formula, beyond redemption.

The criticism was often correct. Many pulps appeared to have been created by an idiot with a rubber stamp. But in others, energy crackled through the pages and the prose spoke in contemporary tones with originality and force.

Perhaps the pulp magazines were too visible to be cooly judged. They represented a phenomena more complex than it appeared. The pulps had not leaped, fully realized, from the Depression. Not at all. Instead, they had evolved from the story papers and dime novels of the late 1800's.

Like the later pulps, the dime novels were cheap, readily available, and without social status. In appearance, they were paper-covered pamphlets, varying in size, page count, and price. Around early 1900, they stabilized as 32-page, double-column, paper-bound booklets measuring about 8 x 11 inches and costing five cents. The colored cover was illustrated by a scene of sweating action. The stories were snorting melodrama.

The first formal dime novel seems to have been "Malaeska, the Indian Wife of the White Hunter." Published in 1860, it was a reprint of a novel serialized some twenty years before. The new, ten-cent edition sold hugely.

Once sales demonstrated a market for inexpensive, sensational fiction, the dime novel era began.

For the next sixty years, the dime novels sold intensely physical adventure, dense with coincidence and purple diction. Through their pages swarmed coarsely-drawn figures—frontier scouts, detectives, boy adventurers, and other fascinating people.

Of all those heroes rising from the teeming dime novels, few are still remembered, other than Nick Carter, Buffalo Bill, and Frank Merriwell. These represent, respectively, detective adventure, western adventure, and adventure around the world, with a heavy emphasis on sports.

These three were superlative men. They stood for high ideals, moral impeccability, and individual insistence on independence and personal integrity. Tough, shrewd, resourceful, they proved conclusively that idealism was manly, that perfection might, after all, be attained in this imperfect world.

But even high excellence at length exhausts itself. About 1915, obsolescent overtook the dime novel. Selected titles lingered on, even into the late 1920's. The form, itself, grayed and glimmered out.

However, the fiction merely took other dress and hastened onward.

Directly into the pulp magazines.

The pulp magazines and the dime novels overlapped by about fifteen years. THE ARGOSY, that first citizen of the pulp magazines, began in 1888. (It developed from the 1882 childrens' paper, THE GOLDEN ARGOSY.) In 1903, THE POPULAR MAGAZINE appeared—the same year that the Jesse James dime novels were discontinued. 1904 saw publication of the MONTHLY STORY MAGAZINE, which changed its name, in 1907 to BLUE BOOK and began a wondrous career.

In 1905, THE ALL-STORY appeared. And suddenly, general-fiction magazines (suitable for the whole family) burst forth, spilling across the years PEOPLE'S FAVORITE MAGAZINE, THE SCRAP BOOK, CAVALIER, TOP NOTCH, ADVENTURE, SNAPPY STORIES. . .

Now specialization set in. The single-theme magazine began (if you stretch the point a little) with the 1906 RAILROAD MAN'S MAGAZINE. Then, in 1915, publishers Street & Smith issued the DETECTIVE STORY MAGAZINE, its dime novel ancestry clinging like the odor of apples in a hot room.

The success of this publication encouraged Street & Smith to try other single-theme magazines. In 1919, WESTERN STORY MAGAZINE appeared, gobbling down the superannuated Buffalo Bill dime novel. Two years later, LOVE STORY MAGAZINE began its long career. By then, BLACK MASK (1920) was on the stands. And SEA STORIES (1922). And WEIRD TALES and SPORTS STORY MAGAZINE (1923).

Once begun, proliferation seemed endless. Within such general categories as western, love, sports, adventure, and mystery, the magazines reproduced merrily:

WILD WEST WEEKLY, GHOST STORIES, LIVE GIRL STORIES, COMPLETE STORIES, FLYNN'S, OUTDOOR STORIES, SECRET SERVICE STORIES, CABARET, ZEPPELIN, SUBMARINE STORIES, ROMANCE, THE UNDERWORLD, THE DRAGNET, FAME AND FORTUNE, CLUES, DANGER TRAIL, AIR WONDER STORIES, AMAZING STORIES, SCIENTIFIC DETECTIVE STORIES.

The dime novel explosion of the late 1800's was being repeated in another form, even to the establishment of small publishers who rode their tiny stable of titles to wealth.

Competition was ferocious, the public fickle. The market-place savagely culled the titles. Under that deadly pressure, story types, narrative styles, characters heated to white incandescence. And changed.

In this competition, the series characters played their part.

2.

The single-character publication was not a pulp magazine innovation. Long before THE PHANTOM DETECTIVE and DOC SAVAGE, there had been weekly publications rejoicing in such names as JESSE JAMES STORIES, NICK CARTER WEEKLY, YOUNG SLEUTH, BUFFALO BILL BORDER STORIES, DIAMOND DICK WEEKLY.

In other dime novel series, strong series characters appeared week after week, although their names never quite made the title. The TIP-TOP WEEKLY was devoted to the Merriwells, as SECRET SERVICE featured the Bradys, and the ROUGH RIDER WEEKLY celebrated Ted Strong.

By the time the single-character dime novels faded, series characters had thoroughly penetrated the general-fiction magazines. They gleamed brightly in the pages of THE POPULAR MAGAZINE, BLUE BOOK, PEOPLE's, ALL-STORY, and particularly in DETECTIVE STORY MAGAZINE. In all these, the dime novel tradition blended with new characters from both sides of the Atlantic—particularly England. Many popular series characters skipped directly from English magazine publication to American magazine reprint.

By 1920, certain specialized classes of heroes had crystallized from the magma of public print.

Consider these selected few:

*The astute private detective in the big, tough city solves problems that hopelessly baffle the police.
Nick Carter (first appearance: NEW YORK WEEKLY, 1888): Educated by his father to become the perfect detective. In short, having ten men's strength. Expert at gymnastics, sciences, languages. A disguise master, carries false hair and face putty in pockets for instant changes. Also carries two guns, which he uses freely, plus tool kit, handcuffs, a special pick-lock. Is moral, upright, honorable. His word inviolable. Radiates integrity, force of personality. Father was murdered. Married once but wife murdered. Through own exertions becomes

wealthy, developing powerful connections in city, state,
national government. Is assisted by numerous aides—young
men, women, boys, girls, plus his adopted son, Chick.
Adventures over the world. Uses each new device, scientific
instrument, vehicle as it is developed. Fights innumerable
criminal geniuses, many doctors and scientists, all ferocious,
none easy.

* An altruistic secret group, branded public enemies,
punish or kill malefactors too powerful for the law to reach.
The Just Men (first appearance: *The Four Just Men, 1905):
Three wealthy geniuses (the fourth was killed by police) have
pooled their fortunes to bring justice to men and organizations
too powerful for usual social mechanisms to deal with. They
warn once. Habitually they kill. For years, they were invisible,
wanted by police of all countries. Were pardoned. Set up a
modest detective agency in London, from which the quiet,
deadly work goes on.*

*A cowboy, supremely fast with the Colt pistol, rights wrongs
and punishes the wicked in the Old West.
Hopalong Cassidy (first appearance: THE OUTING
MAGAZINE,1907): short, bow-legged, red-headed,dexterous
and ambidexterous with the Colt .45. At the beginning of career
was pranking, jesting, relishing chewing tobacco, whisky,
cards. Married and settled down. Wife and child died. Became
withdrawn, cold, calculating, showing extraordinary tactical
ability. Killed multiple dozens face to face. Preferred to out-
think the enemy. From beginning was member of close-knit
ranch group, the Bar-20 men, loyal eccentrics, gifted fighting
men. In later part of life, served as sheriff. In many stories,
wanders alone, or with a friend, correcting evil by shooting it
dead.

* A wealthy amateur and friends operate successfully as
an unofficial intelligence force against their country's enemies:
Sir George Trevor of Diplomatic Free-Lances series
(first appearance: BLUE BOOK, 1910). Trevor is not Trevor but
an American who assumed Trevor's identity when that weak
cluck died. Made a spectacular place for himself in English
intelligence circles. A genius, tall, self-possessed, gifted,
penetrating, concealing these admirable traits under facade of
silly-ass Englishman. Speaks variety of languages, shoots,
codes, flies. Has organized an unofficial group to battle hostile
foreign nationals. Marries an accomplished and effective
woman, has an accomplished and effective son. In time, his
wealth becoming colossal, becomes one of six men to dominate
Western civilization. Maintains own navy and air force. Is a

secret state within England, acting always for civilization.

* An amateur investigator unravels contemporary crimes by use of advanced scientific equipment.
Craig Kennedy (first appearance: COSMOPOLITAN, 1910): A tall, austere professor, the American Sherlock Holmes, solves all manner of crimes with—meters and—graphs— at first. Later he solves everything by intuition. His associate, Walter Jameson, is a newspaper man of refined stupidity. Has friends all over, stands tall in society, police adore him. He enjoys more money than any professor before 1910 or since.

* A feral child becomes Lord of the Jungle.
Tarzan (first appearance: ALL STORY, 1912): An orphan infant raised by odd African apes, grows to intensely powerful manhood. Tall, gray-eyed, of commanding presence, even when eating raw antelope. Of English nobility, he ultimately claims his heritage and his bride, Jane. Retires to Africa, rejecting civilization's snares. His son matures in father's image. Tarzan was skilled at killing large fierce animals with a knife, and large, fierce men in uncomplicated ways. Finds many lost civilizations. Between bouts of amnesia and an unending succession of lookalikes, he has a lively time.

* A fiendish oriental genius repeatedly strikes for world domination.
Doctor Fu Manchu (first appearance: *The Insidious Dr. Fu Manchu*, 1913): Tall and lean. His green eyes blaze hypnotically from a face wrinkled evil. An incomparable genius, an enormous criminal intellect. Oriental evil swarms to his command—dacoits, Thuggs, other sinister specialists. Uses drugs, poisons, scorpions, snakes, poisoned bugs. His plans, forever on verge of success, forever fail. Usually by the activities of Nayland Smith, who dogs the Chinese fiend. Has daughter, intensely beautiful, as usual.

* A wealthy young man, who regrets that he played secretly at crime, uses multiple identities to battle the underworld.
Jimmie Dale (first appearance: PEOPLE'S, 1914): Tall, strong, handsome, very rich. Once very bored. Created the character of The Gray Seal, a merry safe cracker, who broke and entered for fun. His identity discovered by The Toscin, a mysterious young woman. She blackmailed him into doing good and aiding the unfortunate. Dale lived double life—a wealthy idler; also a filthy crook in New York's underworld. Carried a gun but quaked fearfully that he might hurt someone with it. Never quite married the lovely girl.

*A wealthy young idler fight for justice, using a secret identity
and a splendid costume.

Zorro (first appearance: ALL-STORY:1919). By day, Don Diego
Vega, that weakling lounger, languishes poetically within his
father's hacienda. By night, he becomes Zorro, bold rider in
black, who thunders, masked, along Old California's Mission
Trail to punish wicked oppressors. These he whips, carves "Z"
into their foreheads or cheeks. Some few he dispatches from
this sorrowful world, for he is lightning doom with the rapier.
His secret identity revealed at the end of the first novel, he
married the girl. She later dies. His identity as Zorro is
conveniently forgotten by everyone in the entire world. The
series continues . . .

That similarities exist among these diverse personalities is not
surprising. They are, all of them, glorious dreams. Myself as I
should be, if only . . .

No puny bodies here. No flat wallets. The half-trained mind
does not fumble wistfully along the foothills of culture. Wet babies
and unwashed dishes do not intrude here. Nor time's tax on hope.

These heroes live above customary consequences. Not really of
society, they occupy a privileged position outside. They are
guardians, not subjects. It is their self-imposed responsibility to
protect society from those terrible forces that gnaw it. And so
their worlds are taut with melodrama, their opponents ever
unambiguous, their adventures too violent for delicate ethical
shadings. Thus they are spared—as the reader is not—the
annoyance of performing in a difficult world where good and evil
shade from situation to situation, and no man is less than
complex.

Problems at these levels simply do not assail the series heroes.
Their judgments are invariably correct. Their actions are
justified by results. Uncorrupted by power, they tower, excellent
and benign, respected by enemies, admired by friends, models for
us all.

3.

Through the 1920's magazines move ever—increasing numbers
of series characters, richly idiosyncratic. You can hardly count
their numbers. Perhaps over that ten—year period, from 1920 to
1930, 250-300 separate series appeared. Most series contained a
scant handful of stories. To familiar magazine pages would
appear a new theme, a flashing new character, fresh green and
vibrant. And, within a year, as things usually went, both theme
and character withered and were gone.

Steer Lyte, who retired to adventure. Balbane, the magician detective, and Godfrey Usher, who detected by occult vibrations. Commander McTurk. Rosy, the clever secretary. Masie St. Claire, whose heart was of gold, and The Spider (western badman) whose heart was bad, and The Spider (pudgy super-criminal) whose heart was steel or mush, depending on the issue that you read.

Across the years, reader interest flared briefly for all manner of specialized stuff. For there are fads in popular literature, as in popular music.

Railroad adventures with Scientific Sprague

Lip-reading adventures with Judith Lee

Dance band adventures with the Syncopating Kid

World-wide adventures with the Lost Legion

Fire—fight with Holly in BLUE BOOK

Gold-dig with an unnamed blond darling in SNAPPY STORIES

Make silent movies with the Perfect Pictures troop in POPULAR

Or crack crimes with The Camera Chap (TOP NOTCH) and break out of the stir with Big Scar, the tough con, in FLYNN'S.

Grab the dough and run with Big Nose Charlie (DETECTIVE STORY MAGAZINE) and adventure all over, your heart pure, with Janie Frete (ALL-STORY), while solving ridiculous crimes with Professor Armand Macklin (SCIENTIFIC DETECTIVE MONTHLY) and Beau Quicksiler (ARGOSY ALL-STORY WEEKLY).

Their accomplishments run vivid across the page. Soon enough, series featuring diplomacy, humorous baseball, and vaudeville fade in the brighter glare of new series about small-town politicians, clever wives, and doctors who detected.

These, in turn, yielding up their brief eminences and returning to silence and the rich literary loom of pulp magazine fiction.

Within such familiar categories as mystery, adventure, fantasy, love, humor, numerous sub-species rose and fell. Evolution was intense. Specializations developed which would flower profusely across the generations.

As, for example, those many specializations welling up within the mystery story.

Already, the mystery story had created long-enduring types: The husband and wife detective team (The Honeymoon Detectives, ALL-STORY CAVALIER WEEKLY), the first American Scientific detective Luther Trant, (HAMPTON'S MAGAZINE), the occult detective (Semi-Dual, PEOPLE'S), the young woman detective (Nan Russell, ARGOSY ALL-STORY). Eccentric geniuses paced everywhere. Equally eccentric private detectives, lit with Sherlock's fire, saved police from humiliating

failure. Occasionally appeared a scattering of professional
police—some ludicrous (Initiating Noggins, DETECTIVE
STORY); others, like Brady and Riordan (FLYNN'S WEEKLY
DETECTIVE FICTION) ringing like new silver.

A major innovation was the creation of the hard-boiled
detective story, BLACK MASK's contribution to American
letters. By 1926, the classical BLACK MASK story was in being,
featuring economical scenes, brittle with understated emotion,
using images as bright as crystal splinters. In soiled cities, men
contended, their speech terse, their minds disbelieving. Within
the polished glass of this fiction trembled a romantic core,
contemptuous of its own generous impulses. But this was not
evident for a long time.

As the hard-boiled story rose to its peak, the number of pulp
detective fiction magazines rapidly increased. FLYNN's had
appeared in 1924, stuffed with English fiction. In 1927, it became
FLYNN's WEEKLY DETECTIVE FICTION and yearned for the
BLACK MASK sound. By then, CLUES had appeared, followed
by CRIME MYSTERIES, STARTLING DETECTIVE
ADVENTURES, THE DRAGNET, MYSTERY, and the reprint
BEST DETECTIVE MYSTERIES.

Related fictional forms enjoyed hot popularity. One of these,
the crime story, reached its peak during the 1920's, although it
had begun generations before.

Early crime stories groaned under the weight of artistic thieves
and cracksmen, echoing the Raffles and Arsene Lupin themes.
The early pulps fleshed these out by borrowings from sources as
various as Jesse James and Dr. Fu Manchu. Each major figure
was represented by lines of derivative figures through the pages
of DETECTIVE STORY, DETECTIVE TALES, PEOPLE'S, the
early BLACK MASK, and FLYNN'S.

Emperors of crime appeared, directing their voracious legions
(Black Star, Rafferty). Lone-wolf outlaws preyed on society, or
upon other criminals, or dispoiled dishonest white-collar fellows
(Blue Jean Billy, Mr. Chang, the Crimson Clown).

Still other series featured out-and-out crooks, all repentant.
Some were cute (Thubway Tham) and some were not (Barton
Edgeworth). A few practiced the confidence game with beguiling
grace (Mr. Clackworthy). Others were tricky thieves (Red Raven,
Boston Betty). A very few murdered wicked folks gracefully (The
Ringer).

Among the crooks appeared that distinctive class, the
buccaneer, the modern Robin Hood, who pillaged only the
dishonest while doing good (Lester Leith, The Saint). Another
exceptionally large group—among whom are included some
founding fathers—were those who had repented their criminal
pasts (Cleek, The Lone Wolf, Anthony Trent). Some played at

thieving to ease their boredom (Jimmie Dale); other struck because society had done them wrong (The Picaroon). Whatever the reason, as a group, their hearts glowed with repentance; they spent years living down earlier follies and enjoying monthly adventures.

Another group of characters turned to crime as the only means to redress wrongs. Not systematically criminal, they operated behind the law only long enough to punish those who had victimized them—and to dazzle those dullard police. After which they turned again to blameless lives (The Night Wind, Four-Square Jane, The Thunderbolt, Pat the Piper).

Criminal heroes and hard-boiled detectives aside, another major branch of pulp fiction captured a disproportionate number of 1920's hearts. This was the scientific romance—distinguished by being non-scientific and unromantic. It had the familiar history: dime novel roots, European development, and American magazine exploitation.

Those early masters, Verne and Wells, contributed a neat stack of novels concerning moon flights, Martian invasion, invisible men, unchecked growth, monster making, submarine travels, and time machines. In one form or another, most of these ideas entered the Munsey publications. The early ALL-STORY carried heavy doses of such early science-fiction—more accurately, fantasy, as few effects had a laboratory connection. WEIRD TALES always included quantities of science-fiction, and, by the time AMAZING STORIES was issued, vast amounts of material existed. Called scientific romance, sciencefiction, interplanetary romance, or whatnot, it was science fantasy and unrepentant about it.

Edgar Rice Burroughs contributed heavily to this field. His subject was romantic adventure set far enough away that errors in fact could not be checked. He specialized in sword and peril stories, beginning on Mars, plunging into the earth's core, and much later, bounding out to Venus. Other writers followed, industriously re-excavating these furrows—on Mars, the Planet of Peril (O. A. Klein); on Mercury, full of winged maidens (Ray Cummings); and down down into the atomic universes (Mr. Cummings, repeatedly).

Wherever the heroes went, they found blood and battle, and omnious biology. All through the 1920's issues of ARGOSY ALL-STORY WEEKLY, these stories flickered in counterpoint to the endless adventures of Tarzan. The sword and peril stories, numbed by a great sameness, slowly petered out. The Tarzan theme remained fresh enough to generate crass copies during the 1930's.

The interplanetary romance mutated to space opera in Edmond Hamilton's 1928 stories (WEIRD TALES) about the Interstellar

Patrol. Creepy aliens appeared. Spaceships hurled rays and defied physics. E. E. Smith followed with the Skylark series in AMAZING and ASTOUNDING. The theme of interstellar battle, seasoned by alien cultures and scientific heroes, spread unchecked. It would become a staple of 1930's fiction, appearing side by side with Gernsback's didactic efforts to teach science and morality through AMAZING STORIES, SCIENCE WONDER STORIES, AIR WONDER STORIES, and on into 1930 deeps.

More conventional adventure had been developing in the general-fiction magazines of the time: ADVENTURE, BLUE BOOK, SHORT STORIES, COMPLETE STORIES, and ARGOSY ALL-STORY WEEKLY.

Early in the 1920's appeared a burst of superior historical fiction written by Harold Lamb (the Khlit series) and Talbot Mundy (the Tros series), both in ADVENTURE. Readers unmoved by the excellence of these fictions could indulge themselves with tales of adventure in sweaty places. These stories bore a certain family resemblance. The somewhat tarnished hero struggled for riches against the plotting of a villain, characterized in shades of black. The stories ended in a rain of bodies.

Certain of these epics were sited in India (Secret Service Smith) or the South Seas (Hurricane Williams, Red O'Neill) or among the sun-baked tough guys of the Foreign Legion. The Old West was particularly popular, and innumerable gunslicks rode trails first traveled by The Virginian and Hopalong Cassidy. Each enjoyed a speciality, one being a wandering pal of the good (Hashknife), another an outlaw who fought for justice in spite of his reputation (White Wolf).

No sooner did a figure prove successful, than from him, like the tail of a comet, flowed a stream of similar characters. Similar, not identical. Variation was the rule.

Beginning in 1926, the pulps discovered that fine new subject war. The subject became popular following the success of "What Price Glory," which opened on Broadway in the Fall of 1924. The play was bawdy, colloquial, tough-spirited. It brimmed with that sardonic sentimentality, disguised as unsentimental toughness, that brightened BLACK MASK and ADVENTURE fiction.

These qualities did not quite make it into pulp war fiction. This remained firmly chained to the legend of the individual hero, who casually violated orders, got misunderstood by superiors, and excluded an air of disrespect sufficient to earn him a firing squad, given actual combat conditions. You found him in WAR STORIES (1926), BATTLE STORIES (1927), and WAR NOVELS (1928), and there were others.

The individualist reigned even more gloriously in the air-war pulp magazines. During 1927, these burst forth like an epidemic of viral flu. WINGS and AIR STORIES were followed, in 1928, by WAR BIRDS, SKY BIRDS, and AIR TRAILS, and in 1929, by that specialist's magazine, ZEPPELIN STORIES.

The air war pulp swept into the 1930's, hurling out new titles (BATTLE BIRDS, SKY FIGHTERS, DAREDEVIL ACES), and penetrating the single-character magazines (G-8 AND HIS BATTLE ACES, DUSTY AYERS, THE LONE EAGLE, BILL BARNES). Other single-character magazines gladly borrowed the tradition of the intrepid airman who fought alone against fierce flights of Fokkers. This background got spliced into the history of The Shadow and The Phantom Detective, for instance. It often seemed that you couldn't qualify as a magazine lead character unless you had been a World War I ace. Or combat officer.

The air-war pulps, themselves, are beautiful examples of late 1920's popular fiction. They offered individualistic heroes hurtling wildly through adventures which bore only the feeblest connection with reality. But how stylish these fictions are. How brightly drawn. If they are impossibilities, they are impossibilities on the grand scale. And through the years, they grow steadily grander. The same inflation touches the heroes. At first merely extraordinary men, they become increasingly like earth-bound gods, suprahuman and astounding.

4.

The popular fiction of the 1930's used most of the character types and themes shaped by earlier fictions. As before, this was not just restatements of earlier materials, but new growth from healthy old roots.

However, the new characters performed in a world strikingly changed.

During the 1920's, profound changes in social mores shook the country. For all those changes, the great, underlying beams of government, law, business remained stable. The house stood firm, even if a bathtub gin party with a red-hot jazz band roared in the front room.

By the 1930's, however, pieces began to crack away. Beyond national boundries, war thumped and foreign crazies ranted. Depression corroded the national soul. The wind soured with failure's stench, while political and economic institutions reeled forth explanations, promising mightily. But events ignored promises.

In the pulp magazines, those sensitive indicators, the fiction grew darker, more obsessed. The pressures of the decade expressed themselves in fiction that told of violence and death, of struggles against odds. And, because social failure generates social rage, the fiction stiffened with images of violence—blood, torture, widespread slaughter, the small change of the single-character magazines.

Deep national disturbances were dramatized in images that the least astute reader could grasp: Military invasion of the country, criminal insurrection, criminal conspiracy—all products of rapacious geniuses leading legions soaked in gore.

Beneath it all burnt a single theme: Responsible leadership had collapsed. Those oaken beams of government-law-business had rotted while the jazz bands blared. The society was no longer viable.

Pulp magazine fiction gave public form to these private myths. These were emotional responses to the urgencies of the times. Often enough superficial responses. Often enough irrational. But they were felt powerfully and sought powerful outlets.

So, in 1930's fiction, strong heroes rose. Violent men assailing complex problems with simple solutions. Are there social ills? These are the consequence of conspiracy. Is there joblessness, stagnation, the fear of war? These are produced by sinister interests—gangsters, bankers, and other criminals; munitions makers; unstated socialistic influences. All vastly powerful, fatly evil.

Against these evils rose a long series of avengers. Identity concealed, robed, masked, moving by night, they reaffirmed justice with flaming pistols. The Shadow and The Spider strike against powerful criminal conspiracies. The Phantom Detective and Secret Agent X, disguise masters, tear out evil's hidden heart. Operator 5 marshalls his bloody patriots against the invader's polished legions.

These heroic figures continue traditions developed during the two preceding decades of pulp magazine fiction. They are new faces in a line stretching, unbroken, from the dime novels. At the same time, these new faces are unique to their period—fresh, deadly, intense, they are unmistakably of the 1930's.

They did not all come at once. First the single-character magazine had to be re-created.

It began quietly enough.

Each Thursday night, at the end of 1930, a voice throbbed weirdly from the radio . . .

CHAPTER I—
THE NIGHT MASTER

1.

LISTEN
on
THURSDAY NIGHTS
Commencing July 31st
at
9:30 Eastern Daylight Saving Time
8:30 Eastern Standard Time

to your

RADIO

After tuning in on

The Columbia Broadcasting System

And you will

HEAR

A Dramatized Version of One of the Stories in
the Next Week's

DETECTIVE STORY MAGAZINE

(Advertisement in DETECTIVE STORY MAGAZINE,
August 2, 1930 issue)

2.

Competition pressed that grand institution, DETECTIVE
STORY MAGAZINE.

Since 1915, the magazine had stood alone, barely challenged,
its weekly pages faithfully reflecting the faddish tides of mystery,
crime, and detective fiction.

It was, all agreed, a most successful pulp magazine.

But in this sinful world, success does not guarantee monopoly. In the mid-1920's, other detective magazines rose to challenge DETECTIVE STORY's reign. The most serious competition came from BLACK MASK and FLYNN'S—this latter publication being known variously as FLYNN'S WEEKLY, FLYNN'S WEEKLY DETECTIVE FICTION, and DETECTIVE FICTION WEEKLY (Formerly Flynn's), depending on whether you read it in 1926, 1927, or 1929.

After a sluggish start, BLACK MASK developed unexpected sales strength with stories of seedy men tersely injuring each other. And FLYNN'S, full of imported English fiction as dense as English tweed, had unexpectedly become a serious competitor during 1927-1928—jazzing up cover, contents, and title. Regrettably, across its masthead stretched the words

DETECTIVE

Fiction Weekly

thus wilfully seducing scores of readers from their habitual

DETECTIVE

Story Magazine

The challenge was not to be ignored.

DETECTIVE STORY MAGAZINE countered strongly. It imported imposing names: Agatha Christie (with her new detective, Old Miss Marple) and Edgar Wallace (with novels and new short story series featuring The Just Men, the Ringer, and Mr. J. G. Reeder).

Nick Carter was revived in a new series of novelettes.[1] And a brand-new bent hero was created for the occasion—Mr. John Doe, a daring criminal, and his daring criminal wife. New stories appeared of that charming thief, The Picaroon. And additional exploits were added to the legend of Rafferty, emperor of crime; the Crimson Clown, Robin Hood of crime; and that proven crowd pleaser, Mr. Chang.

As a final blow to saucy competition, Street & Smith went to the expense of sponsoring a new radio program.

This, the *Detective Story Hour*, was aired each Thursday night for thirty minutes. In two weeks, on August 14, 1930, it was retitled *Detective Story Program*. Whatever the name, it featured a story from next week's issue, dramatized by skilled "voice-actors."[2] Precisely what went on during those first programs isn't quite clear. Although DETECTIVE STORY MAGAZINE spoke grandly of "actors," other sources claim that only a single voice, the announcer's, read from a magazine.

Whatever the situation, the announcer's role speedily modified. Within weeks, he had become a mysterious voice, the voice of destiny, spectral, deep-toned, sinister.

The agency dubbed this voice, The Shadow. Soon they had provided him with a set of catch phrases, since it is the destiny of a weird radio voice to sound omniscient, as well as chilling. Thus the Thursday night oracle droned to his listeners that "Crime Does Not Pay—The Shadow Knows,"then laughed like a Gothic novel. (That companion saying, "The Weed of Crime Bears Bitter Fruit,"also seems to have been created at this time.)

The result was that customers began asking for "That Shadow magazine"—meaning DETECTIVE STORY MAGAZINE— which was not quite the response Street & Smith had envisioned. Obviously, the Voice possessed public pizazz.

It then occurred to the boys at Street & Smith that The Shadow had accidentally become a valuable commercial property. A property, moreover, they had better secure by copyright—before the competition thought to do so.

As they were a publishing house, the immediate thought was to get The Shadow into one of their magazines. Editor-in-Chief, Frank Blackwell, suggested using DETECTIVE STORY MAGAZINE as the forum for a Describe The Shadow contest.

Henry Ralston favored tieing down the name by issuing a magazine. (Ralston had been with Street & Smith since 1898: he had brilliantly risen through the ranks to an eventual Vice-Presidency, and had, for years, been, unofficially, Ormond Smith's executive assistant.) A single issue would establish copyright without question. Or, on a trial basis, a quarterly magazine might be issued. This was the usual way to test public enthusiasm for a title. Three months between issues gave plenty of time to assess the publication's pull.

If the Shadow's magazine were successful, perhaps the time would be right for issuing other magazines dedicated to other single characters—as in the days of Nick Carter and Buffalo Bill, which Ralston so vividly remembered.

At this point, Walter B. Gibson paid an unscheduled visit to the Street & Smith offices. Gibson was in town to make arrangements about a book. While there, he decided to talk with Frank Blackwell about a possible series of factual crime articles for DETECTIVE STORY MAGAZINE.[3]

3.

In 1930, Walter B. Gibson had been writing professionally for about a decade. Born in Philadelphia, 1896, he early became interested in magic. From 1915 on, he contributed innumerable articles to magic magazines and briefly worked as a carnival magician after his graduation from Colgate. In 1922, he became a reporter for the Philadelphia *North American* and, later, the *Evening Ledger*. Soon he branched into the syndicated series of daily features including *Daily After Dinner Tricks, Teasers, Brain Tests, Numerology, Science Questions*, and crossword puzzles. At the same time, he wrote feature articles on magic. These interested such notable names as Thurston, Houdini, and Blackstone. For all these he ghosted various books and articles— including a 5-part "autobiography" of Thurston which appeared in the 1928 COLLIERS.

Beginning in mid-1920's he began writing books on magic, ghosting some, publishing others under his own name: *The World's Best Book of Magic, Thurston's 200 Tricks You Can Do, Blackstone's Secrets of Magic, Book of Secrets*, et al. In addition to all this, he contributed to GHOST STORIES and TRUE DETECTIVE, and had edited TALES OF MAGIC AND MYSTERY and TRUE STRANGE STORIES.

In 1930, he completed the book, *Houdini's Escapes*, compiled from the magician's notes, and had received permission to proceed with a companion volume.

At which point, he visited Street & Smith and his life irrevocably changed.

Frank Blackwell outlined Street & Smith's thoughts about The Shadow, and Gibson left the editorial offices having committed himself to writing a 70,000-word novel concerning the adventures of that voice incorporal, The Shadow.

Although Gibson was seasoned at writing factual material, his experience with fiction was small. But no matter. A professional newspaper man could write anything. He proceeded.

The speed with which all this happened is mildly terrifying. Gibson began to write the novel in January 1931. To begin the story, he used opening scenes that he had been considering for a tentative mystery novel. It was rather hazy. But not for long.

By mid-January, 1931, Gibson delivered the final manuscript.[4] The working title was "Murder In the Next Room," later changed to the more familiar "The Living Shadow."

Now he received authorization to commence three more novels. At this time, he had no contract. The arrangement was pleasantly casual. Ideas for each novel were discussed with the editor—at this time, Lon Murray—after which, Gibson would write it out, more or less first draft. "The Hand of The Shadow," the second novel (later retitled "The Eyes of The Shadow") was completed late in February. The third novel, "The Shadow Laughs," was submitted a month later.[5]

By that time, the first issue of the magazine had vanished from the news stands. It was an encouraging sign.

Public acceptance of the magazine is most probably because of the radio voice. It's possible that the rather labored promotion of The Shadow figure, which began in January, 1931, may have contributed its might. As Blackwell had suggested, the S&S DETECTIVE STORY MAGAZINE was the focal point for that promotion.

It was in traditional form—a $1,000 contest.

Describe what The Shadow looked like.

Tell his background.

Use 100 words or fewer.

To stimulate your imagination, a series of "clews" were offered, spread over ten weeks. Each was first offered in the radio program, then printed in DETECTIVE STORY. The Shadow, himself, read the "clews" each Thursday night, the first one being broadcast on January 29, 1931, and published in the February 7 issue of the magazine.

The clew was suitable cryptic: "By the mark of the cobra on my chest".

Trailing off, we may assume, in a shuddering laugh.

When the final clew appeared in the April 11 DETECTIVE STORY MAGAZINE, Gibson was half through the fourth Shadow novel. He had seen the clews list before beginning "Murder In the Next Room." Blackwell had suggested that Gibson incorporate as many clews as possible into the story, but, since Gibson's Shadow was rather intangible, not many got adopted.

Just as well. The clews reek of midnight ad agency oil. They led you irresistibly to the conclusion that The Shadow was lean, blond, 40-ish, physically powerful, and decorated with a cobra tattoo.

These characteristics were succinctly specified in John G. Porter's prize-winning conclusion. This, and two other descriptions, were after a long lag, published in the July 25,1931, issue of DETECTIVE STORY. All persons submitting an entry received an autographed picture of The Shadow.

By this time, magazine sales were adequate, if not spectacular. In the Fall of 1931, Street & Smith decided to make the magazine a monthly, a decision which did not get immediately to Gibson. He was then writing his way through the second batch of four novels, assuming that the magazine was still quarterly. On the third issue, however, the magazine became THE SHADOW, A DETECTIVE MONTHLY. (The "A" was dropped beginning with the December 1931 issue.)

The contest was over, but the radio tie-ins remained. The catch phrase, "The Shadow Knows," was worked into every novel. The Shadow's broadcasts were alluded to in every issue.[6]

He lived, you see. He was real. His adventures were occuring right now this minute in New York City.

On the back of the front cover, in that first issue, The Shadow stated that it all was so:

"This is to certify that I have made careful examination of the manuscript known as 'The Living Shadow,' as set down by my raconteur, Mr. Maxwell Grant, and do find it a true account of my activities upon that occasion. I have therefore arranged that Mr. Grant shall have exclusive privilege to such further of my exploits as may be considered of interest to the American people."

He forgot to mention his royalty arrangements with Street & Smith, but then The Shadow would always be reticient about business details.

The novel raised considerable hurrah about The Shadow's broadcasting activities. He did them from a hidden room. He was all in black, his identity a mystery. Watchers attempted to see him and failed. Criminals attempted to trace him and failed.

Oh, he was indeed real. But remote, secret, a "weird creature of the night."

The magazines sold merrily. Once a month, Gibson typed out a fresh 60,000-word story. (Beginning with the sixth issue, it had been reduced to 60,000 words to allow more space for short stories.) But his labors were only beginning.

Surveys showed that most Shadow magazines sold during the first two weeks on the news stands. Clearly, sales could be approximately doubled by publishing the magazine twice a month. The possibilities were interesting. Gibson was given a year's contract for 24 novels, from March 1, 1932, to March 1, 1933. He responded handsomely, pouring out some 1,700,000 words. With the October 1, 1932, issue, "Green Eyes," the twice-a-month schedule began. Again the magazine was retitled, becoming THE SHADOW MAGAZINE.

The great days had arrived. Although no one knew it yet.

4.

THE SHADOW MAGAZINE, that grand institution, stretches like a chain mountain through the time of the single-character pulp magazines, from the beginning almost to the end.

Three hundred and twenty-five issue, plus three annuals, were published: Volume 1, No.1 (April-June 1931) through Volume LV, No.1 (Summer 1949). This produced a stack of publications approximately ten and a half feet high, whole Canadian forests having been consumed to relate the destruction of American criminals.

From October 1, 1932, through March 1, 1943 -- the dates given on the covers -- the magazine appeared two times a month. Fresh stacks arrived regularly as tidal pulse. For eighteen years, you could always buy a Shadow, crisply fresh, to speed away the hours until television was invented.

For eighteen years, The Shadow was part of American life, familiar as Fords and the Flag. You grew up with The Shadow. You were intimately familiar with that darkly cloaked figure, big-brimmed hat pulled down low, the automatics, the fierce profile, the laugh that early passed into folk lore.

From the magazine, that golden vein, poured such treasure as might elate the heart. Unending radio series. Motion pictures. Fingerprint kits. Club lapel pins, rubber stamps, toy pistols. Shadow costumes and make-up kits. Shadow games. Shadow wrist watches. Sheeet music for the piano -- "The Shadow Knows, Ha, Ha, Ha," the cover illustration (informed readers knew) reprinted from the July 15, 1938, "The Golden Vulture." The Shadow's adventures entered the Better Little Books. Comic books. Newspaper strips.

The Shadow's success revitalized the single-character publication, stuporous since that last Buffalo Bill dime novel in 1919. THE SHADOW MAGAZINE stands at the hinge of the 1930's, dominating the period. It locked competitors' imaginations upon the secret justice figure with pistols. It established the format for the single-character magazine -- art, contents, and departments.   It also captured a substantial fraction of the market, ensuring that it would be imitated for years, publishers being eager to sow familiar seed in familiar fields.

By late 1932, after others had absorbed the lesson of THE SHADOW, A DETECTIVE MAGAZINE, the single-character renaissance began. News stands foamed with magazines dedicated to the adventures of deadly justice figures battling evil.

During 1933, seven magazines appeared, among them DOC SAVAGE, THE SPIDER, THE PHANTOM DETECTIVE, NICK CARTER, and G-8 AND HIS BATTLE ACES. The following year, 1934, saw six additional titles, including SECRET AGENT X, OPERATOR 5, and BILL BARNES. By mid-1934, you had a choice of fourteen different single-character magazines. At that point, the number of new magazines issued dropped sharply. While established magazines continued, few new ones enjoyed much success. Obvious exceptions are G-MEN (Dan Fowler: 1935-1953) and BLACK BOOK DETECTIVE (The Black Bat: 1939-1953).

The careers of most single-character magazines were dotted by many different writers. One man would begin the series. He would continue until family matters, illness, or boredom depleted his imaginative reserves. Then other writers fluttered in. Few bothered to read more than a couple of recent copies in the series they were to continue. The result was predictable. Grisly discrepancies occurred. Characters lurch out of character. The dead live. Familiar series places and devices glare strange in strange new light.

Few readers observed and fewer complained. The pulp world existed essentially without memory.

For the most part, The Shadow was spared grotesque deviations from the series line. Three primary writers were involved: Walter Gibson, 282 novels and 85% of the series; Theodore Tinsley, 27 novels; and Bruce Elliott, 15 novels.[7]

Except for the Elliott interlude (1946-1948), when The Shadow got unfocused, the novels are nicely compatible. It is not too obvious which is by Tinsley and which by Gibson. Similar characters, backgrounds, devices unify the stories. They share much the same prose sound. And they enjoyed the presence of a single editor -- John Nanovic, The Shadow's editor from 1932 to 1943.

Consistency in such areas explains only a part of The Shadow's continuing success.

It is notorious that long-duration series characters tend to overstay their times. At last they begin to repeat themselves, like a bell tolling in a cave, and eventually they grow rigid, endlessly caricaturing more glorious days.

Why did he endure? He appeared in cheap magazines. First-draft fiction. Melodramas of action and death, mass produced for a mass audience believed to be predominately juvenile.

As John Nanovic has remarked:

"...WE WEREN'T SELLING ART; WE WEREN'T EVEN SELLING LITERATURE. We were selling excitement; were selling dreams for the average American."[8]

Perhaps that appraisal is true. Perhaps it represents the wisdom of the marketplace, which assumes every diamond to be glass. Regardless. Conventional wisdom predicted that The Shadow soon would exhaust his popularity and be put decently to rest.

Strangely enough, it did not happen.

The Shadow continued across the years. His popularity did not substantially dwindle. Other things changed: The magazine grew less inexpensive. The audience altered. So did the times. The character was mercilessly exploited at the sleaziest levels of merchandising.

Yet The Shadow endured.

In part, this can be explained by skillful narrative pacing and manipulation, adroit editing, clever promotion, and the constant presence of the radio program.

But public acceptance lay at levels deeper than a coin purse.

All inadvertently, Gibson had touched some concealed public need.

In a time of national crisis, failure, and dismay, The Shadow provided an example of high excellence.

Times were complex. No man was trusted. No institution remained blameless. Virtue bled. The evil swallowed wine and rejoiced in high places. Or so it seemed.

The Shadow, disinterested, stood apart from this.

He required neither wealth nor praise. Dispasssionately, with ever-growing lethality, he brought justice to those insulated from justice.

Social mechanisms may falter. The Shadow did not. Cold, remote, perceptive, he was part abstract force, part myth in contemporary trousers. His adventures affirmed virtue in a world without virtue.

A secret force sustained the good.

A popular allegory of the search for justice.

"Dreams for the average American."

And they were successful. Even by the standards of the marketplace, they were successful.

5.

Change makes its sly way through the novels from the first issue. It was unavoidable. Gibson simply had no choice. The situation required that he develop the character of The Shadow from nothing -- from a spooky radio voice.

The Voice of the *Detective Story Program* was in the familiar literary tradition of the omniscient narrator. The weird tones personified Fate or Destiny or some other tingling abstract.

But spooky radio voices provide little substance to sustain the hard reality of a 70,000-word novel. Such voices are inactive. They cackle. They know. They perform little.

For a pulp magazine lead character, inaction would be fatal. The medium required The Shadow to exert meaningful influence on the story. It was essential that the Voice put on flesh.

Gibson solved the matter by postulating a mysterious individual who lurked at the fringes of the adventure, secretly manipulating. Proper activity for a Fate figure.

THE LIVING SHADOW (April—June, 1931): Harry Vincent, a distressed young man, is saved from suicide by a living mystery—a black-garbed individual, whispering, sinister, face concealed in darkness. For unquestioning service, Vincent is promised adventure, travel, money. He agrees—and plunges blindly into a black boil. Murder in the room next to his at the hotel. His own near murder in Chinatown. A near beating by thugs. Another near murder by jewel robbers. From all these embarassments he is saved by

The Shadow, who turns up disguised as somebody else every
other chapter. In spite of Vincent's dubious help, The Shadow
eventually breaks up a murderous batch of jewel thieves. The
leader, Diamond Bert Farwell, spends his time disguised as a
Chinese, thereby justifying the magazine cover. He ends up
caught—and The Shadow melts through a secret wall panel, as
the police clump inward.

"The Living Shadow" and the next dozen novels basically
shape the series. In these, Gibson pulls together basic characters,
basic situations. He creates visual images that will endure for
years. He searches for a prose tone, and for a method of telling
complicated stories, brimming with characters and chapters. It is
a self-taught apprenticeship.

That first novel is dense with beginnings. Among its basics,we
find:

- —that The Shadow heads a secret organization, rather like a
  cell of spies, that has operated for about two years.
- —that he is strong for fanciful communications methods:
  emphasized words and messages in vanishing ink.
- —that he is associated with radio broadcasting.
- —that he might have been a WWI aviator, a spy, that his face
  may have been wounded, that his identity is unknown, that
  most scoff at his existence.
- —that he can disguise himself so thoroughly no one can tell,
  even in broad daylight.
- —that no door or window can restrain him. He slides up sashes
  and picks locks with abandon.
- —and that he has clever ways with safe combinations, codes,
  and cryptic secrets.

While all this is going on, we enter such soon-to-be-famous
locales as:

Joe Cardona's desk at police headquarters.

The Metrolite Hotel, where Vincent will stay for years and
death walks regularly.

The Pink Rat, that evil dive. It is only mentioned, but we will
enter it in time.

Sinister Chinese basements and secret ways.

The Jonas Office on 23rd St., where mail slipped through the
letter slot in that dirt-caked door, always reaches the Shadow.

The Shadow's sanctum, that concealed room, black with a blue
light, where evidence is reviewed and deductions made.

Claude Fellow's insurance office in the Grandville Building.

We also meet those series regulars, Joe Cardona, Harry
Vincent, and Claude Fellows.

*Vincent,*a husky young man from Colin, Michigan, failed to
impress New York City, was jilted by his girl, and decided to

die. He did not. He became The Shadow's foremost active
agent. Self possessed, wearing clothes well, he can
investigate at all social levels.

Cardona, a chunky, dark-skinned, Italian-American detective,
will become The Shadow's favorite police department
contact. Over the years he will rise to the glory that is
Inspector, buoyed by his famous hunches. Joe never solves
anything and must be repeatedly saved from death, since he
is too thick to save himself. He meets The Shadow in issue 7
and admires him forever after.

Fellows, a fat, placid fellow, was saved from ruin by The
Shadow, set up in the insurance business. Fellows is the
contact man, receiving and sending messages. After
awhile, this role dwindles. In "Gangdom's Doom" (Dec
1931) Chicago crooks machine-gun him. He is the only agent
killed in the series. Rutledge Mann, an exact duplicate, will
be reinstated in a similar position a few issues later.

All these people, places, situations, facts are briskly absorbed.
They become part of the Shadow mystique, familiar to the
dedicated reader as his own coffeecup. (Refer to Table I.)

Familiar, even, as certain scenes repeated in every novel. If
they didn't appear, you felt a sense of loss and psychological
disorientation.

TABLE I—Continuing Characters in The Shadow Series: The
First Wave

Novel Written	Character	First Appearance
Jan. 1931	Joe Cardona	The Living Shadow
	Steve Cronin[2] (NOTE 1)	
	Diamond Bert Farwell[2]	
	Claude Fellows[5]	
	*Fritz	
	Inspector John Malone[2]	
	Spotter[3] (NOTE 2)	
	Harry Vincent	
Feb. 1931	Burbank	Eyes of The Shadow
	Isaac Coffran[2]	
	*Lamont Cranston	
	Bruce Duncan[3]	
	Red Mike	
	Richards	
	Stanley	
*Unnamed mobster		
Mar. 1931	Lamont Cranston (himself)	The Shadow Laughs!
	Vic Marquette	

Apr. 1931	Professor Arthur Whitburn[2]	The Red Menace
Aug. 1931	Clyde Burke	The Death Tower
	*George Clarendon[2]	
Sept 1931	Inspector Timothy Klein	The Silent Seven
Nov. 1931	*Henry Arnaud	The Black Master
Dec. 1931	Cliff Marsland	Mobsmen On the Spot
	*Shadow disguise	
Jan. 1932	Rutledge Mann	Double Z
Mar. 1932	Det. Sgt. Mayhew[2]	Hidden Death
	Commissioner Ralph Weston	
Jun 1932	*Pineas Twambley	Kings of Crime
Aug. 1932	Tam Sook	Six Men of Evil
Nov. 1932	Det. Sgt. Markham	The Black Hush
Dec. 1932	Pietro	The Silver Scourge

NOTE 1. Many characters appear only two or three times and are then discarded. This Table cites characters of more than routine interest. The number by their name indicates their approximate number of appearances. Those names without numbers may be assumed to appear with reasonable frequency through significant parts of the series.

NOTE 2. Spotter appears three times only. However, he is the prototype of later similar characters, each bearing a dfferent name and an identical description. Finally the character is named Hawkeye and stabilizes as an agent.

As when—

Cardona ponders at his desk, fingering The Evidence. All around him mops The Shadow, disguised as the janitor, Fritz, glancing at Cardona's evidence, understanding....

Although tough gunmen watch everywhere, The Shadow glides past them, ascends a building wall, listens to a secret gangland conference on the 29th floor....

The sanctum light snicks off. The room fills with a dreadful laugh that rises to a fearful crescendo, shatters to gibing echoes....

As killers dart forward, pistols bristling, a veering taxi whips toward them. A mocking laugh rises. Pistol shots smack them down...

Just as the sneering mastermind has confessed to the assembled cast and prepares to murder all, The Shadow materializes from a dark doorway, .45's bulging from each gloved fist.

These set pieces are strongly visual. They lie worlds away from mystery radio voices. They reflect Gibson's joy in strongly dramatic situations and in the use of atmosphere—thick slabs of it.

In spite of such pleasures, there was never such a rational man, as Walter Gibson. He is all rationality. In his haunted castles, every ghost is electric and manufactured by Westinghouse.

That rationality permeates every shred of The Shadow series. Intelligence underlies it, a delight in intellectual games. The pages are stuffed with codes and cryptograms, mechanical devices, frauds, alibis, magical apparatus, and deductive logic.

The Shadow understands these and manipulates them in high style. He relishes puzzles. He excels at situational analysis. In all the 10½ feet of the magazine, he hardly expresses a single abstract idea. It is all artful analysis, the truth meticulously disengaged from the snares of misdirection. The Shadow's mind is clear as a diamond from space. And as icy.

The Shadow's first recorded action is to prevent a suicide. His second action is to turn a hold-up man's gun on the owner.

In the first chapter, then, appear enduring themes: The Shadow will aid the unfortunate and will fight contemporary crime with its own weapons.

Yes, he would retain characteristics of the radio Voice. He would continue to laugh weirdly. He would have a confoundedly detailed insight into other people's business. He would be associated with radio.

Primarily, however, he would be a figure of action. As the magazine media required.

During the first several issues, Gibson felt his way to the character:

"...a tall, black-cloaked figure that might have represented death itself.... The stranger's face was entirely obscured by a broad-brimmed felt hat bent downward over his features and the long black coat looked almost like part of the thickening fog." (The Living Shadow," Chapter I.)

Early novels seldom reveal The Shadow so clearly. He apears in hints. Shapeless blots move in the dark. Weird shadows melt away. Barely observed motion stirs in the night. Rarely, the cloaked figure appears near a light,then vanishes, "its course untraceable."

By daylight, he could be any man. He is as much a chameleon as Nick Carter or Cleek, The Man of Forty Faces. Whatever the face, whatever the physique, The Shadow duplicates it effortlessly.

The ability is most convenient for Gibson's purposes. Since any character might be The Shadow, he can appear as required by the plot—particularly when the problem can be solved no easy way.

Under these circumstances, there can be little conventional character development. The Shadow is a presence—a mystery figure, a Weird Creature of the Night.

Anything but a man wearing a wide-brimmed hat and cloak. What we know of him comes indirectly.

Agents speculate. Gangsters mouth rumors. Gibson might help but he doesn't. Irregularly he drops enticing scraps to tickle our attention.

It is never enough.

But how do you characterize an individual who appears briefly and speaks little?

There are ways.

You show other characters' reactions to him. You describe him in action. You describe his decisions and choices.

Gibson's first efforts lumber. How to show Holmes in the heat of deduction when there is no Watson? The Shadow manages by sitting in the sanctum, writing to himself. He clips and arranges Fellows' reports, transforming speculation to fact. More often he pens cryptic notes, revealing Gibson's intent for future chapters. Or he writes brief essays, deducting furiously, mounding gigantic theories upon timorous facts, incidentally informing the reader.

All this demonstrates the flow of a master intelligence——or it's supposed to. It gives the reader a private moment with The Shadow. Helps to heighten your identification with him.

Every mote of identification is needed for The Shadow is a most peculiar hero.

His eyes blaze like fire points from beneath the hat brim. The hands are white, the fingers long. An fire opal ring flames on the third finger, left hand. The voice is a whisper, a sinister hiss.

The laugh comes weirdly at unexpected times for unexplained reasons. It is an essential element of the radio Voice. Gibson uses the laugh to express The Shadow's inner thoughts, when it is not a battle cry. Gives the reader a means of gauging The Shadow's intent. Always nice when the face is concealed.

And now, all manner of games begin concerning his real identity:

The Eyes Of The Shadow (1931): Scheming evil Isaac Coffran plots to sieze Russian jewels belonging to Bruce Duncan. This fine young man is menaced by all manner of hulking fiends, deadly gas traps, rooms with closing walls, and such devices as made hearts light at the silent movies. Repeatedly, The Shadow saves our heroes. Then he is lured into a gang trap at the dive, The Shadow gets considerably shot and knifed. While he recovers at the New Jersey mansion of a Lamont Cranston, Duncan and Vincent get into more trouble—caught by a deadly ape-man, strung to the rack. But The Shadow comes through. The ape-man dies, wearing a black cloak. The crooks plunge to their doom in the river. The Shadow saves the jewels. And Coffran gets clean away.

The novel is a fascinating hybrid. Part is early 1920's novel, part silent movie, part mid-1930's action. Scraps of Frank Packard, Edgar Wallace, Nick Carter flick by, with hints and suggestions of dime novel days, back when a story piled up action scenes to the requisite number of words, then quit.

In spite of the melodrama's fragility, the story works. It dances about, shouting exhuberently. It contains too much of everything——heroes, villains, traps.

Still, these are excesses of zeal. The action lures you on and on and the figure of The Shadow intrigues.

Even *he* makes errors.

Slovenly lurking lets his presence be known. If he can't be seen, the movement of his shadow can. Crooks detect him, lure him to a trap.

There follows the first thunderous gun battle with the underworld——the first of many. Blood, death, and escape from a hopeless situation. He foresightedly carried along a gas mask and gas, you see. He is a miracle of foresight.

New faces are showering into the narrative. Both Coffran and Duncan will return.[9] Red Mike, a minor dive keeper, will appear again. And Burbank, the faceless and undescribed, who will coordinate communications for the rest of the series, appears as a radio expert.

A major addition is Lamont Cranston and his servants.

Gibson first considered calling him Lamont Dupont, a name suggestive of vast wealth and agonizingly contrived.   He ultimately settled on Cranston, causing Heaven to sigh with relief. Cranston was a lean, impassive, young millionaire. That's all we learn in this novel. Superficial parallels exist between Cranston and Jimmie Dale, another young millionaire, known also as the Gray Seal, who had a penchant for disguise and underworld adventure. Cranston's subsequent development, however, is in directions that Jimmie Dale never explored.[10]

It should be noted that both Cranston and Dale are mildly aided by a butler and a chauffeur. Cranston's butler is named Richards, who wonders why the Boss acts so oddly. The chauffeur is Stanley, who drives Cranston all over New Jersey and New York City. He is rather a dull stick, seeing nothing, hearing nothing, ——even though Cranston continually vanishes from the limousine and The Shadow garb and weapons reside in a drawer under the rear seat.

In the next novel, the Cranston matter is squarely faced—— and squarely evaded.

The Shadow Laughs(October 1931): Issac Coffran returns, leading a murderous counterfeiting gang. Vincent is trapped and saved very often. The Shadow is repeatedly seen, although all

traps fail. Eventually, the gang is broken with the aid of the
Secret Service and considerable cliff-hanging. Near the ending
The Shadow stars in the first of many Terminal Explanation
scenes——The Shadow explains who's guilty, following by lots of
shooting to save the cost of a trial.

This novel introduces Vic Marquette, a tough stocky fellow
with a heavy mustache. Vic is the resident Federal Agent,
working variously for the Secret Service, Treasury, Justice,F.B.I,
all seemingly interchangeable. He early reaches an
understanding with Vincent. Later he will work closely with The
Shadow. Smart, aggressive, competent, Vic appears throughout
the series.

The prime glory of this novel is the complication surrounding
Mr. Lamont Cranston, "a tall man, with rather pronounced
features, who seemed to carry a very bored expression, as though
life was rather tasteless."

Home after a 6-month absence, Cranston finds that he has been
seen where he wasn't and is considered wounded when he isn't. At
4 a.m., he wakes to see himself at the foot of the bed. It's enough to
make you give up sleeping.

The Shadow has come to explain Cranston's position.

"Some people call me The Shadow.

"That is but one identity. I have other personalities that I
assume as easily as I don my cloak and hat.

"One of my personalities is that of Lamont Cranston.

"In the past, I have used it while you were away. At present, I
choose to use it now. It would be embarassing for both of us to be
here. So you must go."

Quite reasonably, Cranston is put out. Eventually, after some
straight-forward threats, The Shadow prevails.

Cranston: "You have convinced me that there is no use in
  opposing you. I don't know your purpose, or what you intend to
  do; but I wish you the best of luck."

Then he goes back to sleep. Some men are born unruffled.

Later meetings will be less harrowing. Cranston appears
irregularly, always on the spot when needed.[11] The two are
friendly, but Cranston never learns the identity under his face.

The shared identity gimmick works so brightly that the really
outrageous aspects slip quietly past.

Assuming that The Shadow can disguise himself perfectly as
another, why does he select Cranston at this time? What
motivates him to obliterate his own personality, and live
disguised for twenty years, behind another man's face?

In "The Shadow Unmasks" (August 1, 1937), he explains:

"I had once known Lamont Cranston, millionaire globetrotter,
whose hobbies were exploration and aviation. Cranston was

often absent from the country; so I adopted his appearance. It gave me all the advantages that I needed." (Chapter XIII)

And in the "The Hydra,"(December 1, 1942) he remarks to Cranston, himself:

"When I first decided to supplant you, it was purely because you were away from home for such long periods. It was very convenient to be someone who wouldn't show up for a year or more."

The explanations do not explain very much.

The most obvious answer is that the Cranston wealth and social position permitted access to highly influential leaders in the business and political communities. Thus, the Cranston identity permits entry into a world closed to most men——the world of the true insiders...and also, the world of those major criminals who are The Shadow's natural prey.

In practice, these advantages translate to smaller change. Cranston can drop into any social function, unannounced, uninvited, and be welcome. And he can leave as informally, begging a prior business engagement.

Most usefully, the Cranston social position dazzles Weston, the Police Commissioner, who gapes for wealth and admiration. He cultivates Cranston; Cranston cultivates him; and The Shadow learns all the inside details of all major police operations.

Still, these justifications are woefully weak. The truth is that no good reason is ever advanced. The problem is ignored for years. Eventually, The Shadow goes into full-time Cranstoning and the problem vanishes, unsolved, undiscussed.

In his booklet, *Gangland's Doom, The Shadow of the Pulps*(1974),Frank Eisgruber, Jr. suggests that The Shadow gave up his true identity of Kent Allard in order to separate himself from the intelligence agencies that he was associated with during World War I. "He knew an agent cannot quit at any time he wants, especially one as talented as he." This is so sensible a suggestion that we can only regret Gibson did not use it.

A second possibility, based on unexplained scenes in the series, is that Allard's face was mutilated in a battle so severely that rebuilding the features by make-up was necessary. The Allard personality was suppressed because of these wounds. Since he had to rebuild his own face to appear in public, it is a logical step for Allard to adopt another man's features, as needed.

Whatever the reason, the Cranston matter is left floating in limbo:

"In all his years of service, (Clyde) had never become convinced of his chief's identity.

"True, Clyde had associated Cranston with The Shadow, but so had a lot of other people. The further such a quest was pressed, the less it produced; in fact, there were times when Cranston and The Shadow had been seen independently in places so far apart that it seemed certain that two persons must be different individuals. "There were whys and wherefores to that subject, which Clyde Burke, like other agents of The Shadow, had felt it his duty to ignore." ("The Shadow Meets The Mask." October 1944, p. 25)

Since we are not so closely associated with The Shadow, there is no reason for us to ignore the subject.

What seems to have happened is that Gibson accidentally wrote himself into this anomaly while working up a new slant to an old theme.

The Cranston of "The Eyes of The Shadow" is one of those familiar 1920's millionaires whose double identity sometimes serves justice. (This matter is discussed in Chapter 3.) That figure had become a literary cliche, worked to rags by books and periodicals of the times. The type includes such people as Sir George Trevor; Anthony Trent; Jimmie Dale; and those innumerable characters from DETECTIVE STORY MAGAZINE, among them The Crimson Clown, The Man In Purple, The White Rook, and The Thunderbolt.

By the 1930's, the concept was distinctly elderly, a well-worn element of the literary tradition. Gibson sought a new variation, we may speculate. And Cranston becomes merely a guise for someone else.

The twist is typically Gibson: He delighted in such sleight-of-hand techniques. In his work, white is eternally black, and left is right. The suspect is innocent, the benign guilty. Cranston is not Cranston but someone else.

Who?

Doesn't matter. Time to name him later. Mystify now. Let the future explain itself.

So it is possible that Gibson inadvertently saddled himself with a situation whose implications did not bother him at the time. The situation was created in issue number 3. At that time, no one anticipated an 18-year run of the magazine or the character's immense popularity. The novels were written for a brief sales period followed by oblivion.

The wonder is not that there were inconsistencies, but that there were so few inconsistencies.

By the end of March, 1931, the manuscript for "The Shadow Laughs" was submitted and the magazine judged sufficiently well received that it could become a monthly.

The fourth novel, "The Red Menace" (published as the November 1931 issue) was written and submitted in about two and a half weeks. In geological terms, the novel marks the transition from the Proterozoic to the Cambrian.

The Red Menace(November 1931): A cell of Red agents seeks to seize some mysterious plans. They are directed, more or less by a master genius, The Red Envoy, whose identity is concealed by a red mask and red gloves. In the first half of the story, they kill, trap, and work their will. A disguised Russian prince seeks to oppose them but does little. Vincent gets trapped, as usual, this time in The Pink Rat. He is saved by a lovely girl, Arlette DeLand member of the ring; they love each other but it is too early in the series for Harry to take a wife, so she eventually renounces him until she forgets her past. Never comes back. After an abortive attempt to kill Cranston in a tricky elevator, the Reds shift operations to Death Island. There Professor Whitburn has invented something weird. All people on the island slink around suspiciously. Vic Marquette appears wearing a suspicious beard. Vincent sees a suspicious ghost, and is almost killed a couple of times, which is about par. He ends up trapped in a flooding cellar,with The Shadow and Arlette to keep him company. They escape but the Red Envoy has got plans for the aerial torpedo. Fortunately for the safety of all, The Red Envoy murders all members of his cell, then takes off for Russia and glory. However, The Shadow flies the Atlantic in a single bound, intercepts the fiend aboard a train, and saves the plans. The fiend dies, his secret identity exposed, his mission a failure.

The Red Envoy is the first of Gibson's innumerable criminal geniuses whose identity is concealed until the last chapter. Then they are exposed and die by gunfire. Some wear costumes. Others, masks. The rest lurk concealed, vipers in the luxuriant prose.

That concealed identity is one mystery, at least, that lasts the duration of each novel. Other mysteries are of lesser moment—— who killed whom; what's going on. All matters get clarified with reasonable dispatch. Only the identity of the mastermind of crime remains hidden till the closing pages.

The paucity of mystery in these mystery stories is hardly noticed. The chapters reel with action. If Vincent is not about to get bumped off, someone else is. People whisk mysteriously in to whisper and whisk out. The Shadow laughs significantly. Cars whiz about. Menaces rise in the dark night, adjectives rumbling. Misdirection works its slippery way.

Adventure. Excitement. Death, death, death. All strung like beads on the fragile story line. Not much mystery. But plenty of movement, rich atmosphere. And frequent excursions from the story line in what Walter Gibson calls "side tracks".

Gibson: "...they wanted about 75,000 words for ("The Living Shadow")——I don't know why they wanted so many words for the story. They put in quite a few episodes that the story could have done without, but they didn't hurt it fortunately, because I kept the activity... We always called those (added episodes) sidetracks... I felt a little chagrined in doing the stories that I had to spend so much time on those sidetrails. As I went along, I tried to keep the stories more...on a single thing—I tried to have more reason for the side trails."[12]

"The Menace" shovels out interesting chunks of The Shadow's past. He was (we learn) in "Russia during the first months of the War. As the agent of another government, (he) became a member of the Seventh Star." This is a secret order of Royalist Russia and involves passwords and secret signs and good solid stuff like that. The Shadow carries the order's sign——a seven-pointed star—— engraved on the gold bezel under the fire opal. Press a spring to read. The girasol, itself (as we learn in "The Romanoff Jewels," December 1, 1932), was given to The Shadow by the last of the Czars, for services rendered.

Other stories, other explanations. In "Six Men of Evil" (February 15, 1933), the symbol concealed under the opal is The Sign of Chow Lee, a sort of passport to confidence of any Chinese.

By "The Shadow Unmasks" (August 1, 1937) all these stories are out of print. The girasol story is then revamped. Now it becomes an eye from an Xinca idol and was presented to Allard by the Indians of Guatemala.

Since one story effectively cancels the other, Mr. Gibson, very nimble, devised still another story, in 1976, which explained that both girasols came from the same idol. By complex paths, the Czar got one and gave it to The Shadow; the Indians gave the other to Allard.[13] Very neat.

7.

During these early adventures, The Shadow flings around increasing volumes of lead. But it is rare that he kills the most deserving. He hits them in the shoulder, leg, hand——not places where it is desirable to be struck by a .45 bullet, you understand. Not fatal, however. The Shadow is as careful not to kill as any 1920's hero. In the latter part of 1932, he becomes considerably more deadly. By mid-1933, he is dropping the evil right and left. And incidentally, he travels heavy-laden with large calibre weapons, a one-man S.W.A.T. team, blasting away with both hands.

A non-lethal Shadow seems a contradiction in terms. The image of the 1930's Shadow is an ice-eyed avenger who kills without flinching or remorse, and, often, without warning. But he did not begin that way. It was not a trait generally associated with heroes of pulp magazine mystery—adventure stories.

Pulp magazine adventure stories were another matter. Homicide was embedded in their paragraphs. Hopalong Cassidy had burned down opponents since 1905. The Jimgrim associates, and others from the ADVENTURE Magazine, spilled corpses all over the Middle and Far East. And all through the 1920's, Sir George Trevor (of BLUE BOOK'S Diplomatic Free Lance series) executed enemies with unemotional precision. As did his wife and friends.

Certain English series characters gave death long before The Shadow. Edgar Wallace's Just Men, and later, The Ringer, killed promptly, in artistic ways. Nor did Bulldog Drummond or The Saint ever hesitate to bump off in a good cause.

However, the US mystery—adventure tradition not only avoided killing, but its heroes got icy butterflies at the thought.

The Shadow is certainly never that squeamish. While saving Cliff Marsland ("Mobsman on the Spot"), he casually wipes out a couple of thugs. But that was to give Cliff a hard reputation. Normally he disables, only.

That leads to some odd situations. In the "Mobsmen," he fist fights a car load of crooks. In both "The Eyes of the Shadow" and "Hidden Death" (September 1932), he escapes from hordes of hard New York City killers without killing.

All this gradually changes. The Shadow will become one of literature's more deadly heroes. But it takes awhile. Even during the most violent of his attacks, however, he does more hand-to-hand battle than shooting. Drives right into a batch of killers, slugging away with his automatics. This is not to save lives, but to conserve ammunition.[14]

At first, The Shadow carries a pair of small automatics. Later he exchanges these for a revolver of some type or a lesser automatic pistol. Gibson is not particularly specific. In "Mobsmen", the weapon is silenced. Finally, he settles down to the Colt .45, Model 1911A——a beautiful, bulky, inaccurate piece of iron.

Gibson describes this weapon as "huge", which it is not, and pictures underworld figures being overawed by its size and power. Odd, considering that the underworld had been flooded with surplus Army automatics during the 1920's.

In addition to the automatics (up to four of them, carried cocked), The Shadow hauls around masses of special equipment: A lockpick, of course, since all heroes carry lockpicks. A special flat case of tools. Exploding powders sewn into the cloak's hem. A tiny vial of wonderfully reviving medicine. A tiny flashlight that can blink in various colors. A nesting cluster of suction cups for wall scaling. At least once, a boomerang and a cable and hand trolley. Later, a flexible briefcase will be tucked in someplace, after cloak and hat have been extracted from it. And, finally, he carries a vial containing the powders of "The Devil's Whisper."

Two separate powders are used. A light dusting of one on the thumb, of the other on the forefinger. When these are brushed together in the presence of moisture, they explode with loud brilliance. The effect is from stage magic, although it had entered Mystery—Adventure Fiction some years earlier.[15]

"She raised her gloved hand above her head and seemed to snap her fingers. There was a brilliant flash of light that blinded him and made him stagger back. When he opened his eyes again, he could not see her for the golden suns that danced before his eyes; and then he saw a thick white cloud of smoke rolling slowly along the ceiling."[16]

The Shadow first uses the device in "Treasures of Death" (December 15, 1933). Gibson details it sharply, as he does whenever describing magic equipment.

"The Shadow's left hand appeared. It was holding a double-ended vial. The left hand, gloved, approached the ungloved right and performed an operation upon thumb and second finger.

The left hand disappeared with the small glass container...

"...The Shadow held his right hand posed forward, thumb and second finger separated...

"Gripping the window frame with his left hand, he reached forward with his right and snapped his thumb and forefinger. The result was astounding. From The Shadow's fingers sounded a loud report; with it, a flash of blinding flame.

"A stunning reverberation filled the room..."

Throughout The Shadow series, Gibson's abiding affection for stage magic, and his knowledge of its equipment, is constantly shown. The Shadow, himself, has a specialist's knowledge of magic apparatus, gambling devices, and sleight-of-hand effects. Gibson's personal experience constantly surfaces. His familarity with Houdini's seance investigations is reflected in "The Ghost Makers" (October 15,1932). His 1921 experiences while traveling with a carnival are used in "Crime Circus" (April 15, 1934) and "The Freak Show Murders" (May, 1944). Houdini-like escapes frequently occur, as in "The Eyes of The Shadow" (July, 1931) "Green Eyes" (October 31,1932). Magic apparatus may appear at any time: "The Dark Death" (February 15, 1935), "The Unseen Killer" (December 1, 1934), and "The Crime Oracle" (June 1, 1936).

And such feats of magic occur as fire-walking ("The Salamanders", April 1, 1936); the hand unaffected by boiling water ("The Voodoo Master,"March 1, 1936); the vanish in smoke and flame (Xitli, God of Fire," December 1, 1940); a disappearance with mirrors ("Room of Doom," April 1, 1942); and a transparent skull that talks on request ("The Magigals Mystery," Winter, 1949).

As far as magic is concerned, you note that The Shadow has all of Gibson's expertise. And more.

During the next several novels, a blizzard of events, agents, supernummeraries, situations whirl about us.

Claude Fellows gets machine-gunned in Chicago. The story is "Gangdom's Doom" (December, 1931). The Shadow and Vincent come to Chicago to avenge him. Vincent does little more than get into trouble when he does appear, which is not often. The Shadow hardly shows himself as The Shadow; he effectively disrupts all the major criminal plotting and sets two big gangs at each other's throats. Steve Cronin, a hard-boiled minor character, who has appeared in all novels but "The Red Menace," finally is killed off.

In these fictions, at least, gangland still seems simple—— competing mobs riveted together by an overlord. Both Edgar Wallace (*On The Spot,*1931) and Gibson described it that way, reflecting the 1920's experience and mythology. The Shadow is not much strained to get the groups fighting among themselves. He shoots several people in the arms; the gangsters do the rest. Chicago is purged.

Or so it was stated.

Three and a half months after Gibson submitted the story, forty Mafia chiefs were simultaneously murdered across the country.[17] The Shadow had nothing to do with this.

Fellows' death seriously interferes with routine communications between The Shadow and agents which, God knows, were inefficient enough already. Messages transmitted by emphasizing voices, or coded reports in disappearing ink that must be slipped among the cobwebs of an unoccupied office, are gripping devices, indeed, particularly if you are twelve years old. They require an enormous expenditure of time and trouble, far out of proportion to the advantage they offer. Such Micky Mouse devices could be accepted during the first stories. But as the series lengthened out, more substantial arrangements proved necessary—if for no other reason than to smooth the mechanics of telling the story.

As The Shadow's organization grows, orderly transmission of orders and reports is essential and the need for central commmunications becomes more urgent.

It does not arrive all at once. In the novel after Fellows' murder, Burbank is given a minor role. Thereafter, Burbank moves slowly into the communications slot and becomes indispensable. The Fellows' death seriously interferes with routine communications communications activity——not in the center.

The Death Tower (January, 1932): Dr. Palermo is a genius, a

disguise artist, and a sinister plotter, who lives on top of a
building among clouds of criminal intent. He kills for a jewel
and so gets The Shadow on his trail. Clyde Burke, an ex-police
reporter now running a newspaper clipping service, is
approached by strange George Clarendon. For a couple of
months, Burke has been delivering Clarendon's clippings to an
old office on 23rd St. Shortly, Burke finds himself investigating
Dr. Palmino. Vincent helps him. Unfortunately, Palermo has
reasoned out that The Shadow is Clarendon, using a form of
logic that requires no facts. He sets a series of traps. He uses
lovely Thelda Blanchet. A crooked cop. A gang to thugs.
Eventually he captures both agents. The Shadow arrives by
autogyro landing on top of the 40th floor.
The Shadow arrives by autogyro, landing on top of the 40th
floor, from which Dr. P. is swiftly spilled, which serves the old
sinner right.
For almost the only time in the series, The Shadow seems
interested in a woman. He appears as George Clarendon, a rather
more vigorous Lamont Cranston. A wealthy playboy and a
member of the 400, Clarendon will appear only once more
("Hands in the Dark," May, 1932). He wins Thelda's heart from
Palermo. But since she was part crook, she must pay. She is sent
home to mother to grieve out her days in fruitless sorrow. The
final scene between The Shadow/Clarendon and Thelda has
interesting emotional overtones. The Shadow is right annoyed at
first. Whether he is annoyed at Thelda's attempted treachery, or
his impulse toward her you can't quite make out. Whatever the
reason, he suppresses soft emotion and Thelda becomes the first
living individual to see The Shadow clamp on the hat and become
mysterious.
For the balance of the series, The Shadow has no overt
emotional life. Beginning in 1941, he pals around a lot with
Margo Lane. Nothing remotely serious developes there. In the
late 1940's, he speaks warmly to Myra Reldon. She is a competent
professional investigator, who becomes an agent. However,
nothing develops with her, either. Like Sherlock Holmes, The
Shadow seems born to bachelorhood.
This story marks the debut of a major series agent:
Burke: Ex-police reporter. In his mid-twenties. Small, almost
frail, if wiry, but sharp-minded, tough. Has contacts all over New
York in newspapers and police department. Recently lost his job
and opened a clipping service. Will later work (in subsequent,
sequential novels) for the *Evenng Classic* then the *New York
Sun*, then the *Classic* again. The *Classic* is a loud scandal sheet,
rather like the *New York Mirror.* It gives Burke a lot of freedom
and a chance to do special articles and hang around Joe
Cardona's desk, watching for leads.

Both Cardona and Burke appear in the next novel, "The Silent Seven" (February, 1932). The Seven, mentioned briefly in "The Death Tower," is a secret group of hooded fellows who were organized to do good but have gone criminal. They use mystic symbols and signs and have a password routine that is the last word in sophisticated comedy.

The Secret Seven: Learning the secret of the Seven from a dying member, a crook infiltrates the group. He proposes some money-raising schemes which are admirable, if illegal. The Shadow gets on his track and wrecks a plan or two. The Seven attempt to trap him but get Vincent, instead. He gets fastened in a steel room with a lowering roof and The Shadow must battle through hidden passageways and a fierce giant to save him. He must also save Cardona and a police squad. They come to raid the Seven and almost end up as casualties, as they often do. A major gun fight extinguishes this secret society. There will be others.

In this novel, Joe Cardona faces The Shadow for the first time. They meet over pistols. Cardona's gets shot away.

Neither crooks nor cops know what to make of The Shadow. In both "The Death Tower" and "The Secret Seven" the police catch him in suspicious proximity to a dead body. He slides right away from them, however, flinging them about.

Then he slips back to face Cardona:

"Before (Cardona) stood a tall, thin man clad in a close-fitting black suit. The man's arms were folded. His head was bowed, and his face was shadowy beneath the brim of his hat."

Shadow:"Cardona, I am not your enemy...I shall aid you. When I am certain of the murderer's identity and have fathomed the plans of his associates, I shall reveal them to you."

It is the beginning of a long association. Cardona benefits amazingly from The Shadow's help, and comes to rely on the tips hissed from the telephone, the gun stab from darkness at the critical moment, the information-packed fading notes.

In time, Cardona rises to become an inspector, honored by all. He rises on The Shadow's success. It seems what The Shadow wishes. The whole matter bothers Joe.

What bothers him more is the refusal of his superiors to admit that such a person as The Shadow exists. Inspector Klein scoffs and warns Joe that he is emperiling his career by referring to The Shadow in official reports. Later, the Police Commissioner will forbid all mention of men in black cloaks. Could be anybody.

The years ease this position. Comes a point when experienced officers will not fire at The Shadow, even when he is seen near heaps of dead mobsters and blazing automobiles. It is the type of confidence that The Spider never enjoyed.

8.

"Now I am on the threshold of the greatest combat of my career.
I am dealing with a man who is rightfully called The Master."
(The Shadow, speaking as Clifford Gage, to Dr. Zerndorf.)

The Black Master, to be exact. Deadly Red Envoys and
murdering doctors in high towers are all right, if your taste so
inclines. The Black Master is, however, the first of the true
supercriminals that The Shadow will encounter. This particular
genius does not command a mighty horde of gangsters. Still he
does quite well, working essentially alone:

The Black Master(March 32): A murderous genius is blowing
away chunks of New York City. No one knows why. Since
Inspector Burke, Cardona, and the Secret Service don't know
either, they have enlisted the services of a German genius, Dr.
Zerndorff. Wall Street, Grand Central Station, the Evening
Classic——all get ripped up. The Shadow gets another attempt.
(He is disguised as Henry Arnaud for the first time.) Soon he
suspects the identity of the bomb fiend——The Black Master.
Doesn't help too much. The Master runs to gadgets—black
rooms blue with evil light, electric floors, electrical crystal balls
that destroy the will, bombs activated by radioactivity. Vincent
gets his mind cracked and is out of it. The Shadow's identity
of Clifford Gage is seen through. He gets trapped, his face
exposed, himself out of action for a week. He returns just in time
to save New York City from being blasted. The Black Master
dies in an explosion and the only reason The Shadow survives
is by the warm generosity of Walter Gibson, bless him.

The Master has his moments. He solves The Shadow's code and
finds a slick way of beating the disappearing ink. He gets both
Harry and The Shadow with effortless ease. He also introduces a
technological innovation that will run through numerous
novels——the secret message transmitted in blinking lights
around the border of a billboard.

The Shadow borrows this method in "Mobsmen On the Spot"
(April 1932). It appears as a criminal device in "Green Eyes"
(October 1, 1932), "The Circle of Death" (March 1, 1934) "The
Python" (November 15, 1935), and points before and after. It is a
durable idea.

The Master also contrives to be the first supercriminal of
the series to get himself installed in the confidence of the police, as
their personal consultant. Whenever this happens, the fellow is
rotten to the core and you need guess no further as to the identity
of the concealed killer.

The Master appears to be the first individual ever to see The
Shadow's undisguised face. In this story, The Shadow has
appeared as Fritz, the dim-witted police janitor; as Henry
Arnaud, a full-faced eccentric businessman;[18]   and Clifford

Gage, a friend of the millionaire The Black Master is working against.

When The Master jerks away from that slouch hat, The Shadow does not seem to be disguised. There follows an off scene:

The Black Master: "The secret of The Shadow. At last it is understood! The man of many faces——with no face of his own!"

Just what he has seen is not disclosed. In future stories, others see the face of The Shadow and fall down in fits. Not the Master. He is merely fascinated.

And what is this all about?

Gibson calls it the "horror face".

"The 'horror face' was a planted device that could have been picked up for later reference. Allard's own face could have been battle-scared and undergoing plastic surgery; or he could have been testing out a special mask to study the effect. Like the girasol and the finger-snap explosion, these were tests of reader's interest."[19]

If the reader's attention were nipped, he'd write in, intense for information. By such clues, the editor could keep in touch with his public and the magazine would constantly ride the wave. That was the theory.

The "horror face" seemed to have promise. It had been suggested in "The Living Shadow". At discreetly paced intervals, it would appear in "The Shadow's Shadow" (February 1, 1934), before being dropped (at editorial request). It left behind questions as thick as gnats in August. No answers.

On strictly rational grounds, a severely mutilated face explains much that is peculiar in the series. It justifies The Shadow's incredible remoteness. It excuses the constant make-up and the use of other's faces. By assuming that plastic surgery was eventually successful, it accounts for Kent Allard's return. And it explains why The Shadow becomes less spectral and retiring

It is possible. It is also speculation. As a game, you may dig strands of meaning out of the series and attempt to tie them in pretty ways. But it is your game, not Gibson's.

We end with this: a major situational element was introduced, erratically followed up, eventually abandoned. This tells us a good deal about the blatant opportunism of the pulp magazines. Nothing about the character.

"Mobsmen on the Spot" (April 1932) tells how The Shadow cleansed New York City of the rackets. He had done the same favor for Chicago in "Gangdom's Doom"; the New York cleansing doesn't stick, either. The novel focuses on the underworld, showing gangs bloodily at work, crime from the crimnal's viewpoint.

"Hands In the Dark" (May 1932) begins with creepy doings in a creepy old house. The villain is a nice old boy, wreathed in smiles, who plots and schemes and manipulates his underworld helpers. He is out to steal an inheritance. You meet a sweet young thing in trouble and a matter of switched identities. Not the last time you will meet these ideas, either.

"Double Z" (June 1932) is another respectable villain whose helpers are from the underworld. He is a brilliant fellow, this time reveling in the joy of murder. He has ties into Chinatown and with crooks, and murders along toward criminal power until he ends up in a remarkable grave.

These three stories present characteristic themes that bloom energetically through the series. The situation of a young girl endangered in a weird old house——or a young man ditto in a ditto——appears two or three times a year. It is varied in incredibly artful ways.

Through most novels stream thugs and underworld gunmen. From 1931 to 1949, The Shadow spills their gore. The gangsters are tough guys who cock their machine guns and roar away to steal and kill. They enjoy few political ties, little internal organizations, and are easily led. Any mastermind wishing to control the crimeworld, merely kills two or three gang leaders and all the rest fall into line.

That marks the difference between fiction and real life. In our unfortunate world, a mastermind who tried to dominate New York's underworld would shortly find himself at the bottom of a waterway with an earful of bullets.

A more simplified version of life operates in the pulps. The underworld, that frothing mass, is easily lured by fellows who mix secret passages with menacing phone messages. To do this, the supercriminal normally works through one or more lieutenants. These lead the troops and draw pay. Behind them works the darker mind.

That mind is respectable. Gibson's view of millionaires and business leaders is rather depressing. Secret power entices them. No crime repels them. Amoral, avaricious, they represent the free enterprise system gone mad. The more substantial their reputations, the more likely it is that they appear disguised in a weird green light, directing snarling minions.

The situation was not Gibson's invention. It had been so from the beginning of popular crime fiction. Similar situations occur in the Nick Carter stories and in some Jimmie Dale adventures. Fifty years of sensational fiction dimly reflects reality——that the underworld and respectable society are tightly, if secretly, linked. Fiction caught the association, if no accurate detail.

The cynics held that if a man were wealthy, he was a crook. The Depression years reinforced the idea. Obviously, the bankers, lawyers, and politicians caused the whole thing. Just as

munitions manufacturers promoted war for their enrichment—a
folk belief from the early 1920's that would show up in the late
1930's, polished to shining simplicity.

The Shadow stories brim with such fiends. All wealthy. All
respectable. All certifiably insane. They maneuver and crime and
at last they die. The series could not have existed without them.

Meanwhile, The Shadow's organization has been expanding
feverishly. He recruits Cliff Marsland in "Mobsmen" and
replaces Fellows with Rutledge Mann in "Double Z."

Cliff Marsland: Not his real name, never revealed. Met The
Shadow in real identity in France. 14 years before, at end of the
Great War. Returning to States, Marsland took blame for bank
robbery in Brooklyn. Was sent to Sing Sing for 8 years. Robbery
was by black sheep brother of Arline Griscom, Cliff's love
darling and dear. Out of Sing Sing in time for series, he is tall,
broadshouldered man of about 30. Light hair. Blue eyes. Square
jaw and strong impassive face. Self possessed, fleet of wit, he
looks more like an athlete than crook. He is framed by a
murderer, extracted from the plight by The Shadow, gets
reputation of a two-gun killer. Very false. Shadow promptly
recruits him as his eyes in the underworld. At end of novel, Cliff
marries Arline. Last name not given. Marriage is mentioned in
a later novel, then ignored. Cliff spend a great deal of time
drinking in underworld dives. Rotten home life.

Rutledge Mann: Another Claude Fellows in all but name. Of
formerly wealthy family. Established brokerage business. It
failed during the crash. At point of suicide, Mann found himself
confrounted by the figure in black and the usual offer: money
and friendship for full obedience. Agreeing, he finds he has a
checking account and an investment business in Room 909 of
the Badger Building. Mann retains membership in the Cobalt
Club. Grows methodical, fat, incurious. Mind is shrewd and his
knowledge of New York's financial world grows exhaustive.
His office provides a central rallying place for agents, although
Burbank gradually assumes all immediate coordinating and
contact responsibilities.

These men complete the immediate recruitment of agents.
For more than a year, no one will be added to the organization.

The Crime Cult (July 1932): Staid American businessmen in a
Cult of Kali worshippers. The villain sears his victim's
foreheads with a red-hot seal. Joe Cardona wears a luxuriant
false beard. And the heroine drinks a glass of hashish which puts
her in a remarkable frame of mind. The Shadow dominates the
finale, seated on a throne with the dead strewn before him.
After which a raging gun fight in a temple exterminates the
Cult and glorifies the NYPD.

The Blackmail Ring (August 1932): A story of numerous

incidents, characters, scenes, and violence. The hero falls prey
to a benign old man and his peculiar servant. Unbenignly, they
leave him to burn in a flaming old house. Vincent saves him.
From there, plot after plot, as a major blackmail ring endlessly
prepares for operations on an immense scale. But there comes a
chilling chuckle from the shadows and they die, all of them.[20]

This story marks the transition from Gibson's early period into
the mainstream of his work. After "The Blackmail Ring," the
stories were planned out, rather than being improvised, more or
less, as events rushed by.

Through these first novels, Gibson tumbled out his ideas.
Characters, situations, scenes, story types——a lavish flow of
ideas, turned to stories, on the spot, by Gibson's innate skill at
improvising variations.

In some cases, an idea did not jell. Briefly, The Shadow got at
cross-purposes with the Law. Police captured him; he escaped;
hullaballoo. What worked for The Spider, later, was discarded for
The Shadow; with a few exceptions, he remained a recognizable
adjunct of the Law.

Or the identity matters. Many are tried. But somehow they are
not quite right. The Cranston situation is awkward. But all other
faces seem mere variants of Cranston. Of them all, only Arnaud
persists—and this infrequently.

If some ideas did not work, others worked beautifully. The use
of the "proxy hero" was successful from the beginning. Gibson's
original concept of The Shadow was that of an undisclosed figure,
authoritative and all-knowing, who manipulated the action from
behind scenes. He would appear only at intervals, his force not
seen directly.

This figure would be fleshed out by the reactions of the minor
characters——another way of saying that The Shadow developed
himself.

So weirdly vague a hero would produce a weirdly vague story.
Someone had to carry the action. Thus, the secondary, "proxy
hero."

"He is the person, along with others like him, who is matched
against the villains of the piece, in a theme which is really the
personal saga of that all-important lead character, who is
developed through his influence and action toward the lesser
figures.

"The proxy can be replaced by another, even from the wrong
camp. The unity lies in the lead character's identity with the
plot..." (A Million Words a Year For Ten Straight Years")

The "proxy" carries the overt action. He experiences part,
understands part. The meaning of the whole is concealed from
him—and incidentally from the reader. The proxy may be male or
female, a hero, a crook, an agent. He is another point of view and

his experience makes up the story. Or most of it. Or part of it.

In practice, either The Shadow or Vincent keep stepping forward and usurping the reader's attention. The proxy serves Gibson as a way to get into the story. Once there, the narrative veers away. The Shadow disguised escapes from a trap. Vincent, undisguised, plunges headfirst into a trap. Off we go, tangentally.

The proxy's viewpoint is never maintained from beginning to end. This is particularly apparent in "The Blackmail Ring," when the role of the proxy, Stuart Bruxton, fades completely out. He is removed from the field of action, flown hundreds of miles south. The story proceeds and concludes without him.

As "The Blackmail Ring" shows, Gibson could conjure up hordes of characters and fit adventures to each of them. At worst, so many characters clog the story. At best, they permit a complex story development of three or four separate action lines that weave among each other. Some of the mid-1930's Shadows become as intertwined as voices in a Bach fugue.

With the publication of "The Blackmail Ring," Gibson's initial apprenticeship is over. Now he contracts to provide 24 novels a year. He will, that first year, write 28.[21]

9.

Walter Gibson broadly divides his Shadow writing into three general phases: Formative (1931-1936), Expansive (1936-1941), and Established (1941-1946). Which is to say, First, the period during which basic characters and mechanisms of the series were defined. Second, the period during which Gibson elaborated upon this structure and pitted The Shadow against numerous crime geniuses. And Third, straight sailing on generally unchanging seas.[22]

In his critical study of THE SHADOW MAGAZINE, Will Murray remarks:

"While Gibson's breakdown is accurate, it is a very broad one, and *The Shadow* can be further broken down into phases *within* these three. There are several pivotal points at which the series changes course or redefines itself. These pivotal points— specific incidents or novels——denote distinct editorial periods by which the evolution of *The Shadow* can be precisely demonstrated."[23]

That this long sequence of adventure novels can be classified and studied shocks the ardent reader. In that first hot rush of reading, who thought to analyze? The stories were. They ignited the imagination and burnt along the nerves.

But years later, after the heat and passion grow cold, and the coals go white, there is time for review. The prose is then studied which once was swallowed whole, unanalyzed, for pure delight of reading, that sensuous art.

To this long series, we come again.

We have half a century's hindsight. Old streets rise from darkness. Harsh men work out the tangle of their desires.

The Shadow's figure melts through these, a subtle wraith, slowly modifying as months link to years.

The physical bulk of the series puts it beyond detailed discussion. We can only selectively sample, searching out the heart pulse of that long narrative as it rose, twice-a-month, from ten-thousand news stands across America.

10.

New York City near Prohibition's end.

Plunging, leveling, recovering, plunging, the stock market reels. Unemployment whips men aimlessly about the city. These are not yet the worst days.

Damp subway roar, the odor of unwashed clothing. Jazz in Harlem. Long Island mansions.

Liners hoot in black East River. Clusters of taxi cabs——red, black and white, green. Dress racks thrusting brightly among pedestrians.

A rickety office building on East 23rd Street. Dim movement in its darkness.

Bitter-faced men hunch smoking in The Black Ship, The Pink Rat. Between buildings, littered alleys.

White hands beneath a hanging blue light.

Silence in the gloomy Cobalt Club. At the seedy Spartan Hotel, hard-faced men, dirty floors.

A shapeless form glides night streets. Lights glow dim at intersections. Up edges a window, silently. Eyes flaming from the night, a listening presence.

Trick elevator. Secret door. Moving wall.

Across the floor wavered a blot of shadow.

Grimly mocking laughter fades in darkness.

The paper, he saw with a cold thrill, was now blank, the words weirdly erased.

Evil old men ensnare fine young men. Silent mansions. Dry-faced lawyers. Blunt-faced industrialists. Squinty crooks. Wrinkled inventors.

Strident mockery rose to a crescendo of mirth.

Commissioner Weston says that anybody can wear a cape...

He is said to broadcast from a hidden room. No one has ever seen his face.

Dead men seated around a table.

The Cobra. The Crime Master. Charg. Cryo. Zemba.

The power of The Shadow preserves the balance between Law
and Crime.

Penetrates hidden schemes. Punishes those too powerful for the
Law to punish.

As Cranston departs for a forgotten meeting as Weston fumes.
As in the gloomy house terror. And suddenly white flashlight
beam the sapling pulls loose hurling The Shadow doom
thundering freight. Racing cars, black autogyro rolling gun
fights hordes shot dead killed executed punished creepy laughter
The Shadow's justice.

Like a knell.

11.

Now The Shadow plunges confidentally into that most difficult
profession—pulp magazine hero.

The action flicks from place to place: San Francisco,
Philadelphia, Moscow, Atlantic City, Germany, Cuba. A curious
internationalism.

In each locale, The Shadow speaks every language as a native.
His Russian is impeccable. His Chinese dialects, as if home
grown. And French. And Spanish. And German.

Each foreign adventure further reveals his abilities.In "The
Romanoff Jewels," he is intimately familiar with Moscow and
Paris. He strides familarly through Havana ("The Shadow's
Justice," April 15,1933). Elementary complexities of currency
conversion fail to daunt him. Nor is he dismayed by steamship
and railroad schedules.

The Shadow's Justice (April 15, 1933): begins in a decaying
New York City mansion, where a dying multi-millionaire has
set up a cryptic inheritance arrangement. Thereafter, crime
swirls up. The Shadow battles it from Cuba, across the high seas to
the Big City, to the wilderness. After plots and counterplots,
attacks and counter-attacks, the villain gets the hero and
Vincent and the hidden mine full of buried treasure. But
passages, shoots the mobsters unmercifully. The survivors die
beneath loaded mine cars. And "Justice" is equated with
"Death".

Novel stacks on novel. Each reveals The Shadow master of
more   specialized   knowledge.   The   cumulative   weight   is
staggering. Not to put it too finely, The Shadow Knows.

He knows intimate details of Houdini's stage magic. He slides
from a trick packing case ("Dead Men Live," November 15, 1932).
Demonstrates the escape from the Chinese Torture device
("Green Eyes"). Understands the gimmicks associated with the
fake medium racket ("The Ghost Makers").

Instantly, he recognizes a Mexican God's face ("Six Men of

Evil," February 15. 1933). Detects spurious coinage ("The Silver Scourge," July 15, 1933). Is versed in Zeppelin construction and flight path analysis ("Murder Trail," March 15, 1933). Nor do Chinese death traps conceal their secrets from him ("The Grove of Doom," September 1, 1933; "The Living Joss," July 1, 1933). Nor secret poisons ("The Creeping Death," February 15, 1933). Nor trick rooms ("Mox," November 15, 1933).

Equally extraordinary is his penetration into human motives. The reader may be addled by those sudden veers in the story when noble characters become fiends and grinning crooks change to pals of justice. By unlucky chance, the reader may somehow misread the story and be deceived. The Shadow, never.

His performance is dazzling. But no more so than his razoring through those plots that tie, with secret cords, high society with low.

Here, pasty-faced mobsmen, lumpy with guns, mutter over whisky, their manner furtive, their surroundings noisome.

There, jowled business kings, embedded in cigar smoke, boom heartily in walnut-paneled rooms, their mansions opulent, their speech of millions.

These worlds ram together in each novel: the underworld and the privileged world; the black and the gold.

In New York City, it is the difference of one street. In THE SHADOW MAGAZINE, the difference is one paragraph.

Between these worlds, The Shadow slips silently. Down those mean streets, his life is forfeit. Once gangland held him myth. But now he is known as a menace, a hated foe to be gunned on sight.

"Death To The Shadow" is the rallying cry. As once, over the East Side, rang the cry, "Death To The Gray Seal," earlier, "Death to Nick Carter and His Crew."

Some cries seem hereditary.

Hidden Death (September 1932): Letters to Headquarters announce murder. Men die and die. But how? Even the clever consultant to the police is baffled. Commissioner Weston bellows and fumbles. The Shadow, investigating, becomes a nuisance and is lured to a deadly gangland trap, 10,000 pistols cocked for him. Futile. He glides out, guns hot, and shortly all sorts of clever death mechanisms are revealed. The murder master tries a final trap, hoping to obliterate Weston and Cardona, as a start. But it fails, he dies, and The Shadow laughs.

Dead Men Live (November 15, 1932): A band of fiends, snaffling rare inventions, inject the inventors with sinister serum. This causes them to become as dead inventors. Headquarters is in a weird old castle place. The Shadow investigates. Cliff Marsland investigates. After violent action with the fiends' weird gang, The Shadow is presumed dead. Marsland is exposed as a Shadow agent. His doom is nigh. And Cranston, shot full of serum, is thrust into a padlocked box and carried to the castle. Can this be the end? No——only suspenseful sleight-of-hand. The Shadow appears where helpless Cranston lay. With Marsland, he proceeds to shoot the fiends to rags and the story concludes happily——everybody dead.

Repeated failures only whet gangland ferocity.

The Shadow's Shadow(February 1, 1933): Crime leaders seek a fortune in diamonds. To steal safely, they must eliminate The Shadow. How to locate him? Guided by a clever Continental adviser, they decide to send him a letter, via a corpse. A clever underworld tracker follows the letter through Vincent and Mann to the Jonas Office building. But The Shadow is neither seen nor deceived. In quick succession, he blasts a Long Island gun trap set for him. Then, as chapters reel, saves the diamonds, eliminates the gang, eliminates the leaders. A real blood bath.

Such battles take their toll.

At the end of "The Five Chameleons" (November 1, 1932), The Shadow is shot down during a savage gun fight underground. So is almost everyone else. Again, during "The Romanoff Jewels," he is critically wounded while fighting a substantial portion of the Red Army. Like most heroes, he heals with abnormal speed, and revives just at a critical moment.

On a few occasions (so early in the series), he is captured. Orientals are rather better at this than Occidentals. Yet capture happens seldom and is swiftly over. To hold The Shadow is like catching light. Perhaps he recalls his experiences at the hands of The Black Master. You note that he grows wary, suspicious, and violent.

As adventures pass, The Shadow finds an ever-increasing number of scientific devices diverted to crime's use: A drug which, when injected, causes the victim to appear dead ("The Dead Who Lived"); then an amazing poison causing a briskly progressive loss of sensation in the limbs, followed by memorial services ("The Creeping Death," January 15, 1933). Later, intensely poisonous gas enclosed in delicate bubbles ("The Death Giver," May 15, 1933)" The Death Giver, by the way wore a green robe, decorated with skull and crossbones, and colored his face green; he was a sight.

"The Silent Death" (April 1, 1933) was delivered by an electric ray machine, very large, coated with mysterious controls. In contrast, "The Black Hush" (August 1, 1933) is generated by a portable machine,whose projector casts a solid cone of darkness; it cancels all electro-magnetic activity lights, alarm systems, and automobile ignitions.

And high among these extraordinary devices is the machine of the "Master of Death" (September 15, 1933), a sort of super X-ray which throws upon a screen the image of the Master's skeleton, greenly glowing.

During all these adventures, The Shadow gets considerably more exposure than is desirable for "A Weird Creature of the Night". His alternate identities of Arnaud and Cranston are often exposed. All who know swiftly die. Once he is traced to the Jonas office building. His agents show a distressing tendency to capture. Vincent's features and residence at the Metrolite Hotel are known to Diamond Bert Farwell, now tucked away in prison.[24] And since Marsland is repeatedly identified as a Shadow agent, it is an act of God that he survived 1933.

A constant fine rain of facts flesh out The Shadow's personality. His career as a World War I spy is mentioned in "The Shadow's Shadow"——how that daring night-flying ace, The Black Eagle pretended to be shot down over Germany and became a spy. During "Murder Trail," The Shadow——as Arnaud——mentions that he once stowed away on a Zeppelin that was flying a combat strike against London. Before he could sabotage it, a storm drove them back to Germany.

Other details slip in now and again. In "Dead Men Live," we find a description of the device that may——or may not——cause The Shadow to appear faceless:

"The Shadow's hands appeared with what seemed to be a thin mask of wire gauze, no more than a skeleton framework, filled with a few solid patches..."

Fitting this against his face——an action undescribed——he adjusts the mirror and bends forward.

"Into the range of the light came a head and a strange, weird reflection from the mirror. It was the image of a man who seemed to have no face! Guised with the colorless surface of the thin mask, only The Shadow's eyes were visible as they glowed through a plastic mass of grayish hue."(Chapter X)

This is apparently the base upon which certain faces are developed.

By this time, The Shadow uses several continuing identities. One of these is that of a nameless gangster, tall, lean, dirty, wearing a dark sweater.

He also appears as an elderly old boy, Phineas Twambly, who shuffles about, bent over a gold-headed cane. On occasion he can be very spry. At other times, he is terribly hard of hearing or panged with the groans of age. Phineas first appears in "Kings of Crime" (December 15, 1932). He is a specialized identity and used only infrequently. After an extended absence, from the mid-1930's to the mid-1940's, he reappears, this time called Isaac

Twambly. (Gibson explains that Isaac is Phineas' nephew, in the smooth way Mr. Gibson has of patching over inconsistencies.

As the series deepens, Cranston appears more frequently on the stage. The interaction between Cranston and high officials of the Police Department begins early. Cardona meets Cranston in "Shadowed Millions," and is much impressed. "Cranston", (Cardona thinks) "would have made a great detective".

"The Red Blot (June 1, 1933) describes the first meeting with Commissioner Ralph Weston. (Knowing Cranston's big-game hunting reputation, Weston presses him into service against a holed-up crook.) Soon after, Cranston is Weston's personal friend and wanders vaguely onto the scene of the crime, viewing the body with languid eye.

As Weston fumes and Cardona glowers, Cranston glances around, dead-pan as usual. He may drawl a few idle words:

CRANSTON: "Of course, Weston, I would not dispute with one who knows crime as well as you. But if you asked for my opinion——"

WESTON: "It would be?"

CRANSTON: "——that any crook clever enough to have perpetrated tonight's crime is merely at the beginning of his schemes." ("The Red Blot")

His indifferent remarks constantly cause light bulbs to flare over official police heads. Yet neither Cardona or Weston really credit Cranston with much more than lucky surmises.

Ralph Weston: First appeared in "Hidden Death." High-handed, pig-headed, domineering, he has the look of a military man. Short-clipped mustache, firm face. Gestures are dynamic: a man of action with little intellectual rigor. He gets on Cardona's nerves at once, although eventually they become friends——after months of seeking results by threatening Cardona with firing or suspension unless results are realized. Weston's outstanding ambition is to be accepted as a member of the 400. He is a snob and shameless social climber and has got himself elected to the Cobalt Club. The Grillroom, there, slowly becomes an extension of the Commissioner's office, to the great annoyance of members. From late 1934-1936 (publication dates) Weston was in charge of the National Police of Garauca, South America, and had to give up his New York City assignment. He later returned to it, becoming steadily more ineffectual and ridiculous as issues passed.

Through the novels pass a trickle of names and faces that will come again. The Italian push-cart vendor, Pietro, plays a minor role in "The Silver Scourge" (July 15, 1933) and will be seen again. Only one new agent develops, however: Doctor Rupert Sayre, who makes his initial appearance in the September 15, 1933, issue, titled:

Master of Death: Death. Death. Death. Death by carbon-
monoxide ice. By artifical fever ray. Cardona sees and understands nothing. But the Shadow knows that somewhere a mad
killer is perverting medical technology to criminal ends. One
day a doctor in peril speaks with his friend, Dr. Sayre.
Attempting to help, Sayre is abducted by stony-faced criminals,
their brains numb. They serve suave Eric Veldon, who
threatens Sayre with a hideous fate unless he performs illegal
brain operations. Or is it Veldon——this gesturing green
skeleton that speaks from the super X-ray machine screen. And
Cliff Marsland is to be the first brain operation. But then, as a
tip sends Cardona and men to batter down Veldon's front door,
Cliff and Rupert make their break. All are trapped, after
battling the brainless minions. Doom impends. Then Veldon
sees The Shadow for the first time——and is shot dead on the
instant. "Fiend versus Shadow. That had been the climax. The
Shadow had gained the triumph." Zowie.

In "Treasures of Death" (December 15, 1933), Sayre discovers
that The Shadow is Cranston——or sometimes Cranston. This
happens when The Shadow gets full of holes and needs a doctor.
Thereafter, Sayre becomes an occasional agent and tends The
Shadow and his men for the balance of the series.

12.

"...The Shadow was always in a state of flux or new
development. I used to sweat over the plots but once formulated,
I enjoyed the writing and seldom encountered an impass."[27]

Constantly varying stories, all different, all the same. A
continuous rain of incident, people, scene. Calculated efforts to
surprise the reader, to evoke atmosphere, to conceal the story's
true thrust.

If the story is one of mood, the "mysterioso atmosphere" is
plastered on with lavish hand:

"The candles, too, added gloom to the gallery...A full hundred in
number, these candles threw a weird light throughout the room.
To offset the darkness in the center, a candelabrum had been
placed upon a long table..."

"Then, from unseen lips, came the sound of an eerie laugh that
chilled the listeners. The sinister mirth broke like a crashing
wave. The candle flames seemed to waver as the burst of
ghostly mockery swept through the gloomy hall.

"As the laugh died, weird echoes took up the cry. The sardonic
tones reverberated from the very walls of the room, coming in
breaking waves that might well be the merriment of a horde of
invisible demons." ("The Ghost of the Manor," June 15, 1933)
Pure Gothic revival.

"Long Island sound lay blanketed with a dense, sullen mist. From the shore, the heavy fog appeared as a grimy mass of solid blackness. The scene was one of swirling, impenetrable night, for not a gleam of light disturbed that omni-present darkness. "No eye could have discerned the spot where shore ceased and water began. The rocks beside the beach were invisible, and so was the man who stood near them..." ("The Grove of Doom," September 1, 1933)

Build-up of the atmosphere is deliberate, elaborate, rich as German gravy. The density can grow suffocating. It overwhelms modern palates, accustomed to the spartan simplicities of Hemingway-like prose. Gibson's sentences thicken with night. Deep sonorities tremble in them and cadences that evoke menace rising, expanding. This prose is troubled and filled with unease.

At worst, it parodies itself and waddles in a wheeze of fat adjectives. At its best, a scene grows steadily deeper and more terrible, apprehension raised to art.[26]

Other stories play with devices, situations, mixing the mundane with the bizzarre.

Circle of Death (March 1, 1934): The master criminal directs death by color signals displayed on an electric sign. His murder squad is composed of such unusual folk as soda jerks, hotel doormen, street salesmen, and window demonstrators. After numerous chapters, this group is wiped out almost to the man as The Shadow fights in through them to the master at the center of the web.

The Tower of Death (May 1, 1934): is a marvelous murder mechanism that swallows the cast methodically, one by one. Until it swallows Cranston, who is reincarnated in black...

The Key (June 1, 1934): Action from New York to South America and back again. Senor Mendoza (The Shadow) performs subtle wonders on the high seas. While, back in NYC, a secret fiend kills and kills at a group of lawyers, and steals the hidden funds, and other crimes. He finally dies of bullet holes. The novel contains an interesting two-page sequence showing Burbank coordinating the agents while The Shadow is out of the country.

The Crime Crypt (June 15, 1934): The Shadow traces a series of robberies/murders back to a secret room underground. Cliff Marsland infiltrates the gang, is trapped, is saved, as creepy laughter pours from a purloined mummy case.

Spoils of The Shadow (September 1, 1934): The Shadow pre-empts a criminal plot by stealing the loot, himself, before the thieves arrive.

Murder Marsh (October 1, 1934): Back to the creepy old house in the swamp. Outside a pack of disguised crooks. Nearby, a sinister fellow lurking in the woods. Around, a half crazy professor seeking the will-o-wisp. Harry Vincent, highly ineffective, has to be rescued as often as a heroine.

While these varied activities proceed, amid a constant roar of guns and thudding of bodies, The Shadow is meeting new breeds of criminal leader. Some hide themselves. Others mutter in the darkness. Still others don peculiar costumes, hissing and clanking menacingly. All are first-carat geniuses. Their executive ability is extraordinary. Their schemes tower. Their ambitions drink the ocean. Foresighted, ruthless, they customarily deal in mass murder, mass robbery. They coordinate armies of killers. They coat New York streets with the dead as other men salt potatoes.

"Grey Fist" (February 15, 1934) grips New York City, welding the underworld to a unit, his baleful influence everywhere. He sets a trap of immense proportions for The Shadow. Drops a corpse at the sanctum door. Turns out the entire underworld to obliterate The Shadow——and almost succeeds. "The Black Falcon," (February 1, 1934) kidnaps Cranston; that's his first mistake. He pays for it with his life.

"The Cobra" (April 1, 1934) wears a snake costume and hisses and shoots mobsters dead. This is not to destroy organized crime, as the police think, but to destroy the leaders, so that all will rally to the Cobra's cause. "The Crime Master" (August 1, 1934) is a weird old genius whose criminal hordes perform to tight plans. He factors in movements of the good guys and the bad, tracking them on an immense transparent checkerboard overlaying a map of the city. After his mobs are dispersed by that fierce fighter from the dark, the Crime master factors in The Shadow and lays a trap and so forth. The usual happens to him, after a novel of unrelenting action.

"Charg, Monster" (July 1, 1934) hunches behind a translucent screen. Terrible forces are his to command. His victims are mauled; his vengence bloody. The Shadow tracks Charg to his lair, and plunges into a dreadful trap——two killing things of steel stalk him in a closed room. Bullets bounce from them. They clutch at any motion. Escape is impossible. And yet....

Strong action in these stories. They hustle around, banging. Repeatedly, whole armies of gunmen stop whatever they are doing to charge about seeking The Shadow. His death is their top priority.

Frequently now, The Shadow is the focus of the action. The proxy hero is used less frequently. The story lingers over criminals planning. The Shadow strikes. The crooks react and the aides, involved, fumble, are trapped, bravely face death. Then The Shadow's last moment counter-stroke. End scene: New scene begins: Crime prepares once more...

Between violent peaks, the characters talk and spin their webs. After they finish the night's plotting, Gibson recaps. What did it all mean? What will be The Shadow's role? Who why are these what?

Then gunfire again. The bold narrative races onward.

The published sequence of novels seems God-given and inevitable. It is not.

The sequence, as published, differs greatly from the sequence in which the novels were written. There is approximately a six-month lag between time of manuscript submittal and magazine publication.[27] The novels were published more or less in sequence until 1934. Then the order became increasingly broken. (The most significant early exception is "The Grove of Doom," which was written immediately after "The Shadow's Shadow" but published seven months later.)

Through 1935-1936, the as-written sequence is badly scrambled. Gibson was so far ahead in the writing that a bulk of stories was available. The editor could schedule novels of contrasting mood and theme, providing constant variety.

This scattering must be allowed for. It masks the development of the character, as this proceeded in Gibson's head. Major variations in the sequence of written novels continues until 1941. Generally, successful novels appear in clusters, spread over several months as Gibson exploits an idea. Then will follow two or three more routine productions, that, in turn, are followed by another excellent group.

In one brief period, for example, from mid-April to the end of June, 1933, Gibson wrote:

Gray Fist
The Wealth Seeker
The Black Falcon
The Crime Crypt
The Embassy Murders
The Cobra

The first and last stories are superior, and the others of more than usual interest.

From September to early December, 1933, he wrote:

Gypsy Vengeance
The Crime Master
Charg, Monster
Chain of Death
The Key
Spoils of The Shadow
Crime Circus   ·
The Garaucan Swindle

Three fine stories, two routine, three above average. Then the
quality of the stories drops sharply until mid-1934, when new
energy returns to the series and again it flowers profusely.

It should be noted that amid the dreary stretches of "Murder
Marsh," "The Four Signets," and "The Blue Sphinx," appear
single stories of considerable effectiveness: "The Death Sleep,"
"The Chinese Disks," "The Dark Death," and "Crooks Go
Straight," are all from this period.

Crooks Go Straight (March 1, 1935): And which of two
criminals released from jail is going back to crime, the tool of
the usual supercriminal? You'd never guess, unless you were
aware of Gibson's penchant for calling black white. The
Shadow is trapped by a gloating supercriminal who does not
wear a mask. Exposed as Cranston, tied hand and foot, nailed
into a packing case, The Shadow is to be riddled by a whole
basement full of thugs. But he escapes. Ending in a typical
slaughter.

The Dark Death (originally "The Black Death") February 15,
1935. A weird inventor has created a machine which,
accidentally, kills all people of even moderately dark skin. A
slick criminal promptly steals the machine, sets it up here, sets
it up there, and kills kills kills to steal steal steal. Swarthy Joe
Cardona comes within a breath of leaving the series. He is
saved, and all those associated with the machine get theirs.

The Chinese Disks (November 1, 1934): Diamond Bert Farwell,
jailed at the end of *The Living Shadow,* is about to get out of the
pen. Already his symbols, coin-sized disks engraved with a
Chinese character, circulate through the underworld. Farwell
has built a huge organization. To meet this challenge, The
Shadow recruits a number of unlikely aides. He needs them.
Slick robberies commence. Impregnable private vaults gape
eagerly. Truck-loads of diamonds vanish. The Shadow
investigates. Is trapped. Escapes. Traps Bert. Who escapes.
Who is trapped. Who escapes. Then he grabs a million in
diamonds. His mob melts before the bullets of justice and Bert,
his secret identity penetrated, dies at the hands of Lamont
Cranston, or a reasonable imitation.

The "Chinese Disks" is one of the major watersheds of the
Shadow series. It draws together elements from all over the
published adventures. Diamond Bert, the disguised genius of
crime, Chinese death traps, trick vault grills manufactured like a
device of stage magic, diamond robbery, gun fighting through a
hotel, identity substitution, and——finally——an influx of new
agents.

It is as if Gibson had paused here to take stock of his work so
far. And, after braiding together numbers of sure elements, he

gave the series a massive injection of fresh faces——a tonic for readers, series, and himself,

On the whole, the new agents are a credit to the series:

Hawkeye: First appeared as a reformed crook in the March 15, 1934, *Green Box.*However, his prototype——the clever little crook who sees everything and can track even shadows——has been in the series from the first issue. Personally, Hawkeye is a little frail fellow. His face, prematurely old, is sallow, wrinkled. His eyes are beady, quick. So are his wits. He is clever, fast, accurate with a gun, and much afraid of The Shadow.

Tapper: Also first appeared in "The Green Box". Tall, thin, reformed ex-crook. A highly skilled lock man, and an excellent safecracker. He appears irregularly in the series and is not of major importance.

Pietro: First had a walk-on part in "The Silver Scourge." A sharp-eyed, street-wise fruit vendor——he pushed a wheeled cart, Very Italian. He is used chiefly for stake-outs, since he is hardly mobile or even lethal. The Shadow once saved his life from thugs and, therefore, feels he can lay a mild claim for Pietro's aid. It isn't much. He appears now and then, but fades after 1935.

Jericho Druke: One of the happiest additions to the series. Jericho is an enormous negro, immensely strong. Built like a land cruiser, he is used in jobs requiring flat raw violence, or long stake-outs, or penetrations of those occasional gangs involving dark-skinned men. Jericho's fighting technique is relatively simple—grab two opponents and bash their heads together. He is cheerful enough, smarter than admitted, and very dark. His virtues are often qualified by the word "African." These obeisances to the 1930's condition satisfied, plus the inevitable reference to white teeth in dark face shining, Jericho is hardly caricatured in the familiar sterotypes. He is treated as a specialized agent and given the proper jobs, with a minimum of pork chop dialogue and yassuh attitudes.

Moe Shrevnitz: With Moe's coming, The Shadow's transportation problem is finally solved. Magazine heroes have to get all over the map,from point to point and back again. Jimmie Dale did it with a private car. The Shadow did it with Stanley. But the limousine stands out. A private taxi is what's needed. So Moe is a welcome addition. A scrappy, smart cabby, he knows the city alley by alley. He is shrewd and impossible to bluff. The Shadow pulled Moe out of trouble, once, when gunmen forced him to drive to the Bronx, then planned to kill him. Moe is small, tough, joins The Shadow's organization willingly.The cab will be in Moe's name, although The Shadow apparently replaces it when it gets overfull of bullet holes or wrecked, which happens about once a story. It is often a deep maroon color. Much later in the series, Moe's name changes to Shrevvy, an unfortunate carryover from the radio program.

The agent-making carries over to the next novel, "The Unseen Killer" (December 1, 1934), when a final new agent is added. He is:

Miles Crofton: the proxy hero of the story——a young war hero, soldier of fortune, flyer. Personally a lean, deadpan fellow, Crofton was accused of commiting a series of murders (while supposedly invisible) in "The Unseen Killer." He had entered The Shadow's service by "The Plot Master" (the story written immediately after "Unseen Kiler.")

In addition to the agents, three other characters have now been introduced:

Slade Farrow: Sociologist. Tall, grim, lean. Seeks first-hand experience with crime and criminals. Has large professional reputation. Unknown outside. By arrangement has himself jailed to study conditions. This man becomes The Shadow's closest friend. He appears first in "The Green Box" (March 15, 1934), with Hawkeye and Trapper, two brands he has rescued from the burning. He later manages a prison island in the Caribbean to which The Shadow sends criminals he has captured or otherwise illegally removed from New York City, Bulldog Drummond did the same thing in *The Black Gang,*and Doc Savage, by this time, was operating on the brains of captured criminals to turn them into law-abiding types. Farrow is the only living person who has been told the real story of Kent Allard——although The Shadow skimped certain details.

Commissioner Wainright Barth: (September 15, 1934) Barth becomes police commissioner after Weston temporarily leaves the series. Barth must be a political appointee. He is tall, stoop-shouldered, with a jutting hawk nose and a bald head fringed by gray hair. He wears a pince-nez. He does not believe in The Shadow, is a first-rate dolt and idiot of the educated fool variety.[28]

Senator Ross Releston: First appears in "The Plot Master" (February 1, 1935). A gray-haired fellow, hardly the typical politician, being dedicated, honest, and interested in the country's welfare. His face is kind, if rugged. He is physically tough. Whenever the story gets near Washington, the Senator appears and The Shadow will undertake several special efforts on Releston's request. He lives at the Hotel Barlingham, Washington, in a special suite of rooms.

All these people enter the series during a relatively brief period. (Refer to Table II.) Moe Shrevnitz is the most important of the group. He appears almost constantly, thereafter. The others, particularly Farrow, Releston, Jericho, appear less often.

Table II——Continuing Characters in The Shadow Series: The Second Wave.

Novel Written	Character	First Appearance
Feb. 1933	Dr. Rupert Sayre	Master of Death
Mar. 1933	*Wade Hosth[2]	Mox
	Sheriff Junius Tharbel[2]	
	Fritz (in person)	The Crime Clinic
Jul. 1933	Slade Farrow	The Green Box
	Hawkeye	
	Tapper	
Dec. 1933	Wainright Barth	The Garacucan
Feb. 1934		Swindle
	Miles Crofton	The Unseen Killer
	Jericho Druke	Chinese Disks
Mar. 1934	Moe Shrevnitz	The Chinese Disks
Sept. 1934	Sen. Ross Releston	The Plot Master
	Insp. Eric Delka	The Man From Scotland Yard
Jan. 1935	Dr. Roy Tam	The Fate Joss
Jul. 1935	Dr. Rodil Mocquino[3]	The Voodoo Master
Nov. 1935	*The Count of Santurnia[2]	The Gray Ghost

*Shadow disguise

At this point, The Shadow series reaches maturity. Ahead will be other changes and a few surprises. A scattering of other agents will appear, another sustaining character or so. There will not be, however, any further upheaval comparable to 1933-1934——not even when Kent Allard appears and the flame again leaps.

13.

Taste vary so strangely that you, fingering through your shining stacks of THE SHADOW MAGAZINE, may feel a throb of doubt that the assessments so blithely set forth in these pages are always correct.

You may be assured as to the excellence of these judgments. Penetrating, accurate, nicely balanced, they are the epitome of critical excellence. With all due modesty, it is admitted that the wisdom contained here is without peer, the insights uniquely infallible.

If, by error, you disagree, you should reconsider your position.

14.

"Lingo" (April 1, 1935) is one of Gibson's finest novels.

Lingo: The Shadow has planned a major campaign to discredit underworld big shots. His small group strikes as an unidentified mob, spoiling coup after coup. After three or four major failures, Rook Hollister—a sort of minor Capone—is on the verge of being rubbed out. Suspecting some sort of plot, he fakes his own murder. Lingo Queed, a linquistic genius and gang figure, stumbles on the murder scene, takes credit for the kill. He seizes power and attempts to direct the gangs—but also fails, for The Shadow strikes each attempt. Hollister, however, has accidentally captured Burke and Vincent. Intends to use them to trap The Shadow. By this time, Hawkeye and Jericho have been installed in Lingo's headquarters. A massive trap is planned in Chinatown to net The Shadow, Vincent being the bait. Instead, the trap backfires. The mobsters are burned down. The Shadow makes a perilous trip between skyscraper tips to rescue Burke. Rook dies at Cardona's hands. And Lingo receives The Shadow's personal attention.

A beautifully paced story, taut, deceptive, continuously interesting. Five story strands are woven together. Effortlessly, you glide from part to part. The complications are so great that Gibson must pause in the middle of the climax to explain what has been going on. This blemishes the climax. But the shock of explanation compensates for the loss in pace.

Now through a long series of stories, The Shadow moves at the height of his power. No longer is he intangible, a gliding blot, a pair of watching eyes. Become a terrible figure, death's image, he strikes without mercy and without warning. Complex schemes crumble before his mind. At the sight of him, men go cold and fall to babbling and stumbling.

The stories reel with action, devices, tricks:

In "Atoms of Death" (July 15, 1935), criminals have got hold of a disintegrator and merrily crime away. "The Creeper" (August 15, 1935) involves a code and some tricky photography and sinister creeping easing sneaking through the familiar dark old house.

"The House That Vanished" (October 15, 1935) tells of a house that literally vanishes——and what happened to all those tough guys who carried big-city crime tactics out into the innocent New York state countryside. Another vanish——as amazing as if it were on stage——occurs during "The Fate Joss" (July 1, 1935), when a two-ton statue just up and disappears. The ending involves a major war between two Chinese armies underground.

"The Third Shadow" (March 15, 1936) tells the remarkable events occuring when The Shadow seems to take to crime. And not one Shadow, but two. Number 1 is called by Number 2, who continues until he has the misfortune of meeting the true original.

More tricky games with identity in "The Man From Scotland Yard" (August 1, 1935). The story introduces red-faced, sharp featured Inspector Eric Delka, New Scotland Yard. Delka and The Shadow get along fine and work closely together. If a case occurs in England or Europe, Delka always seems to be there.

The Chinese Tapestry (November 1, 1935). Another bit of misdirection concerning the not-too-secret message woven into a tapestry. The Shadow knows which statue the treasure is hidden under.

The Python (November 15, 1935) gives The Shadow fits. He seems to be an old-ragged gray-beard. That's what he seems. He signals his hordes via a flickering billboard——a little device we have met before—and organizes his coups wonderfully. The novel was written because readers clamoured for another Cobra.

After "The Third Shadow", The Shadow went traveling. The five novels written from mid-April through June 1935 (and published through 1935-1936) leave New York City and hie to the great world beyond: "Murder Town" (June 15, 1936); "Mardi Gras Mystery" (September 1, 1935); "The London Crimes" (September 15, 1935); "Castle of Doom" (January 15, 1936); and "Zemba" (December 1, 1935).

The London Crimes: Phineas Twambly and Lamont Cranston visit England to help nab The Harvester. This is a slick thief, murderer, impersonator, and tax evader, who is full of tricks. Tries to have Delka killed. Kidnaps himself. Accuses Cranston of being The Harvester. But foresighted forgery, breaking and entering, and safe cracking free Cranston, and the real Harvester dies under British guns.

Castle of Doom: This evil brother and dark giant with a rifle are hard at it, bringing crime to peaceful English countryside. Or maybe they arent'. The Shadow glides around, through, over, and down into a castle at the end of nowhere, until the final shoot-out in a remote cellar under it all.

Zemba (December 1, 1935): The Shadow pitches into France's slickest criminal. The novel, which seems a universal favorite for inexplicable reasons, swarms with Apaches in blackened Paris alleys. No one is who he seems. Even the mark of Zemba—one finger nipped off at the joint—is no certain clue. There is considerable murdering and rushing about quaint Paris streets in quaint Paris taxis, an unbreakable alibi based on train schedules, and quantities of rough stuff as three factions battle for stolen military plans.

"The Voodoo Master," written immediately after "Zemba," was published as the March 1, 1936, issue. Dr. Rodil Mocquino, the Voodoo Master, specializes in black magic, hypnotism,, zombies, weird chants, tom-toms, and a swell cult practicing murder for profit. It's all tricked out like a television show.

The Doctor is the first big-time genius to face The Shadow and return. You wonder how he does it, since The Shadow shoots him dead at a range of three feet. The body afterward gets dumped in the river. Yet there in the final paragraph it clearly states:

"The weird Voodoo Master was to return again to menace The Shadow, and civilization..."

To this point, no major villain had survived close quarters with The Shadow, But somehow Mocquino managed. He reappeared in the admirable "City of Doom" (May 15, 1936) and once again was apparently dispatched from this life. After a long absence, he returned for the final effort in "Voodoo Trail," (June 1, 1938).

This final story is a joy and a delight. All restraints are removed. Through purple fields, Walter Gibson capers, his hands overflowing with zombies and fire rituals and black magic. Braving a peril a paragraph, The Shadow battles to a roaring climax in which more ammunition is exploded than at the Normandy invasion.

Mocquino is the first of several larger-than-life series villains. These appeared at spaced intervals: Shiwan Khan (1939-1940), Benedict Stark (1940), and The Wasp (1940-1941). They command bulge-eyed killers and all the money in the world. Their crimes are lurid and frequent. True, their schemes have a tendency to collapse on page 85, but this never deters them for long. Again and yet again they return with more killers, more plots, more plans.

At the time Dr. Mocquino appeared, it seemed that every single-character publication stood neck deep in series villains. Through OPERATOR 5, G-8, THE SPIDER, these resilient fiends hustled, blowing up cities, and frying babies. The Shadow's opponents were less gaudy. Uninterested in mere blood wallows or spending their treasure for sadistic displays. they wished only to make a profit or enslave the world. Nice homey justifications. It never entered their heads to kill half a city in order to rob the remaining half. That was stupid business.

Series villains were good business. Their function and justification was to keep the readers interested, bless them. Precisely the same reason, you see, that sent those constant changes sparking through THE SHADOW MAGAZINE.

15.

As we have seen, THE SHADOW remained constantly in flux. No other magizine made so determined an effort to hold reader interest.

That it all hung together so well was a tribute to the accuracy of Gibson's memory, and to his habit of re-reading each novel as it was published. Occasionally, when oppressed by a relentless need for ideas, he reread earlier novels, a habit which accounts for the return of such ghosts as Diamond Bert Farwell.

You wonder that he went to such lengths. The pulps were never famous for consistency. After 1936, some of the major single-character series—particularly THE SPIDER and THE PHANTOM DETECTIVE—reeled through grotesque gaffs and out-of-character behavior. This was caused by heavy doses of new and uninformed authors takng up the series. It is not noted that readers raised much protest.

Of course, the average reader had little access to earlier issues. Some dedicated few zealously hoarded their complete runs. Others traded with friends, or rummaged in second-hand stores on the scabby side of town. And a few who could laugh at cost, secured back issues at 15¢ a copy, direct from Street & Smith.[29]

But only the most dedicated reader actively searched out back issues. You knew that numerous Shadow novels had once existed. But they were remote as the Pearly Gates. Their utter inaccessibility lifted them towering in your mind. While you never expected to read them, mention of those vanished titles in "The Pulse of the Nation" (a department featuring letters from Shadow Club members) filled you with awe:

> I have been reading THE SHADOW MAGAZINE for three years and think it is the best magazine of all. I hate crime and want to fight against it like The Shadow. My favorite stories are "Gypsy Vengence," "Bells of Doom", and "Death Rides the Skyway." I also thought "The Creeper" was great.
> The Shadow really proves that Crime Doesn't Pay. Enclosed is ten cents for the Shadow Club emblem. I will wear it and tell others about it.
>
> Chris Lindsey

"Bells of Doom," you said. And heard their omnious booming from some distant world. Never did you expect to read the story. It remained abstract and glorious, a 10¢ Avalon glimmering out there, forever mysterious.

For the most part, then, readers were bound to the present. They read casually and, it's suspected, without much discrimination. It was appropriate, since the pulps were the epitome of casual literature. All were published to fill the moment.

Read one time and scrap.

"Trade Back Issues 2 for 1 At Wooda's Magazine Exchange"

A pulp magazine was published, read, discarded. Not often was it preserved for re-reading, few enough people being cursed by the need to mound up issues against the coming night. The pulps embodied impermanence. They were not collectibles, as we known collectibles today. They did not even qualify as examples of the American literary tradition.

They were ephemerals. Most issues evaporated after reading. Who cares where they went. SHADOW, SPIDER, ARGOSY, ALL—STORY DETECTIVE, BLUE BOOK—all of them, existed for brief amusement. If the story lines remained fresh, if the action continued to grip, if new material shed its unexpected silver sheen, then the reader would buy, twice a month, on through the years.

And if the format, exhausted, hardens to predictable fiction, then competitors, wild with excitement, stand waiting to offer *their* disguised heroes with smoking guns, ALL NEW FICTION, DARING, EXCITING, THRILLING.

Walter Gibson preserved his back issues and, with conscious art, introduced into the Shadow's story, a constant flow of new faces, new scenes, fresh tricks, ever more extra-ordinary science-fictional machines, ever more powerful villains.

Constant change——in a high-action format.

The action format, itself, introduced certain peculiar problems.

16.

The 1930's pulp magazine novel was a specialized vehicle. Through it rolled unremitting waves of action——characters in deadly conflict and peril, movement and constant crisis. It portrayed an abrasive existence.

During the early 1920's, the pulp action story had lived less spectacularly, reflecting a more formal novelistic tradition. In these stories, the focus fell on the character: How he performed in the face of danger; how he fought; what he believed in and what he did not. This approach was used by such different authors as Talbot Mundy (the Jimgrin and Tros novel series) and Louis Vance (The Lone Wolf novels). Durng a long series, it was possible that the character would change because of his experience. He might even find love and retire entirely from pulp fiction.

By the end of the 1920's, this older tradition was much eroded. As magazines multiplied, competition pressed with ever more scarlet fang. Routine violence began edging into the stories, accompanied by more realistic dialogue and considerably fewer expressions of noble sentiments. The narrative pace quickened. Weapons flamed more often, and lightly sketched-in people began pounding on each other.

It was as if the dime novels were being reborn.

Through the 1920's, as this metamorphosis was underway, elaborately drawn characters began to fade. Slowly they were replaced by much more limited characters, crisply drawn around two or three strong traits.

Johnston McCulley was a major practitioner of this method.

For two generations, he specialized in heroes whose motives were easily understood by the most opaque mind. Indomitable men, they adventured for fun, justice, and perhaps a touch of profit. Their personalities formed by the second or third story; thereafter, the longest career would not alter them. And they would undergo a constant stream of exciting events.

In the formal sense, these are not fictional characters. Nor do they represent complete human beings. They were never intended to do so. They relate to characters of 1920's fiction as a cartoon relates to a painting. Each character is a bundle of traits. These are carefully selected for maximum sparkle. The glittering whole is outfitted with a name, a gun, and is sent forth, an abstract from reality, to do battle through the double-columned pages.[30]

How perfectly these abstracts support the intricate, violent stories. Hardly ever had there existed such non-political, unintrospective, problem-oriented individuals. They excelled in techniques. Deftly they handle automobiles, automatic pistols, motives. No sense of inadequacy troubles their minds, nor lack of money their days, nor lack of purpose their souls. They kill without emotional response. Their love is as sterile. They seldom hunger. They achieve without elation. Emotionally, their lives are desiccated sand. In their simple perfection, they swoop through the fiction like children hurtling down a slide's polished face, elated and giggly with adventure.

Rarely do these characters change. However, if particular abilities are required by a story, these are added with the stroke of the pen. Traits are accrued, not earned. The process is entirely effortless, as is wishing.

But a stock of abilities, no matter how lovingly enumerated, is not character drawing. It is inventory.

In the gaudy blaze of action, such matters are not noticed. The characters are exquisitely adapted to the story. How its probability does unravel in retrospect. Yet how it clutches with iron hands while you read.

That the reader's attention is steadily gripped, while his sense of reality is outraged, suggests that the 1930's action story was a more highly evolved literary form than customarily acknowledged. Its faults are immediately apparent. It is emotionally stunted. Its culture is guff. Its relationship to the time's great issues is usually, not always, superficial. In such extreme form as the 1935-1939 single-character magazines, the narrative grows white-hot, violent, insensitive, dedicated to nothing more subtle than movement and deadly confrontation. In these stories, the characters become mere decals.

On the other hand, the action story speaks eloquently of selflessness and personal sacrifice. It enshrines knowledge for its ɔwn sake, and professionalism for success. Customarily, it emphasizes ethical commitments to social stability and equal advantage for all men. Although often bloodily obvious, the action story constantly makes value judgments that are far more restrained and conservative than the livid textual material. The single-character action story does not, as many feared, incite the reader to violence. Rather, it incited him to excellence. The form was rude but the intent impeccable. As an art form, the pulp action story is flawed. But it is not entirely without value.

17.

Partners of Peril(November 1, 1936): "You will die this evening," says the note. And the victim dies. As does the next. Cardona weaves all the wrong theories. But the Shadow traces evidences of subtle murder, although the police chase him more frequently than the real, hooded killer. Harry Vincent, trapped and clamped into a truth machine, is about to babble forth secrets best left silent. Just in time, The Shadow appears. Blasting gunfire wrecks the secret underground laboratory, embellished by a flock of crooks and a pool of acid. The trail leads to a chemical factory and a secret formula for poison gas. Murder strikes. The Shadow, accused, flees in broad daylight, commandeering a train. This promptly blows apart and he is believed atomized. And now the killer fiend runs amok, capturing The Beautiful Girl, and Cardona, and poor Vincent, still again. Blood flows. Sadistic blows. Cruel devices. Cruel mouths twist cruelly. At the last possible instant, The Shadow saves everyone from everything. The fiend is blown to bits——and the real fiend is exposed. It was all caused by greed, that deadly sin.

"Partners of Peril" breaks the long run of Gibson novels. It appeared without warning, to Gibson's vast astonishment. No one had quite got around to telling him that another writer would be contributing occasionally to the series.

The writer was Theodore Tinsley, who would, from 1936-1943, write 27 of The Shadow's adventures:

"...I appeared on the scene because ot the feeling at S&S that if Walt Gibson in a fit of absentmindedness walked in front of a speeding taxicab, it would be handy to have another goodlooking, cleancut 'Maxwell Grant' ready to present a masterpiece tailored to the image and likeness of the Founding Father. In this I may——and will———say that I did a pretty damned good job in all."[31]

Theodore Tinsley, born 1894, was a native New Yorker. Graduated from City College (Liberal Arts degree), he edged into pulp writing during the late 1920's. First selling to ACTION

STORIES and other Fiction House publications, he became a
BLASK MASK contributor in 1932. Among other work in 1934-
1935, he wrote one or two Shadow radio scripts. In early 1936, at
the request of John Nanovic, he began writing Shadow.

"...I did what seemed to me a logical and simple preparation for
the deal. I got hold of three or four of the early Shadows and
read them carefully for style and content. I listed all the
characters, checked on the method of narration, noted all the
fashions (for example, the atmosphere and coloring of the
routine 'Sanctum' scenes), and then consciously wrote in the
style, manner and color of Walt Gibson. I did this because Walt
had established the setup, and because Nanovic liked what
Walt did to the hilt, and because Nanovic, a canny editor knew
exactly what he wanted; and that is what I tried to give him.
Never once did I think of 'pleasing the reader'. All I wanted to
please was Nanovic. A good editor knows exactly what will
please *his* readers, and if he guessed wrong he won't last long
with the publishers. Nanovic *did* know and he *did* last long..."[32]

During the years that he was writing Shadow novels, Tinsley
also contributed short stories to THE WHISPERER (Bulldog
Black series) and CRIME BUSTERS, later MYSTERY (Carrie
Cashin series).

In 1943, when wartime paper shortages caused sharp cutbacks
in the pulps, Tinsley left pulp writing for a job in the Office of War
Information. After the war, he worked for the Veteran's
Administration as an information and speech writer. In 1960 he
retired and took up residence in Auburn, Alabama. There he died
in 1979.

Tinsley's first novel, "Partners of Peril," closely followed the
Gibson manner. Much closer, in fact, than in later issues. Even in
this first story, certain situations, actions, events appear that will
become characteristic Tinsley trade marks. These promptly
identify him in later novels.

A Tinsley story habitually contained considerable blood-
spilling, torture scenes, escapes by a hair, sexual menace, trial by
fire and water, railroad scenes, vast underground lairs, and
criminals improbably tricked up in costume.

Gibson used some of these elements occasionally; Tinsley used
all of them constantly.

He drew liberally from the pulp writing conventions of the mid-
1930's. These were steadily moving from the rather sober Street &
Smith atmosphere, still influenced by DETECTIVE STORY
MAGAZINE and Gibson's tightly atmospheric plots, to the
excesses of the Thrilling and Popular publishing groups—more
passion, endless action and violence, lose or inconsistent plots
serving forth endless sequences of bloody foam, in worlds remote
from conventional cause and effect. Although patterned upon

Gibson's format, Tinsley's narratives are closer in spirit to Norvell Page's Spider novels.[33]

In addition, Tinsley brought to the single-character pulps a hardboiled strain direct from BLACK MASK.

This appears immediately, if never for long. In one brief scene from "Partners of Peril," two hard cases give the heroine her choice: either give up the envelope that they want or they'll tear off her clothing until they come to the envelope. The scene has a true BLACK MASK glitter. For a moment, the sentences ring shrilly crystalline, stripped of sentiment. Then the prose tone softens again to the more normal single-character sound—— which had little to do with contemporary speech rhythms or realistic attitudes.

This scene was, incidentally, the first time in the history of THE SHADOW MAGAZINE it had been suggested that women possessed a removable outer layer. Or that men thought about such things.

A second Tinsley contribution was a strong sexual element:

Lascivious: "She drew her magnificent evening gown slowly over her head... She allowed her gauzy underthings to slide lazily to the floor. Staring at her slim smoothness in the bedroom mirror, she felt better." ("The Golden Dog Murders") As did all her vicarious watchers.

Suppressed Passion: "Gently, she pushed him away, her bosom heaving under the thin silk of the house coat." (Also "The Golden Dog Murders")

Hardly Suppressed Passion: "His hand caressed her pliant figure." ("River of Death")

Shameless Behavior: She was "Crouched almost nude in the...parked coupe..." ("Double Death")

Not only were women decorative figures clad in revealing flimsy, but they actively entered the plots——as heroines, as wicked blond girls, as misunderstood molls, as deadly murderesses.

Frequently two women star, of contrasting hair color and temperment. One, the good girl, usually a brunette, is sweet, delicately scented, mildly daring. The other, the girl of tainted background, is usually blond, almost always of a lower class; gaudy and tough-natured, she usually loves an unrepentent crook.

Numerous variations spin out.

Two girls become desperate enemies ("Foxhound," January 15, 1937). Or, after lurid adventures, they become friends and assist The Shadow ("The Pooltex Tangle," October 1, 1937). Or the bad girl loves the murdering fiend and gives the good girl fits ("Double Death," December 15, 1938). Often the bad girl dies in the terminal holocaust.

To vary matters, the bad girl is sometimes killed before the story ends ("River of Death," March 1, 1939). In still other variations, she kills and kills and kills, hissing like a cat from Hell ("Gems of Jeopardy", September 1, 1941).

To get in advance of our story, slightly, when Margo Lane appeared, in 1941, she took over the good girl role. Thereafter, it became Margo's fate to endure peril and torture at the hands of assorted blonds and red-heads.

Not only did Tinsley feature hardboiled women but, on one occasion, a woman achieved the high position of resident fiend. She appears in "The Golden Dog Murders," (September 1, 1938). She is magnificent, gliding about apparently nude, her body coated with gold paint, wearing a dog's head mask.

By 1939, Tinsley's spicy additions to the magazine's content had created certain problems for any woman venturing into the pages. At some point in the story, she could expect to lose her clothing. Even Gibson began using the situation in his stories, although his nudes, even when gleaming bare, left the impression that they were decently clothed.

The nudity theme, like the torture and sadism themes, reflected outside pressures. These narrative situations had grown popular No SPIDER or TERROR TALES would have been complete without a scene where the heroine, stripped bare, is hung by her eyebrows and whipped with scorpions. THE SHADOW MAGAZINE'S ventures into these dark ways were relatively low-key. In other publications, pitiful girls, disrobed, fled through a wilderness of sexual aggression. This was ingenuously symbolized as flames or killers with spears or machines with numerous sharp points. It was all threat and no rape. But only because such goings-on might have endangered the magazines' second-class mailing permits.

In addition to beefing his novels up with the feminine, Tinsley brought in psychopaths by the score. Some of these were hired men, deadly people whose hands shook when the blood flowed. They beat victims till the bones snapped and brains ran. They gave pain and grinned at injury. These characters stand out from the story with BLACK MASK sharpness and represent a specific element of the hard-boiled narrative method.

They also may be seen as focal points for that agressive rage and anger which lies close to the surface in Tinsley's work. It is as if he repeatedly strikes a taut steel string; its edged shrilling penetrates the chapters.

Like his hired gangsters, Tinsley's villains also shake with blood lust. They are rather more restrained about it—at least, until they adjust their hoods. In civil life, they seem nice enough

fellows, businessmen and civic leaders. Beneath their Kiwanis
smiles, their eyes are polished metal. They must see death. They
must create ruin in the large scale. At the surface, they strike for
millions. But in their molten hearts, only heaps of corpses eases
the burning. They must have death. They must have such power
over others as to give death, or humiliation and then death.

Their schemes spread immensely. They require vastness. Hills
and mountains are hollowed out to receive their secret empires. At
the heart of the buried labyrinth, they nest luxurious, protected by
pitfalls, sliding walls, mobile floors, doom rays, gas projectors.
Down under swimming pools they burrow. They plate vast
caverns with steel. And there, amid their stolen stuff, they scowl
and think and snap forth commands to kill.

No particular effort is taken to make all this realistic. It would
be an impossibility. While Gibson sought to emphasize the reality
of the situation——here is the true secret history of last month's
events on 8th Avenue——Tinsley emphasized narrowly realistic
character traits in situations of romantic fantasty. He pictures
extremes of pathological power seeking, and his major villains
are mad in a mad world they have personally created.

All are brilliant men. They battle The Shadow at equal
intellectual levels. In this point, too, the Tinsley novels differ from
those by Gibson. In Gibson, The Shadow's intelligence is of an
order so high that he has no equals, excepting, perhaps, Shiwan
Khan. Only chance and temporary bad luck evens the struggle.
bad luck events the struggle.

But Tinsley's Shadow is cut from different material.

To begin with, he is a shrewd, sharp-minded daredevil seeking
adventure. Bored by his millions, Lamont Cranston has donned
The Shadow's robes to battle injustice...

Cranston? Well, yes, Cranston. No one mentioned to Tinsley
that Cranston was an assumed identity, even as they forgot to
mention that The Shadow had unmasked as Kent Allard.
(Tinsley learned of this in early 1939, an interesting commentary
on the frequency with which he read Shadow.)

So the Tinsley novels begin mildly skewed from the vertical.
The hero is that familiar figure——a millionaire bored with
tabulating his assets, who has adopted a secret identity and
fights crime by assassination in the streets. The Spider, that is;
The Thunderbolt; Jimmie Dale; the Hooded Nonesuch.

The tradition was familiar enough. Tinsley had grown up in it
and he flowed it naturally out upon the page. From the beginning,
however, Tinsley saw The Shadow as a man, rather than as the
superhuman Justice Figure which had initially occupied
Gibson's mind.

And from the beginning, Tinsley's Shadow is sized as a human
being, only slightly magnified for the medium.

His lot is sudden peril, traps, false positions, unanticipated menaces. From these, he extricates himself, always by superhuman efforts. Dangers come in waves, endlessly pounding at him. Never is he quite set for them. In consequence, he is always on the verge of being overwhelmed.

The miraculous feats——the escapes, the struggles, the warding off instant annihilation, he does all this, barely.

Gibson's Shadow, strikingly infallible, foresees most situations. He assesses beforehand, understands instantly, always holding something in reserve.

But Tinsley's Shadow has no reserve. It is all there being expended to the final atom:

——Blood gushing from wounds, The Shadow staggers forward....

——Half unconscious, The Shadow lurches desperately through a wall of flame...

Slipping, reeling, staggering across disaster's lip, he saves himself. It is a miracle.[34]

By the same miracle, he constantly saves his agents.

The agents never showed any vast ability to take care of themselves under Gibson. They grow even more inept under Tinsley. Vincent and Burke are constantly helpless, the prey of sadists. Burke, in particular, spends his waking hours strapped down, being fried by hot irons and ornamented by knives. Even the sacrosanct Margo receives the hot iron ("Death's Bright Finger," May 15, 1942). And the usually capable Cliff Marsland is hacked upon and hurled from a racing train ("Young Men of Death," April 1943).

This is all part of Tinsley's method. He is telling stories of flaming excitement. Peril links to peril. The narrative flares past, a wild rush of violence and danger. Vincent tortured at the top of an unfinished skyscraper; Mann kidnapped and tortured and not even all The Shadow's resources can locate him. The Shadow, trapped in a steel room, is blasted full of lightning bolts. A flaming wall collapses hurling The Shadow over a cliff into the fanged rocks from which there is no escape.

Or so you would think.

The complex Gibson plot line, multitudes of characters and scenes interwoven with sudden violence, paced with andantes and allegros, becomes, in Tinsley's hands, one single searing line, beginning in violence and rising, violence by violence, to the terminal violence.

The Shadow, operating by instinct, rather than reason, battles through. And in the final seconds, as the gas pours out, as the ray machine swivels, as the bomb clicks...

He escapes. From flame, from water, from the deadly caverns, spiky with guns. Each time he sustains personal injury that would put you or I on the critical list. But The Shadow continues, although sorely wounded, his cloak smouldering, his hands blistered, his hat shot to rags.

Only one cartridge remains. Beyond that door snarl three dozen killers. Behind, the bomb sizzles. Then, as the floor hisses back, The Shadow reels and with one desperate effort....

"If you conclude that writing The Shadow had something in common with slicing well-made bologna in a delicatessen for a customer who knew exactly what size and flavor he wanted—— you may be right."[35]

18.

During 1936, Tinsley submitted his first three novels, "Partners of Peril," "Foxhound," and "The Cup of Confucius" Gibson wrote the remaining twenty-one novels. Among these, three or four are outstanding.

"The Golden Masks" (September 1, 1936) is another criminal brotherhood whose members conceal their crime-bloated faces beneath twisted golden masks. "Jibaro Death" (September 15, 1936) features a tribe of Jibaro Indians loose in New York City; they stalk and kill and slash and once capture The Shadow, who ends tied to a sapling while the Indians cluster around, looking deadly. He escapes by a device so improbable as to cause fits of sneezing; otherwise, it is a first-rate action story.

"The Seven Drops of Blood" (December 15, 1936) are rubies which bring death death death death. For some reason, the story inflamed the readers. Years later, they were writing in to the magazine and citing that story among the greats. In the face of this immense public outcry, only a hard head would suggest that the story is not quite.... Well.... Still....

During 1936, the action is implacable. The stories move. The Shadow whirls from one violence to the next. Not quite as deadly as formerly, he takes more than his share of licks on the head, stumbles in the dark, near misses in combat's heat. The "mysterioso" atmosphere is not so dense; the prose seems lighter and whisks smoothly along.

Far and far and far has The Shadow come from that weird night figure haunting the early novels. From a half-tangible terror, an abstraction of death, he has grown visible. Many see him now. He enters partially lighted rooms. He bursts in upon crooks and, in turn, is burst in upon. His figure is known: A terror still, but no longer weird.

To certain individuals, The Shadow has appeared more peacefully. He has the gift of soothing fears, which is a fine gift, and which saved Walter Gibson a world of trouble. A single understanding laugh, and the heart of the most terrified girl melts. A mere flash of his eyes convinces others that he is on the side of the righteous.

To some few, he will even drop the cloak and hat and reveal the Cranston face, not to be thought of five years earlier:

JUDGE NOY: "Who are you? How have you learned all this? "In reply, The Shadow removed his hat and cloak. Judge Noy stared at the features of Lamont Cranston."

JUDGE: "...Wait! I have it! You are Lamont Cranston, whose name was mentioned in today's newspapers."

THE SHADOW: "I have chosen that guise...But when I appeared as you first saw me, wearing the cloak and hat that I have just discarded, I am frequently known as The Shadow."

("Intimidation,Inc.," Dec. 15, 1936)

This is, perhaps, the secret of those stories from the end of The Shadow's Golden Age. Once, The Shadow was The Shadow, a mystery wearing someone else's face. Now the mystery has lessened. Hints of marvels still hang about him. Only slowly will they be dispelled, for he remains immensely able. But that superhuman aura that clung about "The Weird Creature of the Night" gradually fades. The human being shows through.

In the stories of this period, other things show through. Now and again, we detect the dim echoes of other, earlier stories rising—a hint of "The Black Master" in "Vengeance Is Mine!"; a suggestion of "The Four Signets" in "The Seven Drops of Blood"; loud echoes of "The House That Vanished" in "Murder House" and "House of Silence."

But hints only. The ideas contained in earlier stories have kicked off entirely new stories. Incredible, what this master of variation can do with the least scrap of an idea.

With "Crime, Insured" (July 1, 1937), we reach a major transition place in the series. Written during the final weeks of December 1936, the story is one of those turning points, like "The Chinese Disks." Immediately after this, "The Shadow Unmasks" was written and, with that novel, matters changed forever.

Crime, Insured; Each time crooks make a big raid, The Shadow stops them in their tracks. Yet they persist. The Shadow suspects a hidden reason—and so there is: some business-like criminal types are insuring the big jobs. If you fail, you still get paid off. Because of their financial losses, the criminal insurers set about to track down The Shadow and his agents. They spot Harry and Cliff, work out the double Cranston secret, trail one agent to another; locate Hawkeye, Burke, Shrevnitz; learn Burbank's secret phone number. Then close in. At one swoop, the organization is captured. The Sanctum is invaded. Even

The Shadow is scooped up—although the successful raiders do not recognize that. The crooks set The Sanctum back up in a Wall Street skyscraper, 40 stories up. With the help of Farrow, Tapper, Sayre, and Jericho, The Shadow begins a campaign to free his agents and crush the insurance ring. This involves a sub-plot concerning a hoard of cash hidden in an old house. This The Shadow saves for the rightful owners. All the rest is deadly action. The crooks are wiped out and Cardona arrives in time to collect the written confessions. But he misses the Sanctum by minutes; the Shadow's agents have carted it away.

A fascinating novel, rather like a combined "The Shadow's Shadow" and "Gray Fist" carried in another direction. No one penetrates this deeply into the Shadow's organization until Tinsley's final novel of the Benedict Stark series, "The Devil's Paymaster" (November 15, 1940). As far as Gibson is concerned, he has worked this idea to its deeps, and will not use it again.

Another matter concerns him: The revelation of The Shadow's identity.

19.

"Who is The Shadow? Why does he not reveal his true identity? At last he does—only to make himself more mysterious because of it. You'll gasp at the reason, and you'll thrill to the excitement and the danger in "THE SHADOW UNMASKS," in the August 1st issue of The Shadow Magazine."
(Ad copy designed to rouse almost unbearable suspense in the hearts of faithful readers.)

20.

During the Kent Allard years, The Shadow's world undergoes its final change. Later modifications will come, but they are slight by comparison. For the next four years, until the advent of Margo Lane, Gibson will not significantly alter those cogs and wheels whirring behind scenes.
To whet readers' interest, new material had been introduced at least twice yearly—new faces, new insights, new narrative techniques. Major changes, that is. Gibson constantly brought in interesting material—codes, use of Esperanto, adventures at the new locales familiar, at least, to New York City readers. These additions were continuous and deliberate and it is difficult fo find a Shadow which does not contain at least one new twist.
Major changes arrived more sparingly. After the arrival of Tinsley and, perhaps, The Shadow's Island, matters had slicked quietly by for almost a year. Gibson and Nanovic had discussed a

new explosion. Revelation of The Shadow's true identity. The time was never quite right for that. It would represent a major shock and needed to be worked up to, trumpeted and puffed until readers gasped, giddy with anticipation.

Gibson, wrote the story, "The Shadow Unmasks," during the first weeks of January, 1937. With the April 1, 1937, issue, the build-up began, and continued for eight issues.

The Shadow Unmasks; A pack of jewel robbers murder a millionaire each time they strike. Their crimes are directed by coded instructions graven into coins. The Shadow gains a lead to their operation. Then, unexpectedly, the real Cranston is injured in an accident which gets into the newspaper. This astounds Weston, who reads this while Cranston, as he thinks, is standing at his elbow. (Cranston's nephew, really, as he is later led to believe.) While Weston puffs, The Shadow walks into a classy machine-gun trap but leaves the trappers in sorry condition. Then while the crooks prepare for their next job, The Shadow vanishes from New York. He has already analyzed crime's method—which is to sell jewels to one millionaire, then rob them back, killing him in the process, and alter the jewels for the next sale and the next murder. Now Kent Allard, a lost flyer, returns to civilization and a NYC fete. That evening, Allard becomes The Shadow and visits Slade Farrow, where he explains—apparently for the goggle-eyed readers—the true story of The Shadow. There-after these startling revelations, he moves violently against the crooks and wipes them out in around 30 pages.

The story is an interesting, minor effort into which the Kent Allard material is inserted, rather like tomato slices laid into a sandwich. It could be removed from the story without disturbing a comma.

The whole gaudy revelation occupies Chapter XIII. "The Shadow's Story," pages 52-55. In this,The Shadow visits Slade Farrow's apartment, principally because revelations of this type come on better in dialogue and Farrow can ask all those questions that the reader has at the tip of his tongue.

The Kent Allard, who reveals himself to Farrow, is a remarkable fellow:

Kent Allard; His face is long and lean with "firm" eyes gazing beneath straight brows. His is deeply bronzed and has rather a solemn look. He is tall, gaunt. His eyes are clear, deep blue, almost hypnotic in intensity. He moves with a long slow stride, touched by a slight limp in the right leg. In later stories, he becomes brisk, crisp, decisive, quick speaking and quick thinking. On his return, he appears quite wealthy and provides lavish accomodations for himself and the pair of Xinca Indians who are his servants. This will later change.

He is an expert in aircraft technology, as is proper to a famous World War 1 ace.

As Allard explains:

"Winning air battles seemed to come naturally to me; and I gained a preference for night flights. The enemy called me the Dark Eagle. They were glad when they shot down my plane.

"But I was not shot down. I landed by design... Wearing a black garb, I traveled by night, on foot, within enemy's lines. I entered prison camps, yes; but never as a prisoner. I visited them only to release men who were held there, to guide them in their escape.

"By day, I adopted disguises; and, working entirely alone, I contacted our secret agents. That was when I learned my facility for penetrating the deepest schemes...

"I became a roving secret agent..."

He destroys an enemy air base just before the war ends and returns, claiming that he was a prisoner in an enemy war camp. After the war, he continued in aviation, making several long flights:

Allard: "...aviation offered part of the life I needed; but it provided neither the action of battle, nor the keen work of the secret agent. I rejected the idea of becoming a soldier of fortune. I considered warfare an uncivilized institution except when absolute necessity required it.

"...Crime was becoming rampant in America... Underworlds were organized with their own hidden battle lines. Only a lone foe could pierce that cordon; once inside, he would have to move by stealth, and strike with power and suddenness. I chose that mission."

He decides to obliterate his identity:

"I flew South and landed purposely in Guatemala. I spent a few months among the Xincas and gained their friendship."

Then he returned home, adopted Cranston's identity and mansion, and began development of his supporting organization at a crisp pace.

If you have not read those 1931-1932 Shadows, Allard's explanation sounds reasonable. It sounds even more reasonable if you read it very rapidly. To the hot-eyed devotee, however, concentrating on tiny consistencies, the story is sadly loose-jointed. In various important details, it differs from those scraps of history tossed to us, sliver by sliver, during earlier novels.

He gives an entirely new account of how he received the girasol, for instance. Not the least hint does he give concerning the horror face, that fascinating matter. Nor does he mention his service to the Czar.

Indeed, he warily avoids any clear statement about his secret agent activities. It is more than probable that his Russian activities, mentioned in "The Romanoff Jewels," were on the behalf of some nation's intelligence. And, if so, he would have been active several years before entering Russia. Continuing intelligence involvement would explain certain anomalies in his story of combat flying. If he were, indeed, a flying spy (in the G-8 mode), his account of faking a crash behind the German lines makes sense. Otherwise, we must conclude that he deserted in order to conduct his private war. That makes no sense either.

Once you begin poking at Allard's story, it fall into ravelings. But then, it was never constructed to be poked at. It was, after all, wonderful, flowing romance, designed to astound the readers. As before mentioned, the pulps lived in the present. Like a woman with a disgraceful past, they existed without history.

"Dreams," as you recall, "for the average American."

It was not really anticipated that readers would recall details five years old. (Those that did would certainly write.)[36] Consistency would be fine, if it didn't interfere with the story.

So Gibson proceeds through Allard's explanation with a light heart. How smoothly he explains all—and nothing. If inconsistencies appear, brush them aside. Inconsistencies, indeed! This is The Shadow's own real story, told in his own real words.

(For those who enjoy trifling with speculative biography, a possible chronology of Allard's early activities is given in Table III. While the events are possible, they are entirely unauthenticated by either The Shadow or Mr. Walter Gibson.)

TABLE III. An Unofficial Chronology of Certain Major Events in the Career of Kent Allard, The Living Shadow

DATE	HISTORIC EVENT	BIOGRAPHICAL EVENT
1893		Allard born
1912		Enters secret service
1913		Attached to (probably) French embassy in Moscow, where he is able to render a service to the Czar. Use of cloak/hat.
1914	WWI begins	
1915		Enters flying service, becomes famous as The Dark Eagle, and becomes an ace, although main activities are those of an intelligence agent

1916		Goes behind lines in Germany as secret service agent. However, may have been wounded in face at this time.
1918	War ends. Russian Revolution	Destroys German air base. Returns to Allied lines. Meets Cliff Marsland in Paris.
1919	Prohibition begins in US	Remains in Europe. Further intelligence work in Russia, Italy, North Africa, Spain
1920		Allard returns to the US late in the year
1921		No work for ex-pilots. Notes rise of criminal element.
to	1st commercial radio broadcast, in 1922 (Aug.)	Early trials of Shadow garb in Chicago. Meets Cranston. Plans initial Shadow campains.
1923		While flying proposed air mail routes to South America, discovers Xincas of Guatamala. In September returns to Central America, on the trip during which Allard is presumed lost.
1924		Feb: Secretly returns to US, sets up operations in NYC. Early operations in Wall Street. Begins radio work and meets Burbank. Moves into Cranston mansion. Begins recruitment of people for The Shadow's organization, beginning with Fellows.
1926		Recruits Vincent and Burke. Begins investments designed to make him independent of the Cranston fortune.
1927		Fellows murdered. Marsland recruited Meets Cardona face to face
1928		Combat with Hand begins

		Meets Weston
		Recruits Dr. Sayre
		Meets Walter Gibson
1929	The Wall Street Crash	Saves Cranston fortune
1930	*Detective Story Hour* aired	To publicize The Shadow, announces a few radio shows
		Agrees to give S&S and Gibson access to his archives
1931	First issue of The Shadow magazine	Meets Slade Farrow, Hawkeye, Tapper
1932		Massive agent recruitment. Establishes island for reformation of criminals under Farrow.
1933	Chicago World's Fair ends Prohibition	Visits France
		Final member of Hand killed
1934		Battles Mocquino and Shiwan Khan
1935		Shadow conducts major attack on NYC rackets
		Meets Myra Reldon
1936	Italians invade Ethopia	Allard returns
		Agreement between Allard and Gibson to allow Tinsley limited access to archives
1937		Meets Margo Lane. Fictionalized radio programs underway.
1939	WWII begins	Death of Shiwan Kahn and Benedict Stark
1940		Chance LeBrue recruited.
1941		Myra Reldon becomes full-time agent
Thereafter		Unrecorded war investigations. In 1946, Gibson leaves S&S. Elliott draws on imagination for Shadow adventures. Nothing known of 1950's operations. Adventures in

1960's fiction, except one case recorded by Gibson.

For the next two years, Allard novels pour forth. Almost, Cranston is forgotten. Allard at once assumes all Cranston's advantages and privileges—membership at the exclusive Cobalt Club (the average wait for membership was ten years), immediate friendship with Commissioner Weston, access to all those wealthy social levels which greeted Cranston, and an apparently unlimited bank account.

Poker-faced, reserved, impeccable in his tuxedo, Allard was hard to distinguish from Cranston. To summarize differences: He was brisker than Cranston; his face was leaner; he had a pair of Xinca Indians to tend to his wants; he limped slightly, this being part of his cover story that he had crashed in Guatamala, broken his leg, set it himself, gained the Indians' confidence, and so for twelve years reigned as the white god of the tribe—a wonderful story.[37]

In the 1937-1938 novels, then, you may write either Allard or Cranston. Makes no difference; the latest adventure's the thing:

Death Turrets (November 1, 1937): It's a weird old place, half a castle, way out among the farmers. Outside, rain pours down. Inside, murder—a killing fiend slaughters one after the other. The sheriff makes sensible noises. But it is Allard/The Shadow who tracks the killer down, saves Burke's life, explores the secret passages, finds the hidden murder weapon, falls through the floor into a deadly pit and escapes again. It's an old-fashioned, English-flavored mystery all tricked up for the pulps.

Crime Over Boston (September 15, 1938): Absolutely secure steel rooms are within rooms. Yet in those rooms, men die, accompanied by a ghostly tap-tap-tap. But that's not all: A stark and isolated Rhode Island mansion, where the floor slides back and forth over a 140-foot drop into the sea and rocks. Gangsters, plotting masterminds, signals by night, G-men—there's all this and more in this issue. Kent Allard starts it off. Before the end, a gang leader has a very good idea who The Shadow really is. You can imagine what a short life he has.

The Dead Who Lived (October 1, 1938): A rework of the October 15, 1934 "The Death Sleep." Jets of yellow gas plunge men into a deep coma—a living death. As The Shadow probes into this, all sorts of things happen to him. Only by the grace of Walter Gibson does he survive at all, as he is most inattentive to business and, therefore:

1. Gets a revolver jabbed into his back while holding crooks at
gun point.
2. Gets knocked cold by a monkey wrench while holding crooks
at gun point.
3. Gets run over by a truck while shooting at crooks.
Through other mishaps, he demonstrates that, for this story, he
can be as ineffective as you or I. For unbelievers, it is
specifically stated in this novel that Kent Allard is The
Shadow.
Allard again appears to begin 1939 in "Silver Skull" (January
1, 1939), a story filled with skulls large and small, some talking,
other ventingpoison gas. The Silver Skull, that fiend of fiends,
gives The Shadow great problems. He gets gassed. The Cranston
identity gets exposed (again). Kent Allard, accompanied by a
swinging airline stewardess, finds an airbase hidden out in the
desert. And shortly thereafter, like the ending in a G-8 novel, the
Skull and The Shadow meet in an aerial combat. One of them
dies.
After "Silver Skull," Allard's role abruptly dwindles to
intermittent sputters. Cranston's face is used ever more
frequently. Perhaps the original has recovered sufficiently from
his accident to go forth globe-trotting again.
When Allard does appear, he is changed. The applause of 1937
becomes the neglect of 1939. No longer does his tuxedo fit like
poured glass. He seems seedy and rumpled. His apartment is less
pretentious. Weston, who once lionized the hero, is now testy, as if
afraid Allard might request a small loan. Nothing is more banal
than yesterday's hero.
Just why Allard was reabsorbed by the series is not completely
clear. The effects of the radio program may have influenced the
magazine at this point, for in the radio program, The Shadow was
Cranston. No two ways about it. The magazine never went quite
that far, and Allard would appear sporadically for years.
But his great days were in 1937-1938. After that, he got only
minor billing, which, perhaps, is what he wanted. As The Shadow
admitted, he had been Cranston so long that he felt odd as Allard.
It is an interesting side-effect of excessive disguise.
Even if you put Kent Allard's adventures to one side, you still
find scores of fine stories published during those final years of the
1930's. In their own way, the 1938 novels (it was a superb year) are
as choice as those of 1939. Through them, the adventure runs
swift and clear and hot. The prose is lean: masses of characters,
side-tracks, extended atmospheric evocation—all are stripped
away. The resulting prose is tight, swift, vividly episodic, bright
with violence and suspense.
Most frequently, the central story works out through a series of

sub-plots. You see this clearly in "Death Jewels," where six
separate narrative strands may be counted. Each strand features
a single character; each character enjoys brief prominence, then
sinks back, secure in knowing that he has advanced the story still
another step. Yet all flows crisply.

Through all excitement, The Shadow works his will. Now he
whispers advice to a hard-pressed girl. Now he fights. For a
chapter, he is believed dead—only to reappear to guide the
innocent, blast the evil. His perfect medium is action; his
thoughts remain as closed to us as Central Russia.

This is the way of it: every story is different, and every story is
the same. A common pulse unites them. You grow accustomed to
Gibson's structural rhythms: introduction, exposition,
complications, first Shadow appearance, first battle, to final
suspense development, final battle. It is all familiar and good.
Yet each incident is new and each grips.

From this golden time, certain issues stand out.

The highly successful "Teeth of The Dragon" (November 15,
1937) pits The Shadow against a ravaging tong and a horde of
gangsters. After extraordinary perils in underground passages,
and equally extraordinary escapes—one down a tube bisected by
a whirling blade—he maneuvers crooks and tong into a collision
course and rescues the imprisoned Chinese dignitary all the fuss
has been about.

This story marks the first appearance of that remarkable
young woman, Myra Reldon. (Refer to Table IV.)

Myra Reldon: an undercover government agent who, in this
case, is assisting Vic Marquette to investigate a smuggling
ring. In appearance she is a small young woman, very
attractive with "the light complexion of a blond"; her
eyes are brown; her hair is medium brown but appears lighter.
Born in Shanghai, she has lived most of her life in the Orient,
learning the language and customs and, apparently, the art of
makeup, exceedingly well. It is because of that ability that she
is employed by the Justice Department or FBI or whatever
agency Gibson assigns her to, when it is necessary to
investigate Chinese matters. On such occasions, Myra stains
her skin, tapes her eyes, and becomes

Ming Dwan, a beautiful oriental maiden: "Her face was
alluring; her slanted eyes, like her eyebrows, were marvelous in
their blackness. Her lips looked pursed..." As the feminine
confidant of some very hard people, she is, in spite of her beauty
no delicate peony blossom. "Her eyes showed a sudden cunning
as a bitter smile crept to her lips. Her features took on a cruel
malice..." And she can watch the torture and destruction of a
Round-Eyes with callous calm—at least, until it is practical to

do rescue work. Ever the realist, she is effective because she controls herself, does not yield to impulse, sees every situation as it is. She is a competent professional whose abilities The Shadow respects. At the end of the first story, he takes her to dinner and later seems to regard her very highly. By "The Devil Master" (September 15, 1941) she is an agent and far more in The Shadow's confidence than the more widely-known Margo Lane.

TABLE IV—Continuing Characters in The Shadow Series— the Final Additions

Novel Written	Character	First Appearance
Sept. 1936	*Jose Rembole[2]	Quetzal
Jan. 1937	Kent Allard	The Shadow Unmasks
	Xincas	
Feb. 1937	Myra Reldon	The Teeth of the Dragon
Dec. 1937	The Hand leaders[1]	The Hand
Feb. 1939	Beatrice Chadbury[2]	The Golden Master
	Paul Brent[2]	
	Shiwan Khan[4]	
Apr. 1939	**Benedict Stark	The Prince of Evil
Apr. 1940	Velma Corl[2]	The Wasp
	Basil Gannaford[2]	
Dec. 1940	Margo Lane	The Thunder King
June 1941	Chance Lebrue	Death Diamonds
Feb. 1945	Glanville Frost[2]	Murder By Magic
	Val Varno[2]	
	*Shadow disguise	
	**Theodore Tinsley character	

In mid-1938 appears a group of linked novels collectively known as "The Hand" series. These are loosely associated with events described in "The Rackets King," written in early May, 1937, but not published until June 15, 1938.

The Rackets King—Someone has murdered the Rackets King, who preyed on other racketeers. And whoever did it will inherit a rich underworld kingdom. Kent Allard, his two Xincas, and a nice girl named Irene, carry the action through this rapidly moving novel. Early, The Shadow takes a good smack on the head. Thus Dr. Sayre sees Allard's face under the slouch hat only ten issues after the famous unmasking. But he never tells. Eventually, the big crook, run to ground, fakes a suicide in a cabin tightly sealed shut. It's a large version of a stage illusion, as The Shadow instantly recognizes. And so another master criminal bites the dust. It occurs to no one to connect Allard with those two Xincas who are helping The Shadow. But, of

course, when Ram Singh helped The Spider, who drew the
obvious conclusion about Richard Wentworth?

As a result, the New York City racket groups are broken up.
Prominent among these is a collection of gangs and leaders
known as "The Hand"—that is, five gangs, each headed by a
hardcase leader known, improbably, as

"Thumb" Gaudrey

"Pointer" Trame

"Long Steve" Bydle

"Ring" Brescott

"Pinkey" Findlen

That is the frame which holds together five gangland novels
having very little else in common.

The Hand (May 15, 1938, written last of December 1937): Maude
Revelle, a hardboiled broad with a heart of gold, loves the
wrong man but learns to love Cranston more. The crooks,
headed by that rackets master, Pinkey Findlen, have developed
a magnificent racket. They blackmail rich folks with the help of
a detective's look-alike. Through a bullet-swept story, their
plans keep clabbering as The Shadow louses up their big hits.
Tricks and traps avail Pinkey nothing; he finds .45 slugs
instead of millions, and departs this world. In the course of the
story, a good girl is introduced to balance off Maude's part. But
since Maude ends up helping Tne Shadow, instead of detesting
him, she takes over the good girl's role and leaves the poor thing
counting her fingers.

That's the way matters go on. In "Murder For Sale" (July 1,
1938), Brescott is selling murder as fake accidents; the scene is
Philadelphia. In Chicago (and "Chicago Crime," November 15,
1938), Long Steve has set up an organization to swindle insurance
companies by fake accidents. Out on the ocean, Pointer is
heisting cargo ships ("Crime Rides The Sea," January 15, 1939).
And among those West Virginia hills, Thumb is going in for
wholesale millionaire kidnapping ("Realm of Doom," February 1,
1939).

In each place, The Shadow appears to chop off another finger,
issue by issue. All novels are the smooth, high-action adventures
characteristic of this period: much plotting, much shooting, and
an air of general exhuberence.

Before he was well into The Hand sequence, Gibson undertook
revision of the only Shadow novel written by Lester Dent. This
had laid in the editorial safe since mid-July 1932. It had been
ordered by Frank Blackwell before Street & Smith realized how
many novels Gibson could write annually. Dent was given a
batch of early Shadow in his first personality as a Weird Creature
of the Night.

Since the novel was paid for, S&S thriftily hung onto it. Finally, in mid-January 1938, Gibson was asked to revise and update the manuscript. He did so, adding agents Dent had never heard of, expanding the content, adding bridges between most chapters. He did not eliminate the *essence de Dent.*Throughout the story, The Shadow performs feats worthy of Doc Savage. He has become immensely powerful, his steel-like muscles rippling, and you wouldn't be surprised if he suddenly burst forth with an eerie trilling.

Almost all the 1938 novels deserve recognition. The following brief comments only suggest the richness of this particular orchard.

"The Crystal Buddha" (January 1, 1938) is a small figure that causes inordinate amounts of shooting, plotting, and murder. At the whirlwind's center is a beautiful girl, a treacherous Hindu, and quantities of Gibson sleight-of-hand with the characters. "The Fifth Napoleon" (June 15, 1938), a fine Tinsley, pits The Shadow against that giant intellect who secretly directs activities of four lesser criminal Napoleons. "Face of Doom" (March 15, 1938) is a benign fellow whose features get all snarly in the proper lighting. He comes to an odd end, shot dead and propped on his chair in an underground lair, his corpse used to trap his followers.

The Voice (November 1,1938): Horrors! The wealthy magnate is kidnapped from his office—before he exercises his week-long option to buy the Green Star lines. Death cuts down each crook involved, just before The Shadow arrives. It's death by order of the Voice—that sinister unknown on the telephone. The bad girl hates The Shadow; the good girl trusts him. But someone (Walter Gibson) is tricking someone (the reader). The Shadow slicks in and out of a gigantic gangland machine gun trap. Thereafter, a trick disguise sucks The Voice from concealment, and thus from this burdensome life. The gangsters are riddled. And, as astonishing as you may find it, the bad girl was good after all.

On a similar theme:

The Lone Tiger (February 15, 1939): The Tiger is possessed of a gigantic nose, more immense, even, than that of The Shadow. Once heading a swell gang of crooks, The Tiger is now killing them off, one by one. And who is the Tiger? Before The Shadow finds out, he is battered, wrenches his knee, is blown up, dropped through a trick elevator, and shot at 1,675 times. Cranston is very active in this story, his eyes glowing weirdly. Of all the cast, only Weston and Cardona fail to realize that he is The Shadow. The Tiger, ultimately recognized as the least likely suspect, gets shot dead in the last chapter.

The Crime Ray (September 1, 1939): Crooks are boring through

steel walls all over town. They melt elevated tracks, buildings,
even The Shadow's car. The Shadow has several hair-raising
escapes, including a race across a collapsing bridge. Late in the
adventure, Cranston is identified as The Master Fiend. (It is all
a plant; Weston and Cardona know.) Cranston swiftly ends in
the Pen. There Slade Farrow and Tapper have fixed him a
special cell. Soon after, The Shadow walks the prison by night,
eliciting information, preventing a jail break, and at length,
tracking down the evil genius, who is burrowed into an
underground hideaway designed to Tinsley's specifications,
regains his good name. Yeah, him; that dead-pan guy.

On September 15, 1939,, The Shadow's most dangerous
antagonist appeared. (Most dangerous as far as Gibson was
concerned.) "The Golden Master" introduced Shiwan Khan, self-
proclaimed descendent of Genghis Khan.

"Wide at the forehead, the face tapered to a pointed chin. Set in
the center of that triangle was a thin straight nose that stood as
sharply as a ruled line. Beneath thin eyebrows that curved
almost to the temples were green eyes that had a catlike glow.
"Thin whiskers hung down from his upper lip, and on his chin
was a slight dab of whiskers....from lips that were thin streaks
of brown dropped slow, well-accented words that broke the
hush like tingles of a bell." (from "The Golden Master, Chapter
VII)

Shiwan Khan is Gibson's Fu Manchu, a heartless plotter and
long-distance hypnotizer, employing arcane Oriental arts and
technical Western science to reach that familiar goal of world
domination. He is aided by a rare mix of Far Eastern killers: great
hulks with stabbers, spidery weirdos who shock you simple,
orientals withered fat glaring snarling. Not a decent disposition
in the batch.

A certain distance separates the concepts of Fu Manchu and
Shiwan Khan. Fu Manchu, a towering intellect and one of the
world's greatest leaders, is, if evil, filled with a sort of lethal
spirituality; he is a corrupted saint and it is this special quality
which fleshes out his character and gives him such long literary
life. Of Shiwan Khan, we have less good to say. Cut from the
blackest possible cardboard, he exists to oppose The Shadow as
strongly as is commensurate with our hero's continued life. He is
an intelligent man who never says anything worth quoting. He is
a perfect, full-time, concentrated, practicing fiend and, therefore,
has not a shred of humanity, and requires the reader to use not the
slightest shred of belief. With great skill, Gibson creates a major
villain. Unfortunately he neglects to bring him to life. Just as
well. He might have eaten us all up.

Three other novels, in addition to "The Golden Master," make up the series: "Shiwan Khan Returns" (December 1, 1939), "The Invincible Shiwan Khan," (March 1, 1940), and "Masters of Death," (May 15, 1940). These tell how The Golden Master seeks to further his dreams of conquest by collecting war materials, deadly gases, geniuses, and the allegiance of the underworld. At the beginning of the series, he plans to become Emperor of the World; at the end, he is willing to settle for Dictator of America. The Shadow contrives to wreck all these schemes, although you wonder where he found the time, for his every minute was spent rescuing one person or the other from Oriental dangers. Finally, Shiwan Khan, snarling in his silver coffin, goes tumbling into the maw of a blazing house. Since he never returned, that may have ended him, although it has been rumored that Gibson may yet bring that saffron-hued rascal back again—perhaps, this time, scheming to become the Mayor of Philadelphia.

The final Shadow to bear a 1930's date was complex "House of Shadows," (December 15, 1939). To unravel its forks and branches is no mean task, but essentially it goes like this:

The head crook is blackmailing the fine young man. The fine girl believes in him and seeks to help him, and they are both remarkably inept. The Shadow is not much better. He falls off the side of a building and is stunned, is blown up and stunned, is trapped by automatic handcuffs and tied up. At intervals, he is aided by one of Gibson's best characters: old Miss Prudence Ralcott, as feisty a tough-minded wonder as ever walked off the page. Once she wears The Shadow's cloak and hat and pots a crook. On the other hand, the nice young girl has a brief appearance in a nightgown, thus fulfilling the spicy obligation for that issue. It is a disappointment when the concealed master crook gets exposed and all his helpful crooks get shot. It is a nice tricky story, with the Cranston identity repeatedly revealed and The Shadow falling down in the dark and missing many shots, as was his custom in so many 1939 stories.

At this point, 1940 arrived, and everything seemed to change.

22.

The spirit lifts at the polished beauty of the 1940 Shadow magazines. How brightly the covers shine. How compact they are, how smooth and full of promise. Graves Gladney covers sparkle outside; and inside shine the graceful felicities of Cartier and Mayan. The paper has a clean woody smell, and the magazine, itself, balances delicately in the fingers, a minor work of art.

(Slightly more minor than you may suppose. The Shadow novel is about 15,000 words shorter than the 60,000 work adventures of yesteryear.)

From the inexact perspective obtained some 40 years after the fact, the 1940's, that new decade, began on the first Friday of December 1939. As far as The Shadow Magazine was concerned, it did. And with that issue, the big old rough paper magazine vanished. In its stead appeared something slicker and, if the truth must be confessed, unaccountably chilled down, politer, tamer.

It seems a subjunctive phenomena. Of the 24 issues published in 1940, 15 of them were written in 1939 and feature the familiar 1939 story style: a multiplicity of sub-plots, constant movement, The Shadow engaging in many small actions that unexpectedly go awry.

Through the 1940's, this condition worsens. Where once The Shadow could out-slug a battalion of Marines, now 80-pound weaklings defy him. He falters. He stumbles. His bullets clang unforseen obstacles. His knowing ways have left him. He seems less wise, less informed, less effective. Repeatedly he is knocked senseless. It seems appropriate that, in the June 1, 1942, "Twins of Crime," he reflects that he will probably die by accident during battle. It is his only recorded private thought in the entire series.

Slowly the novels simplify. By 1942, they are composed of events strung one after the other. Occasionally a proxy hero blunders into sight and must be saved. Constantly, the Cranston identity is compromised. And, equally often, nothing much more happens than torrents of fairly flat talk. No longer do the stories rush grandly about. More often, they focus on one or two locales and freeze there, while characters shuttle back and forth, running about loudly and accomplishing nothing visible.

By this time, the characters have flattened to decals. Their personalities shape about a single trait. They echo last month's hero and last issue's crook. Even the secret criminal genius seems smaller and somehow grubby. His authority no longer grips a vast mob of leering toughs; now he is lucky to control three or four rascals. Whenever The Shadow gets near them, they all fall down together in a heap.

But no one is hurt. Not often, although the heaps of expended cartridges could be clearly seen from the moon.

In all fairness, this generally gray landscape is mainly found in 1942 issues. Gibson had taken on scripting The Shadow Comic book, plus magic, plus short stories, plus two Shadow novels a month, and began to find himself winded.

The condition would ameliorate itself in 1943, change being the norm for the magazine. And in earlier 1940 issues, yet unexhausted, neatly faceted gems appear. If a single issue sags, the next sparkles vividly.

"Death's Premium" (January 1, 1940): In this admirable story, The American Death Insurance company insures your worst

enemy against living. You pay the premium and promptly the death rate rises. Henry Arnaud pays $125,000 to make sure that Lamont Cranston will die within a week. From that point on, Cranston shoots his way from one death trap to the next, and the mortality rate of underworld killers swoops out of sight. The end comes in the grill room of the Cobalt Club. Weston, full of poisoned mushrooms, doesn't see much; but the slaughter around him is marvelous, and those who learn Cranston's ability with a .45 don't live long enough to conclude the obvious.

This is the last story in which Henry Arnaud plays a featured role. It is not that the identity was compromised and had to be scrapped, for The Shadow clearly expects to continue using the Arnaud face. Apparently the true cause is a shortening of the novel length, a reduction in the numbers of characters used, and the coming presence of Margo Lane (requiring a great deal more Cranston) that caused Arnaud to fade away.

"The Getaway Ring" (February 1, 1940) whisks wanted crooks to safety and the story moves in a long furious line as The Shadow splinters the group. "Voice of Death" (February 15, 1940) speaks on phonograph records, a rather weary idea borrowed from days gone by. "Q," (June 15, 1940) is at once a master criminal and a master criminal and a signal to explode something, and New York shudders with explosions, as once it shuddered under The Black Master's heel.

With the April 15, 1940, issue, "The Prince of Evil," Tinsley began a four-story series during which The Shadow battles Benedict Stark—an extraordinarily ugly millionaire with an IQ of about 549. He lives for revenge, torture, murder. He enjoys all these in massive doses through "Murder Genius," (July 1, 1940); "The Man Who Died Twice," (September 15, 1940); and "The Devil's Paymaster," (November 15, 1940).

"The Prince of Evil" stinks with cruelty. The Stark organization is powerful, malevolent, as knowledgeable as Satan. They work their will unchecked. Blood, death, terror: the play of something hugely shining and metallic that squats, listlessly picking apart a living thing. It is the embodiment of the 20th Century nightmare.

Against that implacable force, The Shadow is not conspiciously successful. He fights the Stark organization to less than a draw, losing Rutledge Mann in the first novel, recovering him, badly used, in the second.

In subsequent novels, the air of inhuman fear gradually dissipates. However, each struggle is drawn. The Shadow and his agents take a dreadful beating. By "The Devil's Paymaster," they have thoroughly interfered with Stark's pleasure, and he concentrates his efforts to eliminate The Shadow et al.

He comes within a hair of doing so—collecting all the agents into a mined underground cavern that is to detonate seconds after harpoons pin them to the walls. Considering the unrestrained melodrama, it is a brilliantly sustained suspense piece.

A less effective villian, The Wasp, makes his first appearance in the October 1, 1940, novel of that name. A tall, lean-waisted demon, he affects a buzzing voice, a stinging touch, and identifies his orders by enclosing wasp wings. Aiding his grandiose thefts is Velma Corl, a hard-boiled woman, by Gibson out of Tinsley. She ends up arrested and returns from jail in "The Wasp Returns," (February 1, 1941). In this novel, The Wasp, rigorously disguised, sees through the Cranston secret and The Shadow sees through The Wasp, who is aiding a foreign power preparing revolution in South America. The Wasp dies dramatically, just when success lies in his hands. And after only two issues.

Xitli, God of Fire (December 1, 1940): Features Kent Allard and his Xincas against a Mayan fire god and his Indian followers. All this disturbance gets started near Mexico City at an archeological dig, then is transplanted to a brand-new New Orleans museum. There the God of Fire appears, garbed in flame and smoke and scary sounds, his plans to further. Before he is stopped, the carnage is terrific.

With the June 15, 1941 issue, "The Thunder King," the SHADOW MAGAZINE and the Shadow radio program uneasily embrace, rather like a meeting between long-parted relatives who never did care much for each other. From nowhere steps Margo Lane, girl nuisance. She tenaciously remains over outraged howls from the readers.

Margo is a composite of several 1930's feminine character types that had been established as much by radio and moving pictures, as by published fiction. Part Girl Friday, part dizzy socialite, she has a capacity for headstrong blundering into trouble which compares favorably with an active 4-year old. Her presence effectively cancels the need for the good girl enmeshed in peril; Margo is always in peril, always at the verge of destruction, and thus multiple chapters may be added and the suspense maintained.

Margo Lane: A beautiful young brunette socialite. She has brown eyes, a glorious complexion, no mathematical sense, and a madly adventureous turn of mind that is coupled with very little personal caution. Since she is required to act in such a way that the plot bounds on and on, she is, by turn, irresponsible, foolhardy, jealous, snoopy, indiscreet; in partial compensation, she is also clever, loyal, and a natural actress, who must play up to some intensely idiotic young ladies passing through the series. Margo originally met the real Cranston while on a Caribbean cruise, then returned to New York and met The Shadow, a

Cranston, at a night club. Over a period of time, she gradually learned that either Cranston was The Shadow or that he was not. Slowly she was introduced to the organization, was jealous of Myra Reldon, friendly with Vincent, and acquainted with the rest. Toward the end of 1945/1946, she is constantly with Cranston (Allard) in situations that would be hopelessly compromising were the medium other than The Shadow Magazine. The Shadow relishes teasing Margo but he shows none of the warmth, in the novels, that was so liberally smeared about the radio programs.

ALLARD (as Cranston): "Now tell me, Margo: does Elaine dent Tharn as much as you do me?"
(Translation for those not conversant with 1942 slang; "Has E. made as much a romantic impression on T. as you've made on me?")
MARGO: "I dent you? I've been trying to dent you for...well, let's forget for how many years!" ("Judge Lawless")
Well, life's little ironies, Margo.
CRANSTON (to The Shadow): "...Anyway, you've found Margo useful."
SHADOW: "Very useful. Whenever trouble is coming up, I know it from the way Margo gets into it."
("The Hydra")

The mere fact that Margo sees Cranston don hat, cloak, and whisk out his automatic should nail down the fact that he is The Shadow. She sees this change repeatedly at close range ("Legacy of Death," "Murder by Moonlight," and others). Yet he can baffle her without effort, as when, in "The Hydra," no less that six Shadows appear to rescue Margo, Cranston, and the friendly police form doleful death.

Is he or isn't he. Certain. But then...

The double Cranston explanation does not seem to suggest itself to her, not for years.

Margo's background slowly accretes through scraps dropped during 1941-1946 adventures. At first she is presented only as the beautiful screwball who gets into trouble with—

The Thunder King (June 15, 1941): who is a scientific terror calling himself Thor. He blasts factories, automobiles, buildings with bellows of man-made lightning. Is he the crazed inventor? Is he the fellow who stands to gain so much if that nice industrial leader cannot meet his contractual obligations? The Shadow, of course, finds out. And Margo, although she isn't in the Organization, suspects Cranston of being The Shadow, only she is not certain. And, although she contributes nothing in this story much more than a pretty body in peril, she simply saturates the novel.

The Devil Master (September 15, 1941): Two oriental fiends scheme separately to rule the Orient, and everybody else. Margo intercepts one of The Shadow's instructions to Myra Reldon and ends up a prisoner in Chinatown. Worse—a prisoner shrunken to the size of a doll, tiny and terrified. Serves the dummy right. Both fiends get whipped separately and together, after complicated violence.

Legacy of Death (August 1, 1942): The Shadow and Margo spent a lot of time sitting around a nightclub watching all the odd things that go on. The subject is what must be serial murder among the heirs. Only who can prove that it's murder? Not Joe Cardona. But The Shadow not only can, he does, and also demonstrates how to drink poisoned sherry with no ill effects at all. This story features a proxy hero who is three parts an idiot, and a proxy heroine who, in her nightclub act, does a shimmy that comes off the page at you.

Judge Lawless (August 15, 1942): makes justice a farce down in his concealed courtroom. Plotting, planning, manipulating, he is served by shabby hordes of gunmen, all fairly inefficient. The proxy hero is determined but wrong-headed. He is blamed for theft by the crusty father of the girl he loves—and she is a dim wit who acts as if she were in heat. Judge Lawless turns out to function in two personalities, a fact which The Shadow turns to his advantage. Margo is more effective than usual, and so is Jericho.

Six months after Margo came on scene, zealously sipping a Mirage cocktail, the final agent was added to The Shadow's organization. There seems little necessity to include Chance Lebrue as a matter of fact. Possibly the series needed that added jolt supplied by a new face; less probably, The Shadow could use a driver equivalent to Moe on out-of-town actions. Or possibly Mr. Gibson enjoyed mixing in a less familiar character. Or all three. At any rate, "Death Diamonds" (February 1, 1942) introduces—

Chance Lebrue, a barnstorming automobile stunt driver of the "Hell on Wheels" school. His face is blunt and square-jawed and he is, to be mild, an entirely complete professional with an automobile. No sooner is he in a car with The Shadow than he drives deliberately over a cliff (to escape a carload of thugs) and brings them out safely at the bottom, surrounded by car parts. Thereafter, Lebrue appears irregularly in the series, almost always behind the wheel. He is a limited agent, but most highly competent.

How far we have come since "The Living Shadow." Then Harry Vincent encountered a black-shrouded mystery, featureless, glitter-eyed, full of menace and mystery. What being lurked in that darkness? Goodness knows; something scary.

And eleven years later?

Eleven years later, that sinister figure in black strolls with Chance Labrue along sandy Florida roads. They talk together; they get along fine—which is hardly the point.

The night master, the mystery being, Fate's striking edge, is forever gone. Remaining is a man. He is dressed in black and is of high competence. His mind penetrates; he shoots brilliantly, moves superbly well, is resolute, skillful, incisive.

But hardly is he mystrious.

It's likely that his eyes no longer glow in the dark.

While the Allard identity is protected, the Cranston identity is no longer preserved from the agents' eyes. On with cloak and hat under the eyes of Margo, Burke, Vincent. Jericho carries a neat package containing the garments; Moe sees Cranston slide in and a shapeless darkness slide out...

As the black outfit slips over him, those observing see Cranston wonderfully transformed. That indolent fellow is transfused with vitality; his calm drawl quickens to a fierce hiss; the slow eyes scald: a transformation to chill the skin, as the harmless and familiar grows charged with menace.

Even so, we hesitate and feel our allegiance thin. Would The Shadow linger in night clubs with brunettes? Would the situation so often rush from his control? Would he be so subject to accident? As in "Five Ivory Boxes," (July 1, 1942), a novel of serial murder, during which The Shadow is

    —stunned by an exploding door
    —stunned by a flying telephone
    —stunned in a cab crash
    —stunned by a chessboard

He does, however, save Cardona from an asp, for whatever that's worth.

Lazing around night clubs throws off the reflexes.

The Museum Murders (January 1, 1943): A museum's treasure hoard has been stored in a secret country house. And to this place creep not one but two gangs of crooks, lurking, sneaking, closing in, chapter after chapter. They make a long job of it. Shortly, The Shadow gets both gangs fighting each other and they die in droves. Finally one batch gets into the museum's hoard that has been stored in a secret country house. And to this. Not at all. The crooks haul in as much as they leave—and why they do this reveals this novel's mastermind, who receives the usual punishment for his transgressions.

It is with deepest regret that it is necessary to observe, at this point, how deeply the infamous radio program had sunk its claws into THE SHADOW's pages. Not only is each story Margoed to the exploding point, but Moe's name is altered.

Thus the admirable Moe Shrevnitz, that tough competent,

street-wise cab driver, agressive and smart, is renamed
"...Shrevvy, as some friends called him..." (p. 32)

Apparently the change is to bring into the magazine some of
the familiar radio names. Unfortunately, the radio Shrevvy is a
Brooklynite played for laughs. He is not competent to steer a
Dodgem car, and, as usual with figures from The Golden Age of
Radio, is drawn as a clumsy cartoon, inept and shallow.

The magazine "Shrevvy" is not much changed from the more
familiar "Moe". But it is clear that other forces were acting on the
magazine now. The Shadow's own success was recoiling back on
itself. Not only did the novels show radio influence, but traces
appeared of material that seemed more comic book than pulp-
magazine oriented.

The Devil Monsters (February 1, 1943): Out there in Castle
Chandos lurks a gigantic scientific intellect, determined to rule
the world's future through things of the past. Meaning, less
cryptically, that a fiend named Monstrodamus has recreated
such creatures as the pterodactyl, hadrosaurus, and
diplodocus. Also giant moles, scorpions, earthworms. Also less
familiar creatures such as salamanders and basilisks. The
story is fast-moving, tricky, and a swell example of how to
handle impossible material in such a way that it seems real—at
least,, until it appears out in the light. The Shadow, as a
character, is above such stuff, and so is Gibson. The whole
effort reads like a novelized comic book.

In spite of such experimental failures, other stories worked
beautifully, sans radio, sans comic books. Gibson turned again to
the past and constructed bright new variations on old ideas:

The Robot Master (May 1943): Echoes of "Charg, Monster,"
here. A wild-eyed inventor commands an 8-foot tall robot that
clumps about New York City, smashing cars, ripping up
buildings, demolishing a factory. The nice young man is
framed, saved by The Shadow, framed, again saved by The
Shadow, etc. etc. etc. The wild inventor's beautiful daughter
believes in the nice young man, although she's hostile to The
Shadow. Inventor #2 has perfected an even larger robot and is
competing with Inventor #1 for rich government and is
industrial contracts. Now we learn that some hidden fellow
wants the secret of the robot's brain. And so it goes, back and
forth. You're never sure who's doing what to whom. The action
darts about like a minnow in shallow water until it's time for
the great, robot fight, which has been in the cards since Robot
#2 was introduced. It was and they do. The winner chases The
Shadow through Times Square—an interesting sight. It is a
distinct error in judgment on the part of the secret mastermind,
who does not survive the final action.

"The Robot Master" is the first formal monthly issue of the magazine since 1932. The paper shortage caused by the war is now destroying magazines ruthlessly, oblitering such well-known names as UNKNOWN WORLDS, THE SPIDER, and THE WHISPERER. But matters other than war and paper shortages trouble THE SHADOW magazine.

Street & Smith retrench and the staff is cut. Among those dropped is John Nanovic, a management error of no mean proportions. He is replaced by Charles Moran. (See Table V.) THE SHADOW is cut back to monthly publication. For five months, Gibson writes no stories, while his story backlog is used up.

And more change.

The December 1943 issue, "Murder By Moonlight," is in a new format, a modified editorial policy, and has shrunk to the size of THE READERS DIGEST.

23.

"With this issue The Shadow magazine comes to you in a different-size package. We think it is a better size, war and the demands of the paper situation being what they are. However, we also believe there is a trend in the direction of this size periodical which cannot be stopped. It is a more easily handled publication and is just as readable in type and text as it was before...

"Let us not, therefore, look too closely and too critically at the change. It is progress..." (from "The Shadow Says," editorial department in THE SHADOW, December 1943).

TABLE V. Approximate Editorial Sequences During Life of THE SHADOW Magazine.

DATE	NAME AND COMMENT
1931	Frank Blackwell, Editor-in-Chief, during initial planning stages
1931—1932 (April)	Lon Murray, Editor; John Nanovic, Asst. In 1932 most editorial activities fell on Nanovic, as Murray was handling the illfated HEADLINES.
1932-1943	John Nanovic, Editor, (During retrenchment and staff alignment in mid-1943, Nanovic was separated)

1943 (Jul.)—1944 (Jan.)	Charles Moran
1944-1946	William de Grouchy, Editor; Babette Rosmond, Assistant
Late 1946-1948	Babette Rosmond, Editor
1948	William de Grouchy
1948 (Jul.) -1949	Daisy Bacon, Editor; Esther Ford, Assistant

With this mendacious introduction, the digest-sized Shadows begin their turbulent history. For nearly five years, the magazine will be wrenched by changing editorial winds, diminishing circulation, incompetent art, erratic publication schedules, contractual disputes, and such similar events as enliven the artistic life in a commercial world.

All this was symptomatic of a deeper sickness. With no one being the wiser, the pulp magazine era was drawing to a close. As it did so, the enabling machinery which had, for so long, supported preparation, publication, and distribution of these magazines, was now, beneath the stress of social change, beginning to fail. Paper supplies shrank, readership shrank, costs inflated, and here distribution faltered and there, labor being ever more unskilled and increasingly expensive.

Change. Deadly change.

Most deadly of all, the tastes of the readership were altering. Battles against 1930's-clots of criminals, single-man heroics against machine-guns. Costumes. Strange millionaires...

Cat, that jive's from nowheresville.

THE SHADOW magazine entered its digest phase optimistically. Altogether 48 digests would be published, 33 of them written by Walter Gibson, and 15 by Bruce Elliott.

Not much difference exists between the 1943 pulp magazine and the 1944 pulp digest as far as story content goes. Half a year later, however, you can draw a few cautious conclusions about the digest novels.

In general the digests, like a prize-winning cake, are lighter and smoother in texture. Often they are touched by humor. More stories appear in which Cranston (The Shadow) and Margo are the primary leads. The action frequently strays from New York City to rural communities, far out.

Large criminal gangs and spectacular concealed fiends are downplayed. The novels are also shorter and complications fewer. That brooding atmosphere of mystery and latent menace, richly draping the 1930's stories, had dispelled. Now the paragraphs shine transparently, but the heart no longer catches at each new chapter.

The action moves violently as ever, movement bursting forth afresh every couple of chapters. Yet all that motion does not seem to lead anywhere in particular. Less blood is spilt. Meanwhile, in clouds of dialogue, the characters are meeting, manipulating, discussing, talking, driving here and there. A fine fresh crop of proxy heroes appears. Not all are dull wits, although all are singularly stubborn; they require as much special attention as Margo to keep them from being killed.

Murder By Moonlight (December 1943): A castle-looking mansion separated by an impassable stream and waterfall from a weird-looking madhouse. All this is way out in the country. And there is murder after murder, seemingly by inmates from the asylum, who wander around very free indeed. Dr. Sayre is required to commit Cranston to the madhouse, where he languishes in a straight-jacket and padded cell. But not to worry—The Shadow is in full control, regardless of what Margo thinks.

The Crystal Skull (January 1944): The Shadow traces concealed links in a series of major robberies of private art and curio collections. Each robbery is by a new criminal whose only link with the others is in his momentary possession of a crystal skull This thing has remarkable powers—it hypnotizes: Vincent, Cardona, even Cranston, and others. It also magnifies encoded messages. The gang members identify each other by a peculiar set of pass words (which mean something, for once) Margo is in a pet because of a beautiful blond who darts in and out of the story, gun in hand, whenever things threaten to slow down. All these strands eventually come together within a seashore cave piled with loot. The skull's hypnotic qualities, by the way, are not explained; once they have been built up, the story darts off in other directions. Truthfully, the story never stops darting. Interesting but very loose.

Admittedly, something interesting is constantly going on: "Syndicate of Death" (February 1944) features a machine that sees through walls. "The Toll of Death" (March 1944) is the boom of weird bells, heralding doom to those out in a certain valley at sunset. "Crime Caravan (April 1944) is a fleet of used cars being driven from the East to high-priced California markets; and every mile is marked by gun violence and bank robbery: before the end, The Shadow is considered dead three separate times.

Voodoo Death (June 1944): Serial murder grinds away at those in line for possession of a gigantic emerald. The concealed voodoo master does in his little dolls at $10,000 a throw, on behalf of the unknown heir, and so they die, one by one. The list is extended to include Margo, who barely misses a bath in boiling bronze, and The Shadow, who is to be macheted. But it doesn't happen.

"Town of Hate" (July 1944) takes us to the country again. Out there among the butterflies and ants, we have terror in the darkness, an Indian legend, farmers with shotguns, and a hidden cavern. It's all nicely mixed and The Shadow concludes things by hurling hand grenades about.

Then, in the August 1944, "Death In the Crystal," documentary views of past crime appear in a crystal ball, isn't that extraordinary? All the good guys turn out to be crooks and the crooks who skulk through the story all turn out to be innocent.

For the dedicated reader. "Fountain of Death" (November 1944) is perhaps the cellar of the series. While investigating the affairs of mineral springs spa and its kindly old owner, The Shadow is detected, wounded, chased by crooks, chased by cops, driven back, driven forth, finally escapes by accident, saved only because Moe is smart. By the end of the case, The Shadow, in somewhat better fettle, cleans up a resort full of gun-toting thugs; he is, at the time, totally enclosed in a plaster cast.

"Merry Mrs. MacBeth" (February 1945) works hard hard hard but succeeds in standing still. It is about stageland and murder during rehearsal. "The Mask of Mephisto" (July 1945) occurs at the Mardi Gras, where The Shadow finds the usual amount of trouble and $100,000 skips from hand to hand.

All this is busy minor fiction, skimming engagingly along. It is brightened by sudden humorous flashes and strongly facetious asides—just as if Uncle Walter were watching home movies and commenting from the side of his mouth.

"Carefully Wade drew out a very special bottle (of brandy). This was twenty-year old stuff, imported; not the one-star domestic that he furnished his guests with apologies regarding the brandy shortage." (The Crystal Skull")

The (Galleries) was really something to take one's breath away, without assistance from the stairs." ("The Chest of Chu Chan")

"The vault at Station KDY looked like a section of the catacombs with its interminable lines radio recordings in which KDY specialized. Here were preserved programs that had once held top rating but which now would call for fumigation of the air, if they were ever sent across it." ("Five Keys to Crime")

"Harry...found himself in a grain store which consisted mostly of a counter and a pot-bellied stove." ("Guardian of Death")

"Everything (the auction house) displayed was designed to catch the eye, but none of it appealed to taste.

"The so-called Oriental rugs that hung about the walls were glossy with a sheen that would wear off once the rugs were used on the floor, and the rugs would probably wear out with it. There were tea sets smeared with a gaudy gold leaf which justified a placecard stating "Genuine Twenty-Two Karat" as though the chinaware were made of precious metal." ("The Stars Promise Death")

"...the leopard gave a low growl. In leopard language it was saying that it didn't like something and since Phil was about the only thing in sight, he was probably what the leopard didn't like." ("The Banshee Murders")

THE SHADOW magazine is an odd vehicle for humor. Since around 1939, however, the high solemnities have been punctuated by occasional, very brief, comic scenes. From about 1942 on, deliberate comic elements are introduced into the story. The facetious aside is used ever more. That somber story, "Judge Lawless," contains a minor theme of a fool girl trying to attract an older man's attention: This is played for comedy and flashes like pink light between scenes of determined grimness. In this case, the ending's force is strengthened by the demonstrated fact that the fool girl has been hurling herself at a man obviously demented.

"The Vampire Murders" (September 1, 1942) blandly kids *Vanardy The Vampire* and every vampire movie made. It is happy parody, all the characters intensely serious, moving through a series of planned anti-climaxes which enhance the final revelations. These are not all amusing.

The Taiwan Joss (September 1945): A young writer knows the inside story of the Taiwan Joss and who intends to buy it. But he's a prisoner in a forgotten theatrical museum and so must adopt unorthodox ways of signaling his plight. All those interested in the joss are being slaughtered, one after the other, with the beautiful girl somehow present each time. So is The Shadow and his merry men (six agents appear). They have frequent, violent battles with a gang of Off-Shore Chinese pirates, who stalk New York City like figments of a cheese dream. It's good brisk rowdy stuff, as the trail of blood goes on and on. Isaac Twambley appears long enough to choke a pirate and get himself dropped through a trap door.

Many stories published in late 1945 and early 1946 use large numbers of agents, the action being wild and rough:

The White Skulls (November 1945): Our hero is checking out a skull-faced financier in a small town. And astounding things happen—a warehouse collapses for no reason. A whole string of cars and trucks vanish. A taxi blows to shreds. And the hero meets a great looking red-head. The story contains enough material for an epic. Behind it all is a displaced Nazi cell, dug into the foundations of New York City; they use a new liquid explosive to further their worldly aims, and wear black suits painted with skeletons. The Shadow, Margo, and a full crew, are much in evidence. The Shadow knows where the secret doors in the underpass are, and who the American Quisling is, and how that vibrating machine was used that bores holes through solid rock. Ah, the world is mad.

Even forgotten Kent Allard shows up in some stories: As in "Crime Out of Mind" (February 1946), which is loaded with information about magic and mentalist activities and features a couple of mediocre professional magicians who had first appeared in "Murder By Magic" (August 1945). Myra Reldon, Tapper, and Slade Farrow have walk-on parts, and Allard seems less shabby than in the immediate past.

"Crime Over Casco" (April 1946) again features Allard, very peculiarly. The story is tightly structured around the proxy hero and follows him as closely as in those distant 1931 days when all you saw of The Shadow was movement in the darkness. The subject is another gang of Germans, including a concealed submarine base, a plan to debark a lot of Nazi agents to prepare for WW III, and stolen plans of the Casco Bay fortifications.

For reasons which shall forever be a mystery, Allard once again decides to reveal his identity as The Shadow. This time, he is not addressing Slade Farrow, that close-mouthed fellow. Instead, he faces a group composed of Harry Vincent, the proxy hero, the mysterious girl, and the killer fiend, and

"...Back went The Shadow's hat; his cloak dropped away. Fully revealed...were the calm features of Lamont Cranston...The Shadow's hands went to his face...as they dropped. They seemed to peel away an outer layer of Cranston's features.

"That calm, well-moulded face was changed into the thin, gaunt features of..."

Well, Kent Allard. He's been calling himself by another name for many chapters—Austin Shiloh, if you must know.

THE SHADOW: "I took Shiloh's place... I had known him, years ago, when I was in the Orient, making a round-the-world flight as myself, Kent Allard."

Well, for Heaven's sakes, he didn't have to say that.

"Kent Allard was a forgotten aviator, a man who belonged strictly to the past. People had wondered what had become of him. No wonder, considering that he had dropped his identity and become The Shadow."

As you may notice, all that elaborate fa-la-la about Xincas, limp, White God, and such, are quietly scrapped in these few lines. Not enough room for them probably. Or perhaps Gibson was just giving the readership a solid certification that the radio program was not right—that Cranston, after all, was only a mask.

The fact that he reveals his identity publicly, thereby scrapping twenty-five or thirty years of silence, is just not understandable. It violates the deepest premise of the series—and for nothing. If there is a good reason (other than providing a brief thrill at the story's end) it has so far escaped comprehension.

"Alibi Trail" (June 1946) uses the same title as the January 1, 1942, issue, but is a different story.[38] It recounts those complicated events caused by a young veteran seeking to claim his father's inheritance. The focus remains strongly upon him and The Shadow remains well in the background.

"Alibi Trail" was followed by the superior "Malmorado" (July 1946), which features a French supercriminal running amok in New York City.

Then, abruptly, the tissue of the magazine is torn across. Gibson's contract was up for renewal; he balked at a couple of items, received no satisfaction, and, with no further discussion, a new writer was brought into the series.

His name was Bruce Elliott and he would write The Shadow from 1946 to the beginning of 1948.

24.

In 1946, de Grouchy formally turned over editorship of THE SHADOW to Babette Rosmund. She was a brilliant young woman whose tastes were vigorously modern. She did not much care for the older pulp magazine tradition of orange and blue melodrama, guns flashing all over the place, and creepy heroes and creepy villains.

That day was done. Her tastes favored more contemporary fiction: realistic modern characters developed in emotional and psychological detail. These were not heroes in the sense of archetypes or "masks" but reasonably average people in high-stress situations.

During the several years of her editorship (which included both DOC SAVAGE and SHADOW), she had concentrated on developing a group of writers who worked in these newer styles. Their stories kept cropping up in THE SHADOW and DOC SAVAGE, sharply elbowing the lead novels.

To the time of the contract dispute, The Shadow novel had weathered several years of editorial neglect. However, one a new writer was selected, then change came, sudden and massive, and ice cold. In moved modernism. Away with old outmoded forms. Off with those passe images of deadly justice figure, the image of Fate.

Something fresh new modern. Something reflecting the new fictional way.

The Shadow novel was replaced by the Cranston novel.

25.

Bruce Elliott (1917-1973) had met Walter Gibson in the mid-1930's through a mutual interest in magic. Elliott had written and edited for magic journals, and was deeply into magic, that arcane avocation. Gibson introduced Elliott at Street & Smith. While he sold no pulp fiction there, he worked on the S&S *Super Magician Comics*. Editor de Grouchy liked his work and, on taking over editorship of THE SHADOW, had Elliott do three Nick Carter short stories. (These appeared in THE SHADOW, June, July, and October 1940, with the fine old characters melted to bland facelessness.)

When the contract dispute with Gibson occured, de Grouchy again turned to Elliott, this time for Shadow novels. These were secured on a one-at-a-time basis, without a long-term contract.

His first novel, "The Blackest Mail" (August 1946) brought Lamont Cranston to Hollywood. There he battled a killer blackmailing the movie folk, shot it out by daylight with gunmen, struggled for life under the Pacific, moved effortlessly through the sound stages. All slick, clear fun.

Subsequently, Cranston was involved in serial murder afflicting a fine old rich family ("Happy Death Day," September 1946); voodoo murder and stolen art in New Orleans ("The Seven Deadly Arts," October); the numbers racket in Chicago ("No Safety In Numbers," November); and, in one state and town after the other, death at the U.N., at a Winter Carnival, in a hospital, in London, on stage, at a New York City Alice-In-Wonderland party.

Fascinating locales. The backgrounds are interesting in themselves. The prose, shining like oiled silk, is concentrated to novelette dimensions—tight and graceful murder mysteries, often with Ellery Queen overtones, or an occasional symphonic whisper from Raymond Chandler.

Cranston is the hero—the gifted amateur. At his beck, lawmen from all states fall gaping at his genius and extended the services of their positions; at his call, familiar names from The Shadow's organization appear, eager for service—Vincent, Burbank, and Shrevvie (who is Elliott's spelling of Shrevvy.).

Why Cranston maintains such a group is inexplicable. Elliott doesn't know. He has inherited the series and uses parts of its structure as they suit him, modifying them to fit his need.

Thus Burbank is no longer merely a communications coordinator but a sensitive, if invisible, mind that detects potential trouble and dispatches Cranston to deal with it—when Cranston cannot find trouble himself. Shrevvie (Moe no more) is a comic book figure who talks like a radio program. Vincent and Hawkeye are characterless names, used to speed along the story by collecting minor plot contributions. Of the other agents birthed by the series, none appear. Even Margo is gone.

The Shadow, himself, is hardly present.

Elliott never really understands The Shadow. Or he may have been told to cut out all that cloak and mystery business. Whichever--He succeeds in eliminating The Shadow from his own magazine.

Why does Cranston go on so? What possible reason does an upstanding, respected, craggy-faced criminologist have for slipping about all decked out like a Victorian novel? And laughing? What possible reason does he have to laugh?

"It was a sound that was a composite of bitter malice and graveyard chuckling." ("Room 1313," April 1947)

It is also a sound variously described as rollicking, baleful, jolly, and nerve-tingling.

Elliott sems rather embarassed by the whole thing. Why does Cranston laugh? Why does he slide around in that get-up?

Whatever the reason, he does it less and less. The Shadow is no longer the central figure, dominating the story. He is merely the contents of a briefcase. In Gibson's novels, The Shadow shakes the story's web. In Elliott, The Shadow is an unnecessary intrusion tolerated to justify the magazine's title.[39]

By the February-March 1947, issue, "Murder In White," The Shadow does not appear at all. Nor in "Model Murder" (June 1947), or during early 1948.

The transition is complete; the Cranston story has won.

These are, literally, Cranston stories. The hero is Lamont Cranston. No fooling around here with identity behind identity.Cranston is Cranston is The Shadow. He is not Kent Allard, who occupies no position in this world.

Neither does Twambley, nor Arnaud. Fritz the janitor has never been heard of. Nor have Xincas, World War I air combat, spying, nor mutilated faces. Neither Benedict Stark nor Shiwan Khan breaks the silver shell of Elliott's fiction. A pulp magazine series has no history, but only a present; sufficient to the day are present sales.

It is gone, all gone, The Shadow's rich past. The death of Fellows forgotten. How Mann was recruited, forgotten, as is the name of Slade Farrow and that highly unusual colony on those islands. Who remembers now The Voodoo Master, The Crime Master, Charg, The Red Blot, The Black Falcon.

Three hundred and five issues. And now oblivion. The sleek Cranston story, smoothly flowing, rises fashionable above the rugged foundations. A piercing intellect, this Cranston, his face like Sherlock Holmes, his mind like Ellery Queen. Forever moving. The wandering criminologist, driven by forces greater than himself to solve, investigate, examine, explain.

In New York City, among the police, remain two familiar names, last remnants of forgotten days. Weston is still Police Commissioner. Changed, of course, in the fresh style that informs the Eliott world, where all things are bright, though God knows, not what they used to be.

Weston, too, is changed. Once a brusque, pompous pain in the neck, but an able administrator, he is now sadly reduced. He blows and roars, a bellowing windbag, his face scarlet, his mind vacant: He thunders and gazes fretfully to Cranston for aid.

Cardona? That tough, rather shabby, Italian-American detective, given to hunches and fast gun work, poker-faced, silent, a hard-nosed professional?

Joe Cardona? Cranston's drinking buddy. Fast friends, they lounge together, swapping stories. All the street-wise Italian is washed from Cardona, now; neat and smooth, he is a working gentleman with combed hair and clean fingers. (Oh, the portrait sometimes wavers and his lack of a humanities education is played for laughs, but Cardona, of course, grins, too.)

The stories—they are too brief for novels—hum tightly by. About 35,000 words long, they are so compressed in time that they are over before they are well begun: half a day, three-quarters, a day and a half, finished.

Cranston arrives, insinuates himself with silken grace into troubled lives, enjoys a brief whiff of danger. Before the story is more than half-way over, he knows all—more than the reader knows. The rest is set-up for the end, a final scene, and conclusion.

Not often do guns roar and whole acres of toughs fall bleeding. No, no. In slick contemporary mystery fiction, wholesale killing is pulpy—a mechanical way to infuse an unconvincing ending with excitement.

In these stories, Cranston draws all the surviving cast together and explains. Just as Professor Craig Kennedy once did: Now we will all sit together. I will explain. I will reveal the guilty party. He will leap up and foam and shout. The police will carry him off, while I stand, stern and inexorable.

So the ending. Cranston rarely has any more proof than Craig Kennedy, who was above concrete evidence. All Cranston's effects are by intuition and bluff.

The Shadow!

Yes. The Shadow doesn't know. He surmises.

A slick modern Shadow needs no evidence. He uses nothing but inspired deductions, as in Ellery Queen's early cases, where the evidence was, in the highest degree, intangible, psychological clues that make a jury sneeze and a defense lawyer glow with satisfaction.

Just let Cranston get going, through, and he'll bluff out a

confession every single time. And not a creepy laugh or menacing
.45 to back him up.

Smooth bright contemporary fiction.

Model Murder (June-July 1947): Murder at the hobby club.
Corpses and bits of corpses all about and a strobe light
flickering on dead eyes. Cranston takes 12 hours to solve it,
aided by a child kleptomaniac and a toy robot.

Svengali Kill (August-September 1947): Murder in full view
during the stage show. But who really did it? We begin in the
unidentified murderer's mind, then shift to Cranston
(accompanied by a persistant feature writer), as he works
briskly to the core of a twisted case of revenge, with a very very
loopy motive. Psychological, sort of.

Ten Glass Eyes (December-January 1948): A genial parody of
the tough private eye school. Mystery shooting that just misses
the hard-boiled PI. Three toughs try their guns against
Cranston. Hand-to-hand battle on the dock. The clue of the ten
glass eyes—although the murdered man lacked only one. The
frame. The flight from justice. Can Cranston save the nice
young guy? The struggle underwater. The cryptic dying
message. Takes Cranston a day and a half to cut through the
muddle.

Sleekly agreeable as were the Elliott novels, the magazine did
not prosper. Early in 1947, its publication schedule was reduced
to bi-monthly (with the April 1947 issue). It was symptomatic of
chronic illness.

"Murder On Main Street" (April-May 1948) is a tricky thing
about serial murder for an inheritance, and begins with a killing
in a sealed house. After this novel, written in September 1947,
Elliott did no more Shadows until the end of the year. The three-
month hiatus was not his fault. Editorial change was the cause.

In 1948, Babette Rosmond had resigned. De Grouchy once more
took over the Shadow editorial job. He allowed the back-log of
purchased novels to be used up. After which he reversed the
editorial policy of the last year and a half.

From the editorial introduction to "Reign of Terror" (June-July
1948): "For a period Lamont Cranston has been fully capable of
taking care of the various run of the mill crimes and killings
that have come up. But now the crime pattern is changing and
with that change has come the necessity for the return of
Cranston's other self...The Shadow."

(In less self-serving terms, our previous editorial policies have
failed to halt the obvious slippage of the magazine and, since we
have no better idea, will turn back to the successful formula of the
past.)

Reign of Terror: Crime explodes across New York City.

Fiendish extortion threats. Raw violence. The Shadow's first attempt to sieze a pair of thugs ends in their death. But other ways are open to the fat man, the brain, a wallowing, simpering gobbling horror. A trick causes dissention within the gang, causing the fat man to kill off a perfectly good lieutenant. A second trick leads The Shadow partially to the fat man and directly into an underground maze full of signal devices and death traps. To escape, he must shoot his way through a lion cage. And does, getting more than slightly mauled. Then, bleeding from every limb, he confronts the fat fiend and his gunners. The Shadow is unarmed. He reels. He bleeds. It is impossible that he escape. As the guns rise up, he says conversationally: "..."

Whatever he says, it gets the crooks to fighting among themselves and pretty soon they're all gone. A miserable comic book ending, disgracing a fairly good novel—or, rather, an inflated short story. The structure is very simple, indeed, and almost a quarter of the story is spent in an elaborate build-up before the story begins—very exciting. Bu where's the plot?

After "Reign of Terror" was submitted, no one wrote a line of Shadow for another three months. Once again, de Grouchy turned to Gibson, hoping to halt the magazine's slide toward oblivion. Bruce Elliott, receiving no further novel commisions, turned to other activities—science fiction, books of magic, novels, and the editorship of those magazines for the pulsating male, DUDE and GENT.

Gibson's return was marked by one of the best Shadow novels in the series. "Jade Dragon" (August-September 1948) is about 50,000 words and is rather highly polished. In action and complexity, it stands with the strong 1934 novels.

The locale is San Francisco, above and below ground. The subject is mass smuggling of jade. There is one jade dragon whose possession brings very rapid death. Before The Shadow finds out why, he has involved most of his agents. Ming Dwan and Vic Marquette appear; the heroine is reasonably sensible, and it is all magnificent hubbub. A splendid story, liberally filled with Cartier spot drawings. Unfortunately, since every excellence needs one defect to emphasize its perfection, the cover is an atrocity.

A new editor, Daisy Bacon, was appointed. She had essentially created the field of love pulps back in 1922 and was seasoned in pulp magazine editing. THE SHADOW (and DOC SAVAGE) were returned to the full pulp-sized magazine format. Fine Rozen covers were provided. The first of the old-look issues came out, dated Fall 1948.

Dead Man's Chest: On the trail of ancient gold, a young veteran finds corpses in series, each knifed in the back. Makes the search hard, even though the beautiful girl helps—and The Shadow and numerous agents. (Among others, we again meet Cliff Marsland, teamed up with Miles Crofton, and both of them tough as an IRS investigator.) The secret is associated with the Dead Man's Chest—which does not mean what you may think. To reach this, we find a garbled log-book entry, very old; a stolen ship model; and a really first-order gun fight in a maritime library. Eventually, everyone picks up stakes for a trip way up the East Coast. The secret plotter and his evil gang come sailing a tall ship to grab up sacks of treasure. But The Shadow's agents wipe out the pirates in a rousing ship-to-ship action with antique cannon. John Paul Jones would have applauded. Both Kent Allard and Mr. Twambly appear in this story—a real gathering of kindred souls.

This will be Allard's final appearance in the magazine. Unfortunately, Gibson drops a comment which raises all sorts of confusion to those readers who got in on only the final bars of the symphony:

"...Kent Allard, like Isaac Twambly, was a personality The Shadow adopted when he did not care to appear as Lamont Cranston." (page 92)

An unfortunate remark. It is made in the story's conclusion, just when the narrative pace will not permit slowing down to explain the uninitiated who Allard is. So those who knew The Shadow/Cranston through radio are not perturbed. The rest of us must grind our teeth and wish that, this one time, Mr. Gibson had deleted one of his sentences.

The Magigals Mystery (Winter 1949): Spectacular suicides rock Chicago—wealthy men with nothing in common, except the highly original magic devices that each carried. The Shadow's trail includes a talking crystal skull, a Chinese magician, a hotel packed with young female magicians. As Cranston, The Shadow makes himself a target for murder and succeeds in getting slugged at the Planetarium—but still manages to expose the real plotter and a load of unique magical devices, which were the cause of it all. Walter Gibson is mentioned in one scene and the young girl of the piece is every bit as adroit at making up as a Chinese as Myra Reldon ever was.

The Black Circle (Spring 1949) is a collection of crooks carrying identifying tokens, in the manner of 500,000 other pulp stories. They serve The Voice, who is a completely original device. And they kill. And they shoot. And they scheme and do violence, and eventually The Shadow gets into the very heart of their stronghold, where W. Gibson is masterfully leading the reader astray. The true mastermind is exposed and so is The Voice... Gibson has worked these fields before. The stories are sound

professional work. If they don't blaze and flare with that
excitement which once jerked you from chapter to chapter, they
are still satisfactory productions from the digest era. The format
is larger. The covers again beautiful. But they lack... Heat,
possibly. The intensity of 60,000 words being reeled off every
week. The mystery of a half-seen figure whose background is not
known. More villains of towering malignity working their wills
through twisting plot lines.

But Gibson has poured himself out across the page since 1931.
Although the ideas continue to come, he is tired. When he kindles
the fire, the flames no longer spurt and tower.

But they do still leap.

The Whispering Eyes (Summer 1949): A lone-wolf hypnotist
stalks the New York City darkness. A whisper from shadows,
blazing eyes in a hooded face. Oblivion. And in his wake,
sequential murder, theft, a litter of hypnotized folk,
stiffly moving, vague, strange. Now two other hypnotists
appear—one scientific, the other bombastic. All leave a trail of
hypnotizees, including Cardona, Burke, even The Shadow as
Cranston. Can such things be? No, as a matter of fact. Helped
by a fine Persian cat named Washington Mews, The Shadow
stops the hypnotist flat in his tracks. First he uses mystic
hypnotic power, then bullets, and so the series ends: Cardona
bent over the secret fiend, dead in a gutter. The Shadow's laugh
throbbing from darkness; a light drift of gun smoke rising.
Issue 325, Volume 54, Number 1.

26.

The Street & Smith pulp magazines—those few left—were
cancelled without warning and in one stoke. Shortly afterward,
Street & Smith, itself, which had aimed for new life in the slick
magazines, failed to find it, shuddered, fell, was absorbed.

Gibson turned to the book field—game books, guides to————,
paperbacks on subjects varied as Astrology to Space Travel. And
vast quantities of fact crime stories.

In 1963, he wrote what is, to date, the final Shadow novel for
Belmont Books. It was to be the first of a series but editorial
direction demanded alteration and updating to an extent that
Gibson could not accept. He dropped the effort after one book. An
additional eight novels were written, under the Maxwell Grant
pseudonym, by Dennis Lynds—perfectly competent, tight stories,
in which The Shadow, Margo, Allard, Cranston, and a few
characters from the series were intensely distorted, as it they had
been fed through a high-pressure steam press. The resulting
stories featured material drawn from James Bond's world, as

filtered through. The Man from U.N.C.L.E. As mid-1960's action novels, they were fine. As Shadow novels, they were patent counterfeits.

The last Shadow novel, then, is paradoxically the first from that final series: "The Return of The Shadow" concerns an international abduction ring, where kidnapped unfortunates languish in the dungeons of a remarkable castle on Hudson River banks. Numbers of agents appear, if briefly: Myra Reldon, Vincent, Burke, Burbank, Hawkeye, Crofton, Marsland, Moe (as Shrevvy), and Mann. Even a pair of familiar police appear— Weston and Eric Delka. The Shadow cuts the heart out of all those criminal plans and the whole thing ends in a mob melee through the castle, everybody pounding on everybody in high old style. All complete down to the violent death of the master plotter. And once again:

"...came a strange weird laugh that shivered into fading echoes... It was The Shadow's mirthless knell..."

27.

Art gestures gracefully before the final curtain and is gone. Life, less disciplined, stumbles and sputters and hesitates, its endings ambiguous.

Thus The Shadow series, so long complete, did not stay that way. In the 1970's, two short stories unexpectedly burst forth.

The first of these, "The Riddle of the Rangoon Ruby," was written around 1976. Intended as the first of a syndicated newspaper series, the "Ruby" was a short mystery story, that paused, just before the last chapter, to allow the reader to solve the mystery. Shades of Ellery Queen's challenges to the reader. And perhaps the reader might have solved the problem if he could have flown with The Shadow in an autogyro above the scene of the crime.

Unfortunately, the series fell through. The story remained unpublished until its appearance in *The Shadow Scrapbook* (1979).

The second story, "Blackmail Bay," had been outlined as the second of the newspaper series. It remained unrealized until Gibson finally wrote it out in late 1979, and it was published in *The History of The Shadow Magazine.*

Both stories are in the style of the mid-1940's digests, touched by a light facetiousness and relatively large doses of Cranston. It's pleasing to report, however, that up around Casco Bay, a sinister, black-cloaked figure yet glides the darkness, and the good work goes on.

CHAPTER II—...IN ALL ITS INFINITE VARIETY

What a beauty THE SHADOW was. In an era of inadvertent style, it evolved its own distinctive combination of art, typography, and fiction. The end result was quiet excellence. You were never aware of how tastefully THE SHADOW was put together, unless you happened to compare it to such lines as THRILLING or FICTION HOUSE. Then you realized the silent miracle that Nanovic and the art director had brought to past.

At first, of course, you can't say this. The magazine began as a quick effort to nail down that copyright. It was scratched together with attention to—well—cheapness.

THE SHADOW A DETECTIVE MAGAZINE measured 7 x 10 inches, including the fragile cover edges. It contained 128 pages for 10¢. This bought you a 70,000 word novel, a short story by Walter Gibson ("The Green Light"). And two possibly fact articles, heavily decked out in recreated dialogue: "Crime Detection in the Philippines" by Charles A. Freeman, and "The Bounty Racket" by one Captain Bruce.

On the back page, a brief paragraph, standing all by itself in a field of white (no advertisers as yet) admonished you to "Listen to THE SHADOW on the radio each Thursday night..."

On the back cover, in a little box, appeared the question:

WHO

is

THE

SHADOW

?

How long it would take for that answer to be known.

On the Table of Contents of that first issue, appeared the information that it was Vol. I April-June Number 1931 No. 1. Published Quarterly. Yearly subscription 40¢. Single Copies, 10 cents.

"We do not accept responsibility for the return of unsolicited manuscripts. To facilitate handling, the author should inclose a self-addressed envelope with the requisite postage attached."
STREET & SMITH PUBLICATIONS, INC., 79 7th AVE., NEWYORK, N.Y.

As elsewhere mentioned, the front cover was reused from the October 1, 1919, THRILL BOOK, and had been painted by Modest Stein. To this had been added the words "The Shadow Knows," and the date, "April 1931."

Each story within was illustrated by a single line-drawing. Those drawings provided the short stories look as if they, too, have been salvaged from earlier issues. The novel is provided an illustration which extends across the upper halves of pages 2 and 3. It is neatly boxed in on each page. The artist's name appears to be F. Werl or perhaps Wert.

The second issue, July 1931, is said to reuse a cover from an earlier DETECTIVE STORY MAGAZINE. This has not been confirmed. It features, however, a tumble of eyes looking out and gives the magazine a bizarre appearance, indeed.

With the October 1931 issue, the magazine changed its name for the first of six times. (See Table VI.) It became THE SHADOW, A DETECTIVE MONTHLY, reflecting its popular acceptence. Jerome Rozen painted the cover and would also do the covers for November and December, 1931, and February 1932. Each cover included a 2¼ x 2-¾-inch insert in the lower right-hand corner. This showed a blue-skinned individual, grinning like a madman from within a black cowl, who pointed a blue finger at the title of the story, given in red type.

A modification of this hooded face appeared on both the January and April 1932 covers. This, the first formal portrait, of The Shadow, was by George Rozen. Steel-eyed and smirking. The Shadow stares fiercely from a black hood. His nose is large and solid. His face is not blue but is so shadowed that the left half appears green, which is hardly an improvement. For the January issue, this portrait was placed on a silver cover; for the April issue, the cover was gold.

The hooded figure was also used to illustrate the Table of Contents, beginning with the April 1932 issue. Prior to that, from the April 1931 issue, the Table of Contents had been adorned by a skeletal-looking fellow peering dourly from under a hat brim—Gibson has identified this as a drawing of Frank Blackwell.[40]

The black-cloaked, slouched-hatted Shadow first appears on the cover of "Gangdom's Doom" (December 1931), briskly dodging a murderer's bullet. This cover does not show his face. The first close-up of The Shadow (once he is out from that black hood and under a slouch hat, where he belongs) is provided on the cover of "The Black Master" (March 1932).

Beginning in January 1932, the novel length was changed. First it shrank to 50,000 words. Then, six issues later, it increased to 60,000 words. It remained at that length for many years, only shrinking again when war approached and costs began to rise. (Refer to Table VII.)

Although the early 1932 novels were shorter, the number of short stories increased from two to about five. And a new department, The National Protective League, was added.

Created and written by the editor, Lon Murray, the NPL was a club, of sorts. It sought to rally those opposed to crime, a motive too laudable to fault. Within a couple of issues, it had expanded to fill nine pages. These began with a department containing four or five sincere essays on con games and criminal events and misadventures—an idea lifted from the "Headquarters Chat" department of DETECTIVE STORY MAGAZINE. On the last page appeared line drawings of "WANTED MEN." And between lay three pages of small type which summarized the militant thoughts mailed in by League members—each identified by his personal code number. Thus:

TABLE VI: Variations in Magazine Titling, 1931 to 1949

MAGAZINE TITLE	DATED
The Shadow, A Detective Magazine	1931: April and July
The Shadow, A Detective Monthly	1931: October and November
The Shadow Detective Monthly	1931: December through 1932: September
The Shadow Magazine	1932: October 1 through 1937: August 1
The Shadow	1937: August 15 through 1947: January
Shadow Mystery	1947: February—March through 1948: August—September
The Shadow	1948: Fall through 1949: Summer

Table VII. Approximate word count in THE SHADOW novels.
(Notice that numbers identify novels in the as-written, rather
than the as-published, sequence. Refer to Appendix C.)

Numerical Sequence of Titles As Written	Beginning With	Approx Word Count
1 through 5	The Living Shadow	70,000
6 through 12	The Death Tower	50,000
13 through 141	The Blackmail Ring	60,000
142 through 145	Hills of Death	50,000
146 through 273	The Murder Master	45,000
274 through 305	Murder By Moonlight	40,000
306 through 320	The Blackest Mail	25,000—30,000
321	Jade Dragon	50,000
322 through 325	Dead Man's Chest	40,000

"PENNSYLVANIAN welcomed into League. Calls his city a
pesthole of graft and crime, badly in need of cleaning up. Hopes
for something like the old-time vigilantes or Big Six of Chicago.
Will be glad to cooperate and help police at any time.

A143"

"LONG ISLAND young men eager to join us in the work of
driving out gangs. Started to form a squad of twelve, to stick
together and gather all information possible that will help
League.

B64"

If you find graft or crime, you see, you write a letter to the
NATIONAL PROTECTIVE LEAGUE. This will be kept in THE
SHADOW'S private files (says so on page 125, March 1932 issue)
and things may happen!

"TACKLES FENCES. This member in an Eastern State is
busy gathering evidence against men who deal in stolen
jewelry, and is already working on other cases. He reports his
progress from time to time to local police and to The Shadow as
well.

B320"

All you needed to do was write The Shadow, on a special pre-
printed form:

"I wish to enroll as a member of the National Protective League and add my voice and actions to the concerted effort to help the forces of law and order conquer the criminal elements of our nation."

You were to "Enclose 5¢, coin or stamps." You also got to take the Pledge:

"I, as a member of the National Protective League, pledge to give my aid to the forces of law and order to help bring about the just punishment of all criminals in this country. I pledge, by my own act, by example and encouragement of others, to do all in my power to abide by the laws of the Nation; to teach others to obey them; and to fulfill my duty in preventing the miscarriage of justice."

Amid such cosmic thunders, the NPL stepped forward upon the stage of destiny. It would remain there until October 1, 1932, when it was swallowed by the newly created Shadow Club. The NPL, memberships, pledges, letters, and all, vanished forever from the October 15, 1932, and subsequent issues.

The March 1932 issue included a new entry in the magazine's departments. This was a crime problem: "Who Stole Mrs. Williston's Pearls?" Gave the problem in March and the answer in April. Another problem was promised for May but did not appear. In a slightly different form, under the title of "The Third Degree", the problem would resume with the October 15, 1932, issue, and continue down through the years, issue after issue, to the April 1, 1939, issue, when the last problem appeared. The answer never seems to have been published.

In June 1932, a few more changes crept in. The number of novel illustrations were increased to four, including a full-page line drawing placed on a page to itself before the opening of the novel. Another fact feature was added to the departments; called "Mysterious Murders," this lasted through the next issue, then was dropped in favor of The Shadow Club.

The Shadow Club began very modestly. It was a club without pledge or dues or members. None of these would be added until December. For the time being, it was identical to that part of The National Protective League which printed little essays about graft and crime. (See Table VIII for a summary of magazine departments.)

In the same issue (July 1932) appeared an announcement of the first reprints of Shadow novel.

"READY FOR YOU NOW"

Reprints of the first two Shadow novels, which had been sold out, are now available to all who wish to complete their files of The Shadow's thrilling experiences as reported by Maxwell Grant.

TABLE VIII. Major Magazine Departments

DEPARTMENT TITLE	DATES	COMMENT
The National Protective League	1/32 - 10/1-32	
Crime Problem	3/32 - 4-32	
The Shadow Club	7/32 - 3/1/43	
The Third Degree	10/15/32 - 4/1/39	crime problem; solution in next issue
Codes	8/15/34 - 8/44	
Code of the Month	9/44 - 10/46	
Secret Codes	Wint 49 - Sum 49	
Our Members Write	5/1/34 - 7/1/34	
Pulse of the Nation	7/15/34 - 11/1/38, 9/15/40 - 11/43	
Letters From Readers	8/43	
The Shadow Readers Write	Fall 48 - Sum 49	
The Shadow Speaks	11/1/34 - 4/1/35	Ad for radio pgm.
Open Letters	5/1/35 - 9/15/35	Letters from city police chiefs
Men of the Law	2/15/37 - 5/15/37	1-2 page illustrated adventures
Free Shadow Picture	5/1/38 - 1/1/39	Submit 3 consecutive coupons of 18
Highlights on The Shadow	11/15/38 - 11/43	Letters, announcements about next issue
Protect Yourself	4/43 - 10/43	New home products
My Strangest Experience	5-43 - 1/46	Your true story wins $5
The Shadow Says	12/43 - 1/44	Ed. announcements

80 Seconds to Solve   12/43 - 12/45

NOTE No departments from 1/47 through 8-9/48

"THE LIVING SHADOW"
and

"THE EYES OF THE SHADOW"

"Mailed to your address upon receipt of fifteen cents, cash or stamps, for each novel...." (p. 126)[11]

By September, the magazine has taken on most characteristics of its first high glory: The lovely Rozen cover. Title page listing the novel, four short stories, and two departments. Then six ad pages:

BIG HUSKY MUSCLES ONLY $2.75
FREE FORD TUDOR SEDAN
I WILL TRAIN YOU AT HOME TO FILL A BIG PAY RADIO JOB

Then the novel, introduced by a stiff black and white drawing and, for the first time, illustrations and a brief comment, about characters of the story. The first two honored were Joe Cardona, and Prof. Biscayne, who turned out bad,

The September 1932 issue was the last to use no color on the spine title. To this point, the spines contained this information:

VOL. III NO.2   the SHADOW DETECTIVE   10 CENTS
   (in red)   MONTHLY   (in red)
           (black type; Shadow was in fat white
               letters outlined in black)

Otherwise the spine was white.

With the October 1, 1932, issue came all manner of change. The title changed to THE SHADOW MAGAZINE and the publication began to appear twice a month, on the second and fourth Fridays. In celebration, the word "Shadow" on the spine was now colored either blue or red. (Blue was first.) This continued until the November 1, 1934, issue, when the spine became all black with white lettering.

That format held until April 15, 1935. Then white boxes were added at spine top and bottom to contain the date and such messages of good cheer as 'Detective Stories" or "Book-Length Novel." Although black was the predominent color, two freaks appeared in 1935: the 7/15 spine was mauve and the 12/15 spine, powder blue. Much later, in mid-1941, other color variations began to show. From August 1942 to the digest issues (beginning

12/43), the color varied from issue to issue, white, red, black spines, in no set rhythm.

Back in 1932, the October 15 issue has just come out. In this, the NPL melted away into the Shadow Club. A new department, "The Third Degree," has begun—a brief crime problem with a tricky answer, revealed in the following issue.

In the December 1, 1932, issue, Tom Lovell begins drawing the internal illustrations. His work is superb. The action flows furiously across the page, figures leaping from a melt of darkness to violent action. It is beautiful, balanced work, gloriously composed, entirely satisfying, pure 1930's.

With the August 1, 1936, issue, Edd Cartier's illustrations

TABLE IX: Artists and Illustrators of THE SHADOW MAGAZINE (1 of 2)

COVER ARTISTS

Date	Artist	Date	Artist
1931: April	Modest Stein	1943: Mar 1 - 1946: Apr	Modest Stein
July	Unidentified		
Oct-Dec	Jerome Rozen	1946: May & June	Unidentified
1932: Jan	George Rozen		
Feb	Jerome Rozen	1946: July	Modest Stein (?)
Mar - 1939: Mar 15	George Rozen	1946: Aug - 1947: Jan	Unidentified
1939: Apr 1- 1941:Sep 15	Graves Gladney	1947:Feb- Nov	H. Swenson(?)
1941: Oct 1- 1942: Jul 15	George Rozen	1948: Jan- May	H. Swenson
1942: Aug 1	Charles De Feo		
1942: Aug 15 Dec 15	George Rozen	1948:Aug	S.R. Powell
1943: Jan 1	Timmins	1948: Fall- 1949: Sum	George Rozen
1943: Jan 15 Feb 15	G. Rozen		

INTERIOR ART
(Novel only)

1931: Apr	F. Werl(?)	1945: Nov	Everett Raymond Kinstler

| 1931: Jul - | Unidentified |
| 1932: Nov 15 | |

1932: Dec 1-	Tom Lovell
1937: Oct 1	
(SEE NOTE	
BELOW)	

| 1936: Aug 1- | Edd Cartier |
| 1940: Apr 15 | |

| 1940: May 1- | Earl Mayan |
| 1941: May 1 | |

| 1941: May 15- | Paul Orban |
| 1945: Oct | |

| 1945: Dec- | Paul Orban |
| 1946: Mar | |

| 1946: Apr | Unidentified |

| 1946: May- | R.F. Schabelitz |
| June | |

| 1946: July | Unidentified |

| 1946:Aug | S.R. Powell |

| 1946: Sept | Unidentified |

NOTE From mid-1936 through late 1937, the novel illustration is traded back and forth between Lovell and Cartier. Some early 1936 novels illustrated by Lovell also include Cartier spot drawings. As late as 1938, a Lovell illustration may be found mixed into the illustrations provided by Cartier.

TABLE IX (cont): Artists and Illustrators of THE SHADOW Magazine (2 of 2)

DATE	ARTIST: INTERIOR ILLUSTRATIONS *(Novel Only)*
1946: Oct	Edd Cartier
Nov	S.R. Powell
1947: Jan- 1948: Aug-Sept	Edd Cartier
1948: Fall- 1949: Summer	Paul Orban

begin appearing. (Refer to Table IX.) His style is, at first, so close to that of Lovell that you must squint sharply to distinguish between them.

The subtle beauty of Lovell's interiors was splendidly set off by the technical brilliance of George Rozen. Unlike his brother, Jerome, George rarely painted a cover depicting a scene from the novel. Instead, his work was elaborately composed, shapes and colors contrasting. The story theme was suggested. But more frequently, the cover was a design through which complex shadings played. The Shadow's partly concealed face was often used symbolically.

—"Dead Men Live" (11/15/32): The Shadow distills from a glass retort images of crime.

—"Shadowed Millions" (1/1/33): An immense Shadow lurks behind skyscrapers to observe the violence of tiny criminals criminals below.

Or it was worked into the design of the cover:

"The Ghost Makers" (10/15/32): From a pointing Shadow at the cover's bottom center, radiate three images of himself, green, purple, and blue, from left to right.

—"Six Men of Evil" (2/15/33): On a dark red cover, three villainous faces peer left, forward, and right, while behind them, the silent Shadow, all black, looms.

Rozen painted a great number of symbolic covers involving hands: pointing, pressing, entwined:

—"The Blackmail Ring" (8/32): The Shadow's gigantic hand, easily identifiable by the ring, grips a tumble of snarling, writhings, shooting crooks.

—"The Golden Grotto" (5/1/33): An immense finger (The Shadow's) presses down a writhing crook on the center of a bullseye.

—"The Isle of Doubt" (8/15/33): The Shadow's hand presses a glass-headed pin into a map.

—"Gray Fist" (2/15/34): The Shadow's hand and a gray-gloved hand grip before a Chinese screen.

Or a single theme from the novel is concentrated into a vivid symbol:

—"The Death Giver" (5/15/33): The Shadow extracts a snake's fangs against a background of criminal faces.

—"The Red Blot" (6/1/33): A giant scarlet drop falls across planes of red, purple, green, over which is cast the Shadow's silhouette.

—"The Cobra" (4/1/34): The Silhouette again, this time falling across a coiled cobra.

At intervals appeared a portrait of The Shadow—not often, but frequently enough to make readers quake with anticipation for the next appearance:

—"The Five Chameleons" (11/1/32): View of The Shadow's profile as he writes with a feather pen.

—"The Black Hush" (8/1/33): Close-up view of The Shadow's partly concealed face, about fifty percent nose; as usual, the shadowed side of his face is green. (This picture was used on the cover of the first Ideal Library volume.)

—"Partners of Peril" (Nov 1, 1936): Three-quarters view of The Shadow, blasting with both guns, on white background. This is the definitive portrait.

And occasionally Rozen came up with an idea so spectacular that it influenced pulp magazine covers a decade later, as: "The Creeping Death" (1/15/33): From between dark green curtains peers a skeleton, one bare eye glaring out, while superimposed over skeleton and curtain is The Shadow's Shadow. [42]

It was all far from what is known as pulp magazine cover art. But it was intensely effective, a curious example of fine arts design succeeding in the big bad world. Rozen can be faulted for only one grievous oversight in all his covers. Persistently, he showed The Shadow with an uncocked automatic—must have assumed that the .45 is a double-action weapon. But no.

Nevertheless, there is no Rozen cover which shows The Shadow holding a cocked weapon. It is a lesson to us all.

The September 15, 1933, issue ("Master of Death") showed a semi-transparent fiend on the cover. Inside, the news was equally exciting. Seems that Shadow Club lapel pins were now available—half-inch silver buttons, The Shadow shown in profile, glancing back over his black-clad shoulder, the whole circled by the word "The Shadow Club." All for ten cents. A staggering bargain.

The Club must have attracted considerable attention. It began branching out promptly. First the pin, and then:

(April 1, 1934):

SHADOW CLUB STATIONERY

"Club members have beseeched us for some printed stationery which they could use for their correspondence. Now, after investigating various means of fulfilling this request in the least expensive way for our members, we have, by ordering a huge amount, been able to secure a rubber stamp bearing The Shadow emblem, an exact duplicate of your badge, with the word 'Member' above it, for all Shadow Club members who desire to purchase them."

Price for this stamp was 10¢, postpaid, without ink pad. Only qualified members of The Shadow Club could buy these stamps.

"They can be imprinted on personal stationery, books, or other possessions of our members."

And, gracious, don't you suppose they were.

The stamp was available for long afterwards. Not so another special offer, which must have cost a world of trouble before it was discontinued:

(August 1, 1934): "TO OUR READERS: Those of our readers who wish to get a special message from The Shadow, written in one of his many secret-ink compounds, may secure one by sending name and address to The Shadow Magazine. Members of The Shadow Club are requested not to submit their names, as they receive The Shadow's bulletins automatically."

During 1934, much attention was paid to magazine departments. Great pains were taken to pump up the Club with scalding gas. To assist in the good work, a letter department was opened in the May 1, 1934, issue. "Our Members Write" continued through July 1. With the July 15 issue, the department was renamed "Pulse of the Nation" and so continued down through the years until the column was temporarily dropped with the November 15, 1938, issue.

Many years before, FLYNN'S WEEKLY had instituted a department called "Solving Cipher Secrets." Conducted by M.E. Ohaver, the feature began in mid-December, 1926, and continued through the decades into the middle 1940's.

(For obscure reasons, the 1930's were filled with code play. Every radio program paused awesomely at the middle or end break to murmur a Secret Message that could only be reconstituted by a secret decoder secured from Tom Mix or Little Orphan Annie or whomever.)

Surrounded by such good examples, it is only surprising that THE SHADOW MAGAZINE delayed so long in adding a codes department. This, austerely titled "Codes," began in the August 15, 1934, issue. The department was unsigned for two issues. Then it was credited to Henry Lysing (John Nanovic) and continued in almost every issue through August 1944.

A less long-lived feature began in the November 1, 1934, issue. Called "The Shadow Speaks," it was an enthusiastic reminder to tune in The Shadow Blue Coal radio program (every Monday and Wednesday over the Columbia Network. At these times, The Shadow sent a secret message, an actual message transmitted by emphasized words buried in the final announcement. For instance, the Shadow said:

"On Monday, October 1: Crime Does Not Pay!
"On Wednesday, October 3: The Law Is Just!
"On Monday, October 8: Honesty is The Best Policy!
"On Wednesday, October 10: The Gangster Is Doomed!

In 1934, your moral fiber got reinforced day and night.

All these department changes were shored up by new editorial ideas. The August 1, 1934, issue contained the first story in a series about Grace Culver, girl private detective. She was the first major series character among the magazine's short stories, appearing in 20 issues spread across four years. The stories, signed Roswell Brown, were by Jean Francis Webb.

"Redsie" Culver was small, red-headed, and inclined to violence. She got captured and tied up a lot. After a year of this, she began to shoot people. Her stories are wildly active, wildly improbable, filled with sadistic overtones concerning violence to the head. They are painfully arch about Grace's feminine devices—and linger on such mystic artifacts as lipstick, necklaces, high heels, skirts, bracelets, and such other devices as distinguish women from men. The series ended with the July 15, 1937, "Return Adress." By then, the suspicious reader would believe that other hands were at the typewriter.[43]

Grace's success lead to other series characters being added to THE SHADOW'S short fiction. The magazine was not precisely original in this: THE SPIDER was already developing its own minor characters to back up Richard Wentworth's blood-lettings.

However, once Grace worked out, another character was added. It was done as deliberately as a cat walking a puddle.

"The Tattooed Skipper," by Steve Fisher, in the May 1, 1935, magazine, introduced Sheridan Doome, a Naval Intelligence investigator and full time horror. Doome had got thoroughly scalded when his ship exploded. When they finished patching him up, the scar tissue left him chalk white. He was held together by steel plates, rather like a metal bridge. During the first stories, two iron braces jet out past his coat collar, in the style popularized by Dr. Frankenstein's celebrated associate.

The plates leave Doome bulletproof; the explosion leaves him somewhat demented—although he is pictured as an icy genius, cold, withdrawn. His assistant, Rush Evans, plays Dr. Watson, and is full of animal spirits and boyish good looks and as many brains as could be jammed into a pencil eraser.

Doome appears alone in the first six stories. These are signed Steve Fisher and published during 1935. No stories appear in 1936, although a novel, "Murder of the Admiral," was published and sank without a trace, presumably taking Fisher's reputation as a writer with it. Beginning in 1937, (August 15), the Doome stories reappear in THE SHADOW. This time they are signed Stephen Gould, and are written in the first person by Rush Evans. The series continued strongly through the years, lasting till July 1943. Little in the magazine lasted beyond that date.

As Culver and Doome prepared the soil for the appearance of other series characters, that sly old editor in charge of things had figured out another way to catch readers' attention.

This was another outburst of zeal for justice. THE SHADOW MAGAZINE was strong for Law and Justice and Decency. And in the name of these truths, it went forth to police chiefs all over the country and solicited their opinions as to the most important thing in the battle against crime.

Right off the bat, the police chief of Forth Worth, Texas, hit the right note:

"...I...believe that the constructive program of The Shadow

Club merits the serious attention and support of those interested in youth and the prevention of crime...."

It is not recorded that Nanovic sold Henry B. Lewis, Chief of Police, a rubber stamp and lapel pin, but he printed the Chief's letter on page 94, May 1, 1935. The series ran through September 15, 1935. All the Chiefs came out firmly against crime and had a genial word for The Shadow Club, that powerful social force.

In spite of these good works, the magazine sales seem to have gone off somewhat. In consequence, Gibson was asked to jazz up the action (resulting in the novel, "The Salamanders") and the covers were give a violent shake. Over night, it seems, Rozen's decorative art is replaced by scenes of intense, and wholly unfamiliar, violence:

One man furiously strangles another, thumbs knitted in the unfortunate's throat. ("The Case of Congressman Coyd," 12/15/35).

On a castle battlement, The Shadow throttles some fellow limp. ("Castle of Doom," Jan 15, 1936)

Seared by a costumed fiend's sizzling torch, The Shadow shoots the miscreant dead. ("The Salamanders," April 1,1936)

Sprawled against a wooden yellow door, The Shadow is obviously being shot to death as you watch. ("The Yellow Door," June 1, 1936)

Tied by the wrists, a helpless prisoner, The Shadow contemplates a grim future while savages gruff around him. ("Jibaro Death," Sept 15, 1936)

These covers, for all their new flair, were by no means as frenzied as those appearing on THE SPIDER. (Where, once a month, the black-cloaked hero plunged into a dozen flaming guns to save The Girl from sadistic torture.) Still, Rozen's minor reformation was interesting—if brief. By 1937, he had returned to set-pieces and paintings of hands, although, admittedly, the unrepentent design covers vanished. Not until 1942 would Rozen again paint hard-action covers.

Issue Number 100, "The Man From Shanghai," Vol. XVII, No. 4, was dated April 15, 1936. Written in early December 1935, it had originally been titled "Ku-Nuan's Jewels."

On the cover, a leering Chinese killer assaults The Shadow with a knife. The Shadow is, at that moment, hanging by one hand from the side of a building about twenty stories up. Below the busy street glows golden. Above, matters look hopeless....

The magazine contains 128 pages, costs 10¢. The Table of contents is illustrated by a line drawing of The Shadow looking stern and handwriting the following:

"The Man From Shanghai Complete Shadow Novel From The Shadow's Private Annals As told to Maxwell Grant"

(This format has been used for the Table of Contents since the January 1, 1935, issue.)

In addition to the novel, the magazine contains four short stories, Codes, The Third Degree, The Shadow Club, and Pulse of the Nation. A package of seven ad pages follows after the Table of Contents. On the left page facing the novel appears a full page of prose about The Shadow. It is emotional as a minister defending womanhood:

"...But hidden in a sanctum in New York, a being in black ponders beneath a blue light and chuckles slyly to himself as he pursues reports of his agents. For The Shadow knows!"

And on and on. It isn't Gibson and hardly sounds like Nanovic. Whoever it was, he got pretty worked up.

Altogether, it is a solid attractive magazine, representing the Golden Age at its richest.

In the July 1, 1936, issue, another long-run series character appeared. This was Danny Garrett, the shoeshine boy detective— The Kid, he was called. Danny seems to have been the most popular of The Shadow supporting series characters. He ran continuously for years, the last story appearing in the September 1943 issue.

Danny was another Steve Fisher creation. Later stories were signed Grant Lane—which was a Fisher pseudonym, but used, in this case, by William G. Bogart. Danny was a street waif—always a popular subject around S&S—and was full of character, determination, will to work, and such qualities as would have elated Horatio Alger. Danny specialized in murder cases. He went hustling from violence to violence until he faced the killer's gun. After which, his pal, The Cop/Detective saved him for the second issue.

Danny had just appeared for the third time (August 1, 1936, "Dash of Death") when Mr. Eric Scott, of London, Ontario, Canada, wrote a letter "Pulse of the Nation" and started a forest fire.

In the letter, Scott remarked that, in his opinion, the ten best Shadows published were:

The Death Giver
The Living Joss
The Grove of Doom
Mox
The Green Box
The Cobra
Murder Marsh
Bells of Doom
The London Crimes
The Ribbon Clues[44]

Gratified by such a fine free idea, The Shadow editor remarked that he'd print other letters on this subject. And upon him descended a deluge of opinion.

Worse, there also poured in orders for all those magazines cited. Unfortunately, many were long out of print—from which followed complaints from Accounting or somebody about all those refunds and not a return stamp in the lot.

This explains why the Editor, very sheepish, in the September 1, 1936, "Pulse of the Nation," remarked that no further lists would be published. And they weren't, for a while. Although, for the duration of the Letters Column, someone was always citing titles of best liked stories.

Two additional series characters were added during 1936-1937. First was Hook McGuire, the bowling detective—an officer who found crime whenever he indulged in bowling, his favorite sport. The series began with the December 1, 1936, issue, and continued for 18 stories, the last appearing in the April 1, 1942, issue. The author was George Allan Moffatt, a pen name of Edwin Burkholder.

The final series character to enter the magazine was The Whisperer, just displaced by the failure of his own magazine. Beginning with "Bullet Bait," (December 1, 1937), The Whisperer appeared 24 times in THE SHADOW, once in CRIMEBUSTERS. A further series of novels ran October 1940-April 1942.

The house name attached to these is Clifford Goodrich, who was Laurence Donovon for the first two stories, and Alan Hathway for the rest.

The Whisperer was a tough little hardcase, with a whispering voice, a projecting jaw, and silenced automatics. He was known as Dunk Smith and was a dimmed, reduced Shadow figure.[45]

As usual, The Whisperer was a disguise for another fellow—just as you suspected. In this case, the other fellow was the Police Commissioner, a human circus named Wildcat Gordon. Wildcat was stocky, red-headed, and had a bright taste in clothing. He felt police methods too slow and created The Whisperer from a handful of gray powder and some dental plates. These distorted his jaw, thereby disguising him beyond identification. How easy things were, then.

Other interesting change came in 1937. First, a brief feature began in the February 15 issue—"Men of the Law" was a double-page cartoon story of how certain sheriffs and detectives broke their big case. Oddly enough, a fellow named Stookie Allen had been doing roughly similar features for ARGOSY ("Men of Daring") and DETECTIVE FICTION WEEKLY ("Illustrated Crimes"). "Men of the Law" marched along till May 15, then quietly vanished, another casualty.

But by this time, the Century Club promotion was underway,

trumpets shrilling. This got started in the March 1, 1937, "Pulse of
the Nation" (Issue No. 121):

"...Maybe you are one who's read a hundred or more issues of
The Shadow, or who's read every single one that's been
published. If so, let us know, and we'll add your name to our
'Century' Club." (page 126)

This was another theme that continued to the final days of the
Letters column. Some subjects just cried to be talked about.

The August 15 issue announced that the magazine's
publication dates were being advanced and that, henceforth, you
could look for your copy on the first and third Fridays of each
month. It seemed indecent—monkeying with dates made
sacrosanct by long usage. But it hardly mattered. You bought
SHADOW every other week and only that long gap between
issues mattered.

The Shadow was now more than a magazine. It was significant
business. A new radio program would begin in the Fall. This
would feature Lamont Cranston (The Shadow) who clouded
minds with a Tibet-based hypnotism, and palled around with a
woman! Good grief, *a woman*!! Faithful reader's minds clouded
with rage at this defilement of The Master!

But little radio cared for that.

In 1937, the first moving picture featuring The Shadow was
also released. Titled "The Shadow Strikes," it was a ghastly
travesty, sluggish, improbable, and demeaning. Supposedly it
was based on the June 15, 1933, "Ghost of the Manor," an
intensely atmospheric novel from the "Weird Creature of the
Night" period. The movie reflected no atmosphere; it was simply
appallng. Later film improved slightly—but only slightly.[46]

A further cultural triumph was celebrated the following year,
1938, when the Lewis Music Publishing Company, Inc. released a
piece of piano music titled "The Shadow Knows." The lyrics gave
enterprising singers the opportunity to go

"Ha Ha Ha" (weirdly)

The cover of the music was a reprint from the July 15, 1938,
"The Golden Vulture." This shows The Shadow beaming a
flashlight upon a sheet of paper, across which is inscribed

The Shadow Knows

How persistently that catch phrase held on.

The January 15, 1938, "Hills of Death," reflects a new round of
cuts and reductions. The novel drops to 50,000 words, 10,000
below the usual word count. It is not evident what the extra space went
for. One month later, another 5,000 words were knocked off. In
compensation, the page count was increased to 130, beginning
with the June 15 issue and remained at that figure through the

November 15 issue. The following issue plunged to 114 pages and stayed there until 1943.

Perhaps to distract attention from these violent spasms, a new promotion began in the May 1, 1937, issue. You were offered a free picture of The Shadow. Only mail three consecutive coupons— clip them right out of the magazine and mail them off. Eighteen coupons would be offered. The promotion ended in the January 1, 1939, issue.

"Highlights On The Shadow," a new department, began November 15, 1938. This department occupied itself with enthusiastic recommendations to read the current novel and short stories. These puffs were followed by enthusiastic eye rollings about the next issue:

"One of the best, brightest, most entertaining Shadow novels we've ever had is scheduled for appearance in our next issue... when we say that it is a story that you will really like, we mean just that..." And so forth. (from Highlights on the Shadow," October 1, 1939, p. 6)

Those magazines issued during 1939 show a lot of format fiddling, as if S&S is conscious that something has drifted awry but are not sure what or where. So the changes begin.

To begin with, the January 15, 1939, novel is split into two pieces. The final chapters are placed at the back of the magazine. In the space thus made are crammed the short stories, departments, and commercial announcements, very much like the filling piled between two halves of a submarine sandwich.

Then "The Third Degree" is dropped. That long-lived crime problem has by this time shrunk to a single column. Its final appearance is in the April 1, 1939, issue and no answer is ever provided for that last riddle.

Other changes:

George Rozen is dropped from the cover. In his place, appears Graves Gladney, whose first art shows The Shadow, as Cranston, accepting a light for his cigarette from a lemon-and-green Japanese, ("Death Ship," April 1). Gladney's work will appear through September 15, 1941, at which time he left the magazine, pronouncing anathema on art directors. His covers included a number of remarkable character studies:

Shiwan Khan—"The Golden Master" (Sept 15, 1939)

Hawkeye—"Wizard of Crime" (August 15, 1939)

and action scenes:

Caught in a night alley by a flashlight, The Shadow fires back. ("Shiwan Khan Returns," December 1, 1939)

The Shadow, Cliff Marsland, and Hawkeye in a blazing gun fight. ("The Getaway Ring," Feb. 1, 1940)

and beautifully designed covers, sleek and brilliant:

A dark blue and purple Shadow with *cocked* .45 before an orange background of flaming buildings. ("Q", June 15, 1940) Ten Shadows fire away at varying angles. (This is for the tenth-anniversary issue) ("The Time Master," April 1, 1941) Death as a flower woman, skull peering from a shawl, as across the figure and flowers fall the Shadow's shadow. (This cover was awarded recognition as the best pulp cover of the year.) ("The Scent of Death," June 1, 1940)

While Gladney polished his cover style, certain physical changes occurred to the magazine. First, the page edges were trimmed (November 1, 1939)—the beginning of a series of related alterations.

The page count was severely cut back to 114 beginning December 1, 1939, and continuing through March 1, 1943. At the same time, a progressive shrinkage of magazine size began. Between January 1938 and January 1940, the magazine width was reduced ⅝-inch. The rough page edges vanished. The cover overlap was gone. And 14 interior pages evaporated.

By the 200th issue, the fine old magazine had undergone a major facelift.

Issue 200. "Q" dated June 15, 1940. Vol. XXXIV, No. 2. On the Table of Contents, the writing Shadow is gone now—has been since May 1, 1939. The undecorated Table of Contents lists the novel, one Sheridan Doome short story, and three departments: The Shadow Club, Codes, and Highlights on the Shadow. At this time there is no letters column, per se, although some letters appear in "Highlights." However, "Pulse of the Nation" will resume September 15, 1940, and continue unchecked through July 1943.

The internal art is by Earl Mayan, now. The magnificent Cartier illustrations last appeared in the April 15, 1940, issue, although several of his spot drawings remain scattered through this issue. Mayan, who would later do SATURDAY EVENING POST covers, sleekly beautiful, will remain with THE SHADOW through May 1, 1941.

His illustrations, while far different from those of Cartier, are brilliantly executed. They concentrate violence, movement, emotion, all caught in a micro-second, the pencil recording as passionlessly as a lens. Wearing a modified cloak, The Shadow is captured in the instant of wheeling, firing, among mobs of snarling, sneering, shouting thugs. Facial expressions are strongly developed. The silent illustration pounds with sound.

Elsewhere in the magazine, you notice numerous ads for S&S magazines—UNKNOWN, CLUES-DETECTIVE, MYSTERY MAGAZINE, SHADOW COMICS, DOC SAVAGE. But the massed advertising is gone, leaving behind only a smattering of the mighty appeals from the 1930's.

By this time (1940), the 15-chapter movie serial, "The Shadow," had been released. So had the first Better Little book. (Refer to Appendix B.) The initial Shadow comic book was issued, dated April 1940; its cover reused the fine November 15, 1932, cover of "Dead Men Live." The magazine, itself, was stuffed with familiar S&S characters and Gibson would soon be contributing scripts for the Shadow story.

In 1941, one of the rarest of all Shadow items was issued. This was an unillustrated paperback reprint of the 1940 novel, "The Voice of Death" (February 15, 1940). Retitled "The Shadow and the Voice of Murder," it was published by Bantam Books of Los Angeles. (Refer to Appendix B.)

The Shadow art was further heaved around in 1941. Mayan was replaced by Paul Orban in May 15, 1941. Orban would continue illustrating the novel through March 1946. Thereafter, he was switched to the short stories, drawing for most of them through October 1946.

Orban had illustrated science fiction, mystery, single-character, western—dozens of interiors for dozens of titles. As a result, all his characters had a family resemblance. He rarely drew a gun that didn't look like a stick of wood, and his girls were delicious non-entities. Some of the illustrations he did in mid-1946 are extraordinarily graceful and well realized. More usually, they resemble mass-produced bland.

Gladney had left, to complete the art shake-up, and George Rozen returned to do the covers, beginning with the October 1, 1941, "Garden of Death." It is an inept cover for a minor story. Rozen would paint all but two covers (as shown in Table IX), until Modest Stein took over with the March 1, 1943, issue. These latter Rozens are characterized by slick bright-colored moments of violent action. The Shadow blasts away at close range. Men sprawl from bullet impact. Others dash about brandishing gleaming blades. Skeletons appear on various covers, their single eye staring. It is a thoroughly high-strung period.

Modest Stein, who followed, had been painting covers for about thirty years and had worked in every medium and every art style known. During the mid-1920's he contributed some outstanding realistic protraits on ARGOSY ALL-STORY WEEKLY covers, including several splendid paintings of Semi-Dual, the occult detective. During the late 'Teens,' he painted action covers for PEOPLE'S MAGAZINE. For THE SHADOW, he provided a series of low-key covers, soft of color, soft of line, decorative but low on action. After the magazine shrank to digest size (December 1943), the action vanishes. The covers become increasingly decorative and dim, like a misty evening. Finally they melt inconspicuously away, perhaps with the April 1946 issue, perhaps earlier. It's hard to say.

The year 1943 was constant uproar. The magazine reeled under change and all those familiar policies and methods which had so long sustained its spirit, now turned to vapor and fled. In almost no case was change an improvement.

What remained was unfamiliar and less pleasing.

"The Black Dragon" (March 1, 1943) would be the final twice-a-month issue. Since October 1, 1932, a new Shadow novel had been available every other week. Now four weeks would intervene. The breath of something cold ran across the sky.

Worse, someone went stomping through the departments in steel boots.

March 1: The final Shadow Club appears. The number of short stories jumps from one to four.

April: Five short stories. Five departments, including an essay on "Palm Prints" and a new department, "Protect Yourself," advising you to use press-on tape, waterproof matches, and to buy war bonds. The magazine price increases to 15¢; the number of pages increases to 162.

May: The department, "My Strangest Experience" begins: Write in your dreams, peculiar events, hard-to-explain incidents, and the magazine may pay you $5 for your letter.

June: The page count shrinks to 146, the price remaining at 15¢.

July: About this time, Nanovic is relieved of his editorial burdens, but receives 6-months severance pay. His replacement will be Charles Moran, former S&S SPORTS STORY editor, who will soon begin a massive modernization and refurbishment of The Shadow's image and his stories.

Aug: "Pulse" becomes "Letters From Readers," which appears in this issue only.

Sept: An exceptional month. No change. No "Pulse."

Oct: Again the page count is cut, now sinking to 130. This is the final appearance of "Protect Yourself."

Nov: Last appearance of "Pulse of the Nation." No hint of the surprise that December will bring.

Dec: The first digest issue. The size reduced to 7-⅞ x 5-⅜; later, it will shed another ⅛-inch all the way around. (Refer to Appendix A.) Two new departments are added: "The Shadow Says," a sort of editorial catchall, which lasts one more month. And also "80

Seconds To Solve It," the crime problem in the same issue. Pages remain 130.

At this point, the hurricane of change that has ripped the magazine slows. Until late in the year, no further format alterations, no hacking at departments.

The only peculiar thing that shows up is the appearance of Walter Gibson's name as author of the June 1944 issue.[47] This error has been ascribed to an assistant editor who was helping Rosmond, who was, at the time, helping de Grouchy.

In September, "Codes" changes its name to "Code of the Month". It will continue thus until October 1946.

Through the beginning of 1945, matters remained calm. Then the devil seems to get hold of The Shadow. Sudden convulsions wrack it, sure sign that Editorial feels heat from somewhere.

In April, 1945 ("Death Has Gray Eyes"), the novel moves bodily to the rear of the book. There it will remain until March 1946 ("Mother Goose Murders"), when, without warning, it is jerked forward again.

Meanwhile, departments begin to drop dead. "80 Seconds to Solve It" is dropped after the December 1945 issue. "My Strangest Experience" appears in January and is gone forever, strangely enough, in February 1946.

Amid these sullen mutters and dark-red flashes, issue #300 is released.

"Crime Out of Mind," February 1946, Vol. and number not given (Vol. 60 #6). 130 pages, 15¢. The magazine measures 7⅝ x 5⅝ inches, has a blue-black-yellow Stein cover, like an old bruise The title page is lightly illustrated by a sketch of The Shadow, the contents being printed on the back of his cloak. One novelette, three short stories, two departments. The novel begins on page 51 and ends on 129. It is illustrated with ten Orban drawings (probably all Orban). Including the covers, only 4½ pages of commercial ads are included, which suggests large revenue losses.

It is, in this trimmed, diminished form, a sorry child of those gigantic days gone by.

Now chaos hits the interior art.

After the March 1946 issue, Orban is replaced by various unknowns who deserve to remain that way. One can draw women's faces; another can draw nothing. The art professionalism disintegrates. In July, the novel is illustrated by scraps of art apparently extracted from comic books. In August, two or three artists are at work, one of them rather good. The others should have had their pencils broken.

Cartier returns in October. Then, in November, Powell does the interiors. He worked the *Shadow Comics*, where an inability to handle proportion was not disasterous, but to use his material in THE SHADOW, where masters had walked, is embarrassing. Cartier illustrated one short story in November and the contrast between his work and Powell's ignominious crudities is rending. Cartier takes up the novel in January 1947 and continues until the end of the digests, 8-9/48.

From this point on, the story is quickly told.

The January 1947 magazine contains no departments—six short stories. We are now in full retreat from THE SHADOW and into Rosmond's vehicle for modern crime stories.

The magazine becomes bi-monthly with the next issue, February-March 1947. The title is changed to SHADOW MYSTERY, so remaining through August-September 1948. The cover is decorated by a sketch of a bust with a skull superimposed; it is done as a decoration. Subsequent covers will be increasingly abstract, increasingly peculiar. The number of pages increases to 162; the price rises to 25¢.

An Edd Cartier decoration is added to the Table of Contents, April-May 1947. The novel and each short story receive an illustration each: Cartier handles the novel and, from August-September 1947 on, the short stories as well.

The August-September issue also begins a freak series of covers by Swenson—they are abstract, arty, often witty, and have as much to do with pulp magazine art as a marshmallow rabbit.

During this period, the novel progressively shrinks. No more than a long short story, 25,000-30,000 words, it is often crowded in its own magazine by novels by Frank Gruber, or Lester Dent (as Harmon Cash, 2-3/37, or Bruno Fischer. Three to six short stories are used—good, sound, solid stuff, contemporary and smoothly competent. The magazine might as well be retitled MYSTERY or DETECTIVE STORY. It no longer has anything to do with The Shadow.

All this terminates with the August-September 1948 issue. This has an inept Powell cover and contains two novels, one of them being the first Gibson Shadow in ages. This is profusely illustrated by Cartier, his final effort for a Shadow novel.

And, with the next issue, we return to the past.

Tha magazine, retitled THE SHADOW, is now a quarterly. Dated Fall 1948, it costs 25¢, measures the familiar 7 x 10 (cover edge to cover edge). There are 130 pages. The Table of Contents lists a "Complete Shadow Novel" (40,000 words), four short stories, and a department: "The Shadow Readers Write—".

The cover is by George Rozen, showing the caped, hatted Shadow pointing a .45 at you, while a white ocean liner looms behind him. Orban illustrates the novel; Cartier illustrates the short stories.

In this format, the magazine proceeds to the end.

With the Winter 1949 issue, the department "Secret Codes" by Henry Lysing is added. The number of short stories rapidly increases, reaching six by Summer 1949. But except for a pair of ads for the S&S AIR TRAILS, the only commercial advertising is on the outside of the back cover.

In March, the Street & Smith management issues an order to buy no more fiction. The surprise is complete and stunning.

From the cover of Vol. LV, No. 1, The Shadow gazes out, steel-eyed and muffled to the nose. He holds a crystal globe reflecting two eyes. By the globe sits a richly furred white Persian cat, last seen living with Margo Lane.

The magazine spine is white with black lettering. Across the front cover appear the words, THE SHADOW, bright red against bright yellow. And so the series ends, in brave primary colors, standing up strong, and vanishing in full regalia, proud and confident.

CHAPTER III—THE GRAND TRADITION

1.

During the final decades of its life, THE AMERICAN MAGAZINE (1905-1956) closed with a complete mystery novel— or as close to a complete novel as a 30,000-word novelette could get.

When you leafed through those back pages, you noticed a small, illustrated insert reading "The Month's American Mystery Novel," as if to assure readers that the mystery had not been accidentally omitted. That insert was decorated by a sketch of an individual in black cloak and slouch hat who pointed a gun. His features were not drawn in.

This sketch was used into the 1950's. During that period, any drawing of a black-cloaked gunman would promptly suggest The Shadow. For, by then. The Shadow's image was firmly embedded in the public mind.

But we can also assume that THE AMERICAN MAGAZINE was making no serious effort to publicize The Shadow. If the magazine used that sketch, it was because a black-cloaked figure meant mystery-adventure. It might suggest Shadow. But that was secondary to the primary message...sinister doings and concealed identities and shots amid peals of thunder and such rich ripe events.

A mystery figure, no less.

When you stop to think about it, you note that The Shadow, that powerful personality, is a great deal more than a figure in a black cloak and slouch hat. He has all sorts of strongly defined attributes: He uses weapons with skill and enthusiasm. He has bright red adventures, shooting it out with the underworld and destroying master criminals and helping the dopes of the Police Department. He uses a small army of agents. He expresses himself by weird laughter and a hissing voice. His eyes gleam. He is not bent by Margo Lane. He revels in codes and secret messages, flies airplanes, is a master at various sciences and technologies, speaks innumerable languages, is a disguise master, owns one or two fire opal rings.

An astonishing individual.

None of these characteristics can be predicted from the

observed fact that The Shadow wears a black cloak and slouch hat.

All these characteristics are improvements that Walter Gibson laid on over the life of the magazine. He had eighteen years to tinker. He added an ability here, a scrap of history there, a more elaborate twist elsewhere, never ceasing to modify. The Shadow grew through the years. In time, he even became two Shadows—The Shadow of the magazine, and also that upstart usurper, The Shadow of radio (a transparent fellow who laughed funny and traveled about with his secretary, solving mysteries).

The radio heresy to one side, the character of the magazine Shadow was built by stacking sophisticated traits upon simple traditional elements, then melting all this in the imagination. He began as a sterotype for the ears.

2.

At first, there was a weird voice laughing as it narrated *The Detective Story Hour*. That voice knew. It said so. Nothing was concealed from it. To human hope and human folly, it reacted with sardonic mirth. That first radio Shadow was the voice of Fate or some other awesome abstraction. Rozen's hooded figure, blue-skinned and jeering, catches the essence precisely.

The implication is, of course, that this figure understands what the people of the drama do not—that they cannot alter their destiny. Predestination clutches them in immutable talons. Their fevers of emotion are wasted. Their future is fixed; as they wiggle unwillingly toward it, Fate watches and laughs.

The Shadow, the ad agency called that voice.

Just where that name came from is uncertain.

"The Shadow," as a name, had long since passed into common usage. At various times, in various literary veins, it stood for evil incarnated, or for the ghost of the returned dead, or for the image of death. This latter usage was employed by Edgar Allen Poe in his sketch, "Shadow,—A Parable" (1835). In this prose poem, seven mourners, drinking wine by the corpse of a friend, see something most unsettling:

"And lo! from among those sable draperies...there came forth a dark and undefined shadow—a shadow such as the moon, when low in the heaven, might fashion from the figure of a man... But the shadow was vague, and formless, and indefinite, and was the shadow neither of man nor God..."

This is representative of that customary usage of "A Shadow" or "The Shadow" to suggest the shadow of death, an image viable in this society, at least. If the meaning is obscure, it will usually be clarified by the text in which the reference appears. However,

"The Shadow," when used as a title, almost always carries overtones associated with death.

Almost as strongly, the title suggests secret observation.

Consider the suggestion made by Charles Dickens in a letter, dated October 7, 1849, to John Forster. Dickents was soon to begin publication of a periodical titled *Household Words*. He was searching for a unifying gimmick to tie together the magazine content—essays, poems, social commentary, and short stories:

"Now to bind all this together, and to get a character established...I want to suppose a certain SHADOW, which may go into anyplace, by sunlight, moonlight, starlight, firelight, candlelight, and be in all homes, and all nooks and corners, and go everywhere, without the least difficulty...a kind of semi-omniscient, omnipresent, intangible creature. I don't think it would do to call the paper THE SHADOW: but I want something tacked to that title to express the notion of its being a cheerful, useful, and always welcome SHADOW. I want to open the first number with this Shadow's account of himself and his family. I want to have all correspondence addressed to him. I want him to issue his warning from time to time, that he is going to fall on such and such a subject; or to expose such and such a piece of humbug; or that he may be expected shortly in such and such a place...I want the compiled part of the paper to express the idea of this Shadow's having been in libraries, and among the books referred to. I want him to loom as a fanciful thing all over London; and to get up a general notion of 'What will the Shadow say about this, I wonder?... Is the Shadow here?' and so forth...it presents an odd, unsubstantial, whimisical, new thing: a sort of previously unthought of Power going about...(It) sets up a creature which isn't anything of the kind: but in which people will be perfectly willing to believe, and which is just as mysterious and quaint enough to have a sort of charm for their imagination, while it will represent commonsense and humanity. I want to express in the title,..that it is the Thing at everybody's elbow, and in everybody's footsteps. At the window, by the fire, in the street, in the house, from infancy, to old age, everybody's inseparable companion..."[48]

At first glance, this seems a tolerably accurate description of several familiar Shadow characteristics. That appearance is deceptive. Mr. Dickens is toying with a character (melodramatically named) who has many of the personal characteristics of Isaac Bickerstaff, the commentator whose presence unifies Addison's *The Spectator* essays (1711-1714).

BICKERSTAFF: "Thus I live in the world rather as a SPECTATOR of mankind than as one of the species...I cannot yet come to a resolution of communicating (my name, my age and my address) to the public. They would indeed draw me out of that obscurity which I have enjoyed for many years, and expose me in public places to several salutes and civilities which have always been very disagreeable to me; for the greatest pain I can suffer is being talked to and being stared at. It is for this reason, likewise, that I keep my complexion and dress as very great secrets..." (from *Spectator* No. 1, March 1, 1711)

So Dicken's proposed Shadow, like Isaac Bickerstaff, observes and comments, does not actively participate, is anonymous in the crowd, and has decided opinions.

As it turned out, Dickens dropped his plans for The Shadow. The concept, considerably modified, was altered to The Uncommercial Traveler, traveling for "The great house of Human Interest Brothers...always wandering here and there...seeing many little things, and some great things, which, because they interest me, I think will interest others." His observations appeared in the periodical *All The Year Round.*

It is evident that we are here dealing with elements of a literary convention—an anonymous observor who comments on the society about him. It is the articulate invisibility of The Spectator and The Shadow which is the point. The names have relatively little significance.

Because of those weird harmonics hovering about the title "The Shadow," the name continued to be popular. It was used, quite independently, by many different writers for many different purposes.

"Shadow" was, for example, the pseudonym of S.T. Hammond, an essayist, who, in 1858, published:

"Midnight Scenes and Social Photographs Being Sketches of Life in the Streets, Wynds, and Dens of the City (Glasglow)"

(Again, as you notice, the articulate, secret observer.)

And The Shadow was soon to become one of the most popular names in the vocabulary of the dime novelist.

The dime novels were peppered full of references to "The Shadow," meaning one who follows secretly—as "I shadowed the subject to a motel where he met a woman identified as Mrs..." Something about the shadowing situation—the unseen individual gliding silently, unseen, undetected, but watching, noting every move...something about that situation set the dime novel people quivering with delighted horror.

Thus, the annals of dime novels are stiff with such titles as:

"Watch-Eye, The Shadow," *Beadles' Half-Dime Library,* #96 (1879)

"The Shadow Detective," *Old Sleuth Library,* #7 (1888)

"Shadowing A Shadow," *New York Detective Library*, #462 (1819)

"A Successful Shadow," *Old Sleuth's Own Series* #112 (1897)

"Buffalo Bill's Spy Shadower," *The Buffalo Bill Stories* #69 (1902)

"Bob, The Shadow," *Brave and Bold* #199 (1906)

"The Shadow," *New Nick Carter Weekly* #586 (1908)

"The Shadows of New York," *Old Sleuth Weekly* #74 (1909)

"The Bradys and the Black Shadow," *Secret Service* #513 (1909)

There were dozens more:

"A Lady Shadower"   "A Puzzling Shadow"   "The Haunting Shadow"   "The Shadow Scout"

All stories testified to the popularity of concealed followers trailing behind, watching, lurking.

In less raffish publications than the dime novels, the name "The Shadow" appeared in a variety of contexts. "The Shadow" was the title of a literary publication (four issues, February-June, 1898) issued by the Cambridge University Press.

It was also the title of at least five novels by:

H. Begbie (1911); E. Phillpotts (1912); A.J. Stringer (1913); L. Rogers (1929); H. Bedford-Jones (1930).

"The Shadow—(a pastoral)" was the title of a 1914 poetry collection. It was also the title for two separate plays (minus "a pastoral"): one by N.G. Glover in the early 1920's; the second by P.J. Skarga in 1924. In 1929, "The Shadow" appeared as the title of a short story collection by J. Farnol; it received horrible reviews.

And in other wonderful and various ways, the name flickered and flashed down years of literary productions:

"Shadow" by M.W. Ovington (1920)

"The Shadowy Thing" by H.D. Drake (1928)

"The Shadow Flies" by R. Macauley (1932)

"The Sinister Shadow" by Henry Holt (1934)

"The Shadow In the House" by M. March (1936)

During 1928, F. Scott Fitzgerald, the soul of the Jazz Age, published two short stories in THE SATURDAY EVENING POST. Each referred to "The Shadow." But don't let your hopes lift. The first story, "The Freshest Boy," (July 28, 1928) opens in the heart of a 14-year old boy's daydream. He imagines himself a suave gentleman burglar named "The Shadow"; the story is set in 1911.[49]

In the second story, "The Captured Shadow" (December 29, 1928) the same young hero, now age fifteen, has written a play about this same gentleman burglar. The play and the short story share the identical title, which also happens to be the title of the play that Fitzgerald wrote when he was about fifteen. This particular literary chain seems to have begun with the stage production of "Alias Jimmie Valentine" (1910), which established the gentleman burgler as a wildly popular type that endured until the end of the 1920's.

Fitzgerald's use of "The Shadow" has occasioned speculation that "The Freshest Boy" was the probable source in naming that radio voice.

"All that remained for the Ruthrauff and Ryan agency man, Walter Gibson, and a S&S executive or three, was to put the readily recalled Fitzgerald concept...into their own varied pattern of use—which, with some more equally naked borrowing from the prominent source of the double-identity crime fighter idea...they very assiduously did."[50]

Still other commentators will not settle for F. Scott Fitzgerald but will insist that The Shadow's proper origin is in the February 1929 issue of Street & Smith's FAME AND FORTUNE MAGAZINE. In that issue appeared a novelette title "The Shadow of Wall Street." This was written by Frank S. Lawton (pseudonym for George C. Jenks), who told how a group of crooked financiers were foiled by an extraordinary fellow who concealed his actual identity in a monkish robe and cowl and so manipulated things that those Wall Street wolves were trimmed. After which, Compton Moore (The Shadow of Wall Street) laughed weirdly.[51]

It is certainly possible that the name, "The Shadow," comes indirectly from either Fitzgerald or FAME AND FORTUNE. It is equally possible that someone in the ad agency was reading Poe or H. Bedford Jones or a dime novel, or that Ralston had suggested the name, or none of these.

As these pages have suggested, "The Shadow," as a title, had appeared in print for a hundred years and was securely a part of the literary tradition. By 1930, "The Shadow" was not only a familiar symbol, with numerous meanings, but had been used almost to extinction.

Nothing is more delightful than speculation about literary origins. The game is played incessantly. Correct solutions are sometimes stumbled upon. But how are you to know, in a welter of solutions, which is correct? How disagreable it is to report that you cannot. Unless specific documentary evidence is available to support your sugared webs of logic, you cannot know. That a thing could have happened is no evidence that it did happen. By all means let us speculate with airy joy upon the many possible reasons why the agency called that anouncer "The Shadow." But, honestly, we don't know why.

Until more substantial facts are disclosed, the story of naming that radio voice is not known.

What Walter Gibson inherited, then, was a deep-toned, weirdly, inflected voice—like that of the usual omniscient fate figure. No matter how great a stir that voice made on radio, it was strictly from literary boiler-plate—a cliche' in sound.

Since fate figures, in the usual course of things, laughed weirdly, so did The Shadow.

At this point, Gibson began his novels.

3.

Before he became involved with The Shadow, Walter Gibson had toyed with the idea of a mystery novel. His idea, only partially formulated, concerned a mysterious figure—an enigma in black—who exerted profound influence, all unseeen, upon the lives of those about him.

These preliminary ideas were transplanted bodily into the new magazine, admirably fleshing out that vaporous radio voice. Gibson's mystery figure inherited the radio voice's name and creepy laugh. That accounted for two of the voice's three characteristics. As for the third trait, the mystery figure was, in Gibson's mind, already virtually omniscient.

In developing The Shadow, Gibson borrowed liberally from the literary convention of the period—which is to say, that store of familiar images and symbols that have, by constant repetition, become embedded in the readers' minds. Gibson mixed in significant memories from his early reading and added effects from professional stage magic.

These factors all reacted, somehow, to produce the figure of The Shadow as we now know him. But they did not react all at once.

Much character formulation appears in "The Living Shadow," but it does not jell until later. Other important features were tacked on in subsequent novels. The process was of steady addition, until certain critical proportions had been reached and Gibson's creative imagination reshaped these many images into the coherent figure of the 1932 Shadow.

It was a slow process. Gibson not only had to teach himself the art of novel writing, but he faced specific technical problems in materializing a solid magazine character. To begin with, he had to

—establish a visual image of a voice,

—dramatize characteristics of a superior individual,

—and, explain realistically, that individual's omniscience.

Development of the visual image was rather more complex than it looks. The ultimate figure was a synthesis of the cloaked mystery figure and a terror shape that loomed from the darkness. This latter image derived rather specifically from Gibson's early reading:

(We begin in the bedroom of a haunted house, where the narrator of our story sees a horror forming:)

"It was a darkness shaping itself out of the air in very indefined outline. I cannot say it was of human form, and yet it had more resemblance to a human form, or rather shadow, than anything else. As it stood, wholly apart and distinct from the air and light around it, its dimensions seemed gigantic; the summit nearly touched the ceiling...

"...As I continued to gaze, I thought—but this I cannot say with precision—that I distinguished two eyes looking down on me from the heights...

"Opposed to my will was another will, as far superior to its strength as storm, fire, and shark are superior in material force to the force of man."

This terror appears in Edward Bulwer-Lytton's "The Haunters and the Haunted or The House and the Brain," a story first published in BLACKWOOD'S MAGAZINE (1859) and remaining continuously in print, ever since. In the afterpart of the story—not often reprinted—the narrator meets a strange magnetic man who is possessed of incredible powers:

"...about the man's whole person there was a dignity, an air of pride and station and superiority that would have made anyone...hesitate long before venturing upon a liberty..."

And a later observation:

"...there was even a smile, though a very quiet and cold one." Further: "(his) laugh was inward, sarcastic, sinister—a sneer raised into a laugh."

And finally: "...he fixed my gaze so steadfastedly that I could not withdraw it—those fascinating serpent eyes." As a matter of fact, this awesome being places a hypnotic command on the narrator, who is forced to obey it in spite of all.

The image of the physical form associated with darkness yet separate from it reappeared, generations later and intensely reworked, in Gibson's novels. So did the dominating will, the almost hypnotic ascendency of The Shadow over those he met; the laugh that was a partial sneer; and, in particular, the eyes.

"But from between the hat and cloak glared two eyes that shone like beads of fire."

And later:

"The figure seemed to dwindle as it merged into darkness. Two burning spots glowed dull and disappeared... A sound followed (Steve Cronin) from the room—it was a mirthless, mocking laugh!

"He had seen The Shadow! It was real! It had spoken! It had looked at him with its eyes of fire." (from "The Eyes of The Shadow")

In the natural world, it is hard to account for the flaming shine of The Shadow's eyes. At different times, they are described as burning or glowing, as if attached to a dry-cell battery. Later in the series, it is commonplace that, when guised as Cranston, The Shadow's eyes will suddenly ignite, sparkle, flash, then return to dullness—all this indicating that he has suddenly taken a profound interest in something.

Since human eyes do not customarily perform these fiery tricks, unless provided with a biologically improbable reflective layer, the only explanation we have for the phenomena is that Gibson has borrowed it from an earlier tradition.

Eyes of weird creatures of the night blaze and flame appropriately. This feature they share in common with hypnotizers and Chinese menaces, and, less fortunately, with feral types.

In popular fiction, the phosphorescent eye is a code symbol for humans with strong animal natures. If the eyes of that nice young man glow red, he is undoubtedly a werewolf and hell on woman. If they glow yellow, or green, or glare like flame, he is a vampire.

Gibson has remarked that his conception of The Shadow was influenced by the stage play, "Dracula." (This was presented in London, 1924; then in New York, 1927, with Bela Lugosi.) The moving picture lifts scenes and dialogue bodily from the play. It is a curious experience to watch the film with The Shadow in mind. The Count winds himself sensuously within that black cloak. He is given to all manner of old-fashioned hypnotizer gestures and his eyes, by some moving-picture miracle, do certainly flame. Occasionally you receive the unsettling impression that The Shadow's ghost has momentarily flickered across the vampire figure—an illusion, but an unexpectedly strong one.

Dracula dominates the screen. He is the embodiment of that fine old cliche, the mystery figure, which has spooked about these many years. Essentially, the mystery figure is a sliding, half-seen form, well wrapped in black coat and wearing a wide-brimmed black hat that obscured its face. It lurks and spies and vanishes silently into the darkness. Often the eyes flame.

It is a familiar figure, most certainly. Muffled figures by night go back as far as stories are told, and many a child has gone chilled to bed with thoughts of creepy laughter from the dark. The image has been extraordinarily durable—note the back pages of the American Mystery Novel.

Similar figures slip menacingly through such ancient prose as Walpole's *The Castle of Otranto* (1765). These figures became conventional suspense devices in subsequent Gothic novels, those tales of murder sadism torture madness hatred revenge and terror which still wink like blue fire, on literature's distant horizon.

(Those essential props, the cloak and hat, date at least 200 years earlier. Their ancestry is respectable, for they were articles of protection in ages when overcoats were not easily come by and a wide-brimmed hat kept off the weather.)

Through distant Gothic thunders, the black-cloaked figure glided. It was never up to much good. A stock figure then, it was a stock figure in the later penny bloods and half-penny dreadfuls published in England in the mid-1800's.

Finally, it became a stock figure in the American dime novels. "...she looked over the balustrade, intending to call. Not a word left her lips...a man was going slowly down, wrapped in a cloak, with a shadowy hat drawn low over his brows. A slender hand shone white against the dark cloak, and as he reached the hall below, he glanced over his shoulder, showing...the same colorless face...and glittering eyes that had frightened her before..." ('A Marble Woman or, The Mysterious Model," 1875.)[52]

And similar figures moved through other dime novels, as "The Man In The Black Cloak," *New York Detective Library*, 362 (1816) or:

"The Haunted Churchyard," *New York Detective Library*, #371 (1890); thus: "...a tall man wearing a heavy cloak and a low slouch hat..."

The figure ignored the assaults of time.

It appears in Nick Carter or Buffalo Bill adventures. It glides through a 1912 POPULAR MAGAZINE. In the 1919 ALL-STORY WEEKLY, it appears, calling itself Zorro.

And in Chapter 53 of Edgar Wallace's *The Face In The Night* (1924):

"He wore a long coat that reached to his heels; his head was covered with a black slouch hat."

You find the figure in a 1926 FLYNN'S, peering through the window of a Digby Gresham story. Down across the years, it flits, a dark phantom, appearing in such detective and adventure fiction as requires a mystery figure's strong visual stimulation to maintain suspense and keep the paying customer from lapsing into a coma.

So common was the mystery figure that Lon Murray, editor of THE SHADOW DETECTIVE MONTHLY, seems to have briefly considered another outfit for The Shadow—this being the monk's cowl mentioned in an earlier chapter.

This idea did not last long. A figure wearing cloak and slouch hat has certain associations with lurkng, suspense, and danger.

The monk's cowl is more frequently associated with supernatural adventures. Death as a skeleton in robe and cowl was a familiar symbol during the Middle Ages, which had their own troubles. When the Gothic novels arrived, the figure was already a conventional symbol of menace and horror, and Matthew Gregory Lewis used it to evoke those emotions in his novel, *The Monk* (1795)

Radiating the usual fear and horror, the cowled figure plays a feature role in Dickens' *A Christmas Carol* (1843):

"It was shrouded in a deep black garment, which concealed its head, its face, its form, and left nothing of it visible save one outstretched hand. But for this it would have been difficult to detach its figure from the night, and separate it from the darkness by which it was surrounded.

"(Scrooge) felt that it was tall and stately...and that its mysterious presence filled him with a solemn dread...behind the dusky shroud there were ghostly eyes intently fixed upon him, while he, though he stretched his own to the utmost, could see nothing but a spectral hand and one great heap of black." (Stave Four: The Last of the Spirits.")

Like the mystery figure, the weird cowled figure persisted into modern times. An image almost identical to the Ghost of Christmas Yet to Come appears in Edgar Wallace's short story, "The Ghost of Down Hill" (1929). In this, the phantom is provided with a skeleton face. A similar phantom comes stalking through Wallace's 1929 play, "The Terror," and gives the heroine blue fits.

The cowled figure sputtered out at the Shadow works—possibly because Murray transferred to another assignment. The black-cloaked mystery figure, as you know, went on, ever more brilliantly. It furnished the core upon which The Shadow's other traits and capabilities were precipitated. And so it began.

4.

The formulation of The Shadow as a mystery figure, well obscured in cloak and slouch hat, is accompanied by tons of gaudy characteristics dumped recklessly into "The Living Shadow."

—He is the mysterious leader
—of a mysterious organization
—that is engaged in dangerous work.
—He demands absolute obedience.
—His will is law, his grip steel, his purpose will prevail.
—He communicates by mysterious disappearing messages, all coded up, and uses a most peculiar maildrop to receive communications from his agents.

—He occupies an unknown office, very theatrical

—He writes out his thoughts, thereby permitting readers to follow and marvel.

—He is constantly alert to save agents from the consequences of their own folly, and

—He does this by being constantly in disguise.

—At the slightest pretext, he laughs weirdly and mocks futile efforts to balk his will.

—He prefers that his activities remain anonymous, even when credit is due.

All the above suggests how you go about making a mystery figure mysterious.

First, tell the readers that they are witnessing a mystery.

Then let Harry Vincent marvel and gasp.

Then allow the crooks to be nervous.

Then show The Shadow laughing—The Shadow detecting in his mystery room—The Shadow saving that poor simp Vincent, who needs saving about every three chapters. These rescues throb through the novel like the strokes of a gigantic heart. At each deliverance from doom, Harry gapes, quakes, wonders.

So, by proxy, does the reader.

Here in a weird room, The Shadow sits beneath a blue light. He wears a blue-stone finger ring, and in all ways is highly mysterious, not to say very very strange.

Observe the setting well. In only two years, all major pulp magazine heroes will have their own secret rooms—their sanctums and labs and fortresses of solitude, where, to their heart's delight, they measure the bursting vigor of their intellects against the current problem.

At this point in time, The Shadow's sanctum holds only a light, a table, a chair, a wastebasket, and a pair of scissors. Who empties the wastebasket is not stated. Perhaps a little old masked lady.

At any rate, it is a proper setting for high-potency deducting.

The Shadow shares many characteristics once displayed by Sherlock Holmes—the lean face and high sharp nose, the long thin body, with muscles of elastic steel, the usual piercing mind and deductive ability. Like those other great detectives after Holmes—The Old Man In The Corner and The Thinking Machine—his mind slices a problem into neat chunks and answers. In certain respects, he is as great an arm-chair detective as Dupin, although—as you remember—The Shadow early turned to blood sport.

Some of The Shadow's deductions seem very thin and how he is always right is not easily answered. Through the pulp magazines, since Nick Carter's time, detectives have deduced with one eye on the plot and the other on the reader. The Shadow deduces with more elan than most. If you can't figure out how he gets his results, it is because he has a special ability for drawing forth the truth from no evidence at all. It is a gift.

In other ways, he dazzles the reader with his superiority. His physical strength is unusual. His mental abilities stun. He seems without fear, and his actions are sudden, forcible, harsh. All these characteristics applied to so many other popular heroes that it would be tedious to list them. Nick Carter possessed them. So did Don Diego Vega (Zorro). As did Jimmie Dale and all those anonymous gentlemen—the Gray Phantom, The Rook, The Picaroon, The Black Star—whose adventures glint vividly as emeralds set in yesterday's prose.

Let us accept The Shadow, particularly in his early appearances, as possessing those traditional qualities familiar to hero figures through time. Let us proceed to other qualities, introduced in "The Living Shadow," which boom through the entire series.

About one important thing, both Gibson and the radio agreed— The Shadow Knew!

And how so?

In a number of ways.

He is there listening, clinging like a huge bat to the wall outside the window. Or he stands in that shadow-filled corner between the bookcase and the wall. Or he is there among the participants, his face treated to look like Earl the Killer.

His listening devices dangle behind the radiator. His friends and agents are part of the secret discussion, remembering every word spoken. Or, if they are absent, The Shadow deduces what went on, for that icy mind, unencumbered by error, reasons as crisply as a solid-state device.

The Shadow was preceded by years of knowing figures who glided by night, unseen. Their numbers are very classy, including that deadly genius, Fantomas (a brilliant French murderer, escape master, and disguise artist.) Blackshirt (a zestful English thief shaped from the clay of Jimmie Dale, and dressed all in black), or that fellow Zorro.

All these are virtually invisible by night. No one sees them come or go. Their paths are—well—untraceable.

Each contributed his bit to the traditional figure of the unseen listener in the shadows. It is, however, less likely that Gibson was influenced by that tradition than by his memory of that tower of shadow hulking up in Bulwer-Lytton's house of horror. It is equally probable that he recalled that device from professional magic when the stage is plunged into darkness—and across it glides an unseen assistant dressed in black and moving against a black background. For certain effects, such invisible helpers are invaluable.

Just as the terror and the magician's aide, The Shadow rises wonderfully from shadow and dwindles back into it. It is a useful ability. Nothing so aids your omniscience as to be present at private conversations.

Present either unseen or in disguise.

The perfect disguise is an old dream. Thousands of authors have disguised tens of thousands of characters, and rarely have those disguises held a flaw. It is not so in crass common life, where a painted face shows its artificial surface by an absence of pores, and light reveals the tell-tale putty, the palpably false hair, the outlines of the altered face.

Not so with The Shadow. Apparently he relies upon large quantities of putty, or something dense and malleable. We know that once, at least, he used a sort of gauze-base upon which the artificial face was erected. And the stories are filled with remarks about Cranston's masklike face. He doesn't seem to be able to smile largely, possibly because the face is solid plaster.

Like all else in these stories, the disguised face has a long long history. In the remote past, back in Bill Shakespeare's era, it was already traditional that if you assumed a disguise, hey, presto, you were disguised. Most usually, if you were a girl wishing to disguise yourself as a man, you donned a doublet and a sword and strode forth to the greenwood, all unbeknown.

In the gothics, disguise was rampant, if rather simple. You merely got into someone else's clothing and, when necessary, applied quantities of false beard. This had the effect of making you appear whoever you said you were—from which we gather that many people looked like masses of hair with eyes.

The dime novels leaped lightly over a great number of problems, their wonders to perform. In these, the mechanics of disguise were, as in Shakespere's time, simply ignored. When Nick Carter or other members of his crew wish to disguise themselves, they do so instantly—whipping out a mustache and a reversible hat, or blacking up with burnt cork, or sticking on a scrap of beard.

For serious business, Nick Carter was able to change his face entirely. Adopting the mannerisms of another, together with his face and voice, he could so disguise himself that if the imitation and original stood side by side, Carter would always be accepted as the genuine article.

Other people shared this ability. Colonel Clay, the famous swindler, was a human chameleon; Cleek of the 40 faces (he was a gentleman crook turned police helper to the Scotland Yard commissioner) had a rubber face that could be kneaded like

dough. So unexpected a figure as Buffalo Bill could appear as a
greasy border thug or evil Indian, then reappear, in moments,
with his famous long flowing hair and white pants. Jimmie Dale
did not attempt so much and was content to transform himself by
seedy clothing and handfuls of dirt, well rubbed in, thus
producing a drug addict or a thief where stood, but moments
before, a wealthy young man.

The Picaroon existed as a slight disguise which totally
transformed the man who donned it. The Gray Phantom once
seems to have worn a slight facial disguise but gave it up. The
Ringer (Edgar Wallace's genial murderer) melted into each part
he undertook and was utterly undetectable, whether in play,
novel, or short story.

Arsene Lupin—a major Shadow influence—arrived late in 1907
and continued into the early 1930's. A gentleman burglar with a
sunny sense of humor, he was a consummate disguise artist.
Through whole novels, he frolics in disguise. No one, including
the reader, suspects that he is there. Yet he is constantly present,
blazing with inward laughter.

A trace of the Lupin situation transferred to The Shadow novel,
minus the high good humor. Like Arsene Lupin, The Shadow was
there, in the text, all the time, perfectly disguised, and watching,
watching.

As a disguise artist, The Shadow performed easily at the level
of perfection required by Nick Carter, Fantomas, and Arsene
Lupin. Indeed, The Shadow places even more violent demands
upon himself. His characterizations often folow one hot after the
other, each wildly different. His appearance may change from
that of a Chinese killer, to a hungry-looking thug, to a German
janitor, and conclude as an immaculate millionaire.

How he hides that great beak of a nose is never explained.
Sherlock Holmes managed a similar feat—but in London, you
could get away with anything, it seems. It's the consequence of all
that fog, no doubt.

5

In the following novel, "The Eyes of The Shadow," Gibson adds
two more ideas that persist to the end of the series.

He specifically identifies The Shadow with wealth
He introduces gangsters and the underworld scene.

The wealthy hero is another traditional element. It justified so
much with so little effort. For years, it had been a favorite ploy of
the urban adventure story; at one blow, it explained how the hero
was able to get off work to go warring against crime. It also
accounted for his ability to endure the massive expenses a

magazine hero must face in pursuit of his destiny.

Let the hero be a sort of reclusive millionaire, and at once he goes where he wills, comes when he wills, wrecks his Stanley Steamer or jet transport without fear of the finance company's wrath. Like The Shadow, he can use up whole cases of cloaks, slouch hats, and .45's. He can operate private laboratories and nest away in fortified apartments.

More, he can pay princely salaries to those associates whose lives are made perilous by his presence.

The magazine millionaire bears little resemblance to the millionaire of stale reality. Those single-minded gentlemen thrill to no powerful altruistic vibrations. They are wary and lead formalized lives, with scant free time and much ritualized sniffing.

But the magazine millionaire is a young jolly fellow with a wicked smile and such winning ways that his friends, devoted to a man, yearn to bind up his wounds and accompany him on midnight excursions to Slum Alley.

The advantages of wealth are considerable. One particular advantage is to maintain a chauffeur who will drive you about the city and never wonder about gossip. Late in his career—and early in the automobile age—Nick Carter started this. Jimmie Dale followed Nick's good example and allowed his chauffeur to drive him to the verge of the Badlands. Johnston McCulley's irritating detective, Terry Trimble, did the same; he also carried disguises concealed in a secret compartment beneath the rear seat of a taxi.

Use of a driver was a grand idea. It eliminated the parking problem. And your machine was always waiting patiently when you suddenly appeared, the recovered jewels under your arm.

The alternatives are dreary. Think of the hero hunting a parking space; the urchins who steal his hood ornament; the low battery; the search for the ignition keys among the lockpicks and nose putty.

When W.R. Burnett published *Little Caesar* in 1929, his success exploded a fad for gangster novels. Through the early 1930's, the gangster novel, the gangster film, the gangster magazine were madly popular. It was not necessary to be authentic; merely violent.

The craze fed on material which crudely restated what BLACK MASK had been publishing all along. But fads do not honor true prophets. Although BLACK MASK said it first, and stylishly, Burnett got the royalties.

Little Caesar was a new version of the old underworld novel. Before the first World War, Frank Packard has introduced underworld scenes and characters into his serials and connected short stories, including *The Miracle Worker, The Wire Devils,* and the various adventures of Jimmie Dale. In his work may be found characteristically razor-edged descriptions of conditions down in the Badlands:

An underworld dance hall: "...there was the usual hilarious uproar, the usual close, almost fetid atmosphere that mingled the odors of stale beer and tobacco...a dozen couples swirling in the throes of the bunny-hug..."

A slum hovel: "It was a squalid place, a miserable hole, in which a single, flickering, yellow gas jet gave light. It was almost bare of furniture; there was nothing but a couple of cheap chairs, a rickety table-unpawnable ."

The people, the scene "...he hurried, talking in the accepted style through one corner of his mouth to hard-visaged individuals behind dirty, reeking bars that were reared on equally dirty and foul-smelling sawdust strewn floors."

The subject matter is dated, but Packard has his own power. This world he displays is soaked in filth, choked with matter rotting in the darkness and the stink of dirt-fouled cloth in airless places. All symbols of moral corruption.

Equally graphic descriptions appear in earlier stories about Nick Carter, Old King Brady, and those other hard-punching dime novel detectives. These men, impressively disguised, move through photographically-rendered scenes down the Bowery, Chinatown, the docks, where the toughest of the tough lounge. Here appear views of New York City from the underside—bars and restaurants, slums, back alleys, gyms and railroad stations. The descriptions of underworld hangouts differ in no great way from those described by Packard ten years later and Gibson almost twenty years later. Only the clothing and dialect change.

English and French fictions of the early 1900's included similar descriptive jaunts. Down in the dens of Paris (so it was said), Cleek and the Lone Wolf fought Apaches. In *Limehouse Nights* (1916), Thomas Burke explored the crime fringes of London and served as an inspiration to Edgar Wallace and the later Bruce Graeme "Blackshirt" novels.

Long before Burnett, the underworld novel was a living entity. But Burnett did feature the new gangsters, no matter how imperfectly seen, and his influence is felt in THE UNDERWORLD, GANG STORIES, UNDERWORLD ROMANCES, and inside the less heady covers of CLUES and SHORT STORIES.

Between Burnett and the hardboiled tradition, gangsters got into The Shadow story and were never afterward dislodged. The gangster mob became an essential plot element, although Al Capone might not have found much realism in the fiction.

"The Shadow Laughs," includes more new material and

continues to transform the old. In this novel, The Shadow's dual identity is established and will never be given up. We learn that he is definitely not Cranston. His true identity seems unimportant at this time. Enough that this astounding figure can impersonate Cranston so effectively that the millionaire must relinquish his own identity. Sets you on the edge of your chair that does!

As with most major themes added to The Shadow saga in these early issues, the dual identity was a traditional strain from the popular mystery adventure story. To recite all those heroes who employed a double identity would be as tedious as waiting out low-grade pain.

But consider only a few crumbs from this immense table.

To begin with, Nick Carter...

Behind much of the popular fiction written during the 'Teens and 'Twenties, and some of the fiction in the 1930's, looms the immense figure of Nick Carter. He radiates a powerful, if not uncelebrated, influence down the generations. His series was long and included the ideas of many writers not afraid to experiment in forms often remote from the mystery adventure.

Nick gives us a classical introduction to the dual identity field. At the beginning of his career, he remained constantly in make-up. Lord knows why. It's never convincingly explained: To conceal his real features so that evil men will not recognize him. Other heroes used the same argument later, with a similar lack of credibility.

In less fantastic moments, Nick was in the habit of disguising himself as a hayseed. A farmer caricature, which would lead to widespread social protest if attempted today, he was called Old Thunderbolt—Thomas Bolt, the countryman detective.

The characterization is appalling:

"A mass of shaggy and unkempt gray hairs covered his head and a long chin beard of the same hue half concealed the high collar and stock which he wore.

"His coat was so long that it swept the floor around the chair in which he was sitting, and he wore...checkered pants.

"On the floor...was a broad-brimmed slouch black hat and on the other side was a carpetbag of the 'daown-east' pattern."

CLIENT: "Are you Old Thunderbolt?"

OLD T.: "Sometimes, when I hev' fits; ordinarily I'm only plain T. Bolt."

CLIENT: "You are a detective?"

OLD T.:"Waal, some think so, an', ag'in, some don't."

(*Nick Carter Library,* No. 17, November 28, 1891)

That dialogue really stretched them out, down at the barber shop.

But we are not considering the development of rural comedy. The thing is, for his own reasons, Mr. Carter elected to spend his days covered with grease paint and false hair. He was not the first to do so, even in the dime novels.

Other dual identities were pursued with much less trouble. In the April 1911 issue of BLUE BOOK, readers were let into the secret of one of the longest-term impersonations in the history of pulp adventure.

You see, after an unfortunate love affair, a wealthy young English Lord (a Deputy Commissioner) left England for the wild places:

"Subsequently the Deputy Commissioner died of enteric in Mysore, but the fact was never known. With him at the time was a man so nearly his double that—believing some relationship to exist between them—the young baronet described minutely his affairs and his personal history. The stranger took up his life where the dead man left it—returning to England as Sir George Trevor..."

And, as Trevor, he continues in a series of great variety and complexity. The stories appeared monthly in BLUE BOOK from 1910 to mid-1933, the longest continuous pulp series written. The title was "Adventures of a Diplomatic Free-Lance," by Clarence Herbert New.

Although that unknown stranger was American, in all honesty he made a better Trevor than did the original. He got the family mansion out of hock, rebuilt the family fortune, established the first international industrial-financial complex, spent decades in the British Secret Service until his personal organization became so strong that he was conducting private wars. And, at last, he was operating as an independent nation, tucked away in the heart of London.

Fortunately, "Trevor" was benign and invariably knew what was best for the world. His example seems to have strongly influenced such giants as Clark Savage Jr. and Richard Wentworth; both borrowed from Trevor's work such material as improved their own operations.

Such long-term adherence to a dual identity was seldom seen in the pulps. Nick Carter eventually gave up Old Thunderbolt and began appearing as himself, with no disguise at all. But Trevor was impersonated to the end of the series.

There are specific differences between the dual identity and the secret identity (either for crime fighting or crime commission.) The dual identity requires either that a man assume another's life, or that he create a fictitious personality of dimension and duration. The dual identity is intended for the long haul. Unlike the more transient faces of disguise, it is not discarded after a few uses.

Thus Jimmie Dale creates the characters of Larry The Bat and Smarlinghue the artist and maintains these, if thinly, over a period of time. Richard Wentworth establishes the character of Blinky McQuade, which has duration, if little else. Cleek lives the quiet moments, after his reformation, in the character of a retired sea captain.

If the dual identity is relatively passive, the secret identity is not. For purposes of these comments (and understanding that nomenclature varies on this subject), the secret identity is the disguise adopted when the hero goes out to battle. The disguise is often symbolic, frequently in costume, and, in all cases, carries a strong charge of agression and violence. The secret identity radiates anger. It may support those grand intangibles, Right, Justice, and Law; or it may be committed to violence against people and property. Either way, it's the raw Id out for a prowl.

A hero-criminal such as The Crimson Clown or John Doe, steals from the rich and defies the world. Such beyond-the-Law heroes as the Just Men, Zorro, The Spider, or The White Rings, combat crime with a brutal directness that the Law cannot countenance.

In both cases, strong emotion glows about the secret identity, in the same way that the corona gleams from behind the eclipse's black disc. The Spider shows these emotions in constant eruption. The Shadow shows nothing; we can only surmise, from our own experiences with men, the white churning hidden in his heart.

The Shadow combines the dual identity and secret identity. Allard is Cranston is The Shadow. It is unique. In popular literature, it is common for one man to be two people. But it is decidely out of the ordinary for one man to be three. And all at once.

6.

At about the middle of 1932, The Shadow takes an altogether astonishing step for a major series character in an early 1930's pulp magazine. He becomes lethal.

In "The Crime Cult," he guns down the villain. In "The Blackmail Ring" and "Hidden Death," he turns his guns on the gangster hordes, themselves, and shoots without regard to whether he wounds or kills.

It is a major change.

The detective story was rather inflexible about not shooting folks dead. Hopalong Cassidy and all those quick-gun western types could cut down their man. Heroes of adventure stories could spill blood and still retain the reader's affection.

But in the mystery adventure, few enough American characters would permit themselves to be seen with a gun in hand, let alone pull the trigger. Matters had tamed considerably from the days of Nick Carter, when that master wore two pistols up his sleeves. In 1929, only a few characters would willingly shoot to kill: Race Williams and The Continental Op (BLACK MASK), perhaps; Ranger Calhoun and Satan Hall (DETECTIVE FICTION WEEKLY), and the later John Doe (DETECTIVE STORY MAGAZINE). (Four years later, no hero's pistol would ever cool.)

The English were not nearly so dainty about deadly heroes. Edgar Wallace, for instance, presented a fine long series of lethal men—from The Just Men and J.G. Reeder to The Ringer. Bulldog Drummond and, after him, The Saint, had most elastic ideas about the sacredness of human life—at least on the public page. Even Dr. Eustance Hailey, a very very very fat doctor-detective, was known to shoot the wicked or nudge them off a high place.

But back in the United States, a hero would go all over shivery if he thought of letting off a weapon. Once, when it seemed inescapable that Jimmie Dale must shoot a fiend, Mr. Dale hemorrhaged words of despair for a full chapter; then he didn't do it.

Since the magazine mystery story did not permit a hero to shed sacred living blood, he was forced to subdue foemen by curious substitutes. By superb marksmanship, he shot the gun from their fingers, or wounded them in the shoulder or arm. Or he sent them to sleep by drug injections, or pressures on the neck, or guns that jetted sleeping gas. Johnston McCulley was very active in so equipping his heroes and villains, and both The Crimson Clown and The Black Star thunder about over rows of snoring victims.

At first, The Shadow reflected this watery attitude. In his second adventure, "The Eyes of The Shadow," he does carry a pair of pistols of microscopic caliber. Through the next year of stories, he fiddles with silenced pistols and attacks thugs with bare fists and behaves as if he had never heard of self preservation.

Around the middle of 1932, The Shadow begins to reflect the violence of the gangster novel, then at its peak. As blood gushed audibly from every paragraph of BLACK MASK, DIME DETECTIVE, SCOTLAND YARD, and DETECTIVE DRAGNET, The Shadow donned a pair of .45's and began using them with deadly precision.

At first, he merely bumped off the Big Brain in self-defense. Later this type of defensive murder is abandoned and The Shadow enters the well-marked path of the Justice Figure.

He executes.

True he gives the opposition a chance. The leader and his minions are armed. When The Shadow cuts them down, he has the justification that they were attempting to kill him. If he wishes to excuse it that way, fine.

But there has been a quiet reversal of philosophy beneath the rushing prose. No longer does The Shadow attempt to corral The Master Murderer and his pasty-faced killers for the Law. Now his cases end as set-ups for major blood-lettings. Trapped and exposed, The Genius of Crime whirls, weapons blasting—and The Shadow drops him.

By the end of 1932, The Shadow is firmly set upon that road celebrated by The Just Men back in 1905. He is the detective, the judge, the jury, and the death cell, all in one.

The usual justifications are trifled with—powerful criminals escape because of wealth or political connections or because their lawyers pry new holes in the fabric of justice. We understand that Law and Order has broken down. The forces of Evil dominate. Justice reels, dismayed. Therefore, avenger, arise.

The Shadow arose. And, as he did so, the series found its own true focus and its own true voice.

7.

In getting his series underway, Gibson was not only influenced by traditional literary materials but by the attitudes and techniques of professional magic.

As practiced, professional magic interleafs two realities: The way things are and the way they appear to be.

On one hand, reality is a firm surface, solid, orderly, repeatable, and untroubled by ghosts.

On the other hand, reality is exceedingly slippery. Perceptions err. The imperfect human senses may be tricked, and so illusion may be created from emotion, visions from hopes, impossibilities from inner needs.

This double vision is fundamental to The Shadow series. The tension between actual and perceived reality is used by Gibson in constructing his stories, in handling clues and devices, and in the situations he builds around his characters.

Every element of The Shadow's world is touched by double or triple meanings. Facts are illusions. These conceal deeper illusions. What is real may seem incontestable, but there seems no limit to the weight of deception it will support.

Beneath The Shadow's hat brim is Arnaud's face. Beneath that, Cranston's. Beneath that, Allard's. Eventually we work down to reality. But it is a long trip.

We have spent some effort detailing some of the characteristics

Gibson used in developing The Shadow. But don't suppose that anything has been said about the real process of character development. We no more understand that process than a bin checker in a parts warehouse, making inventory,understands the engineering design considerations that created those parts.

Consider the situation when the writer—no names please—is asked to produce a 70,000-word novel featuring a mocking radio voice—and get it done soon as you can; we need it right now.

To begin with, assuming that it is at the end of the 1920's, the chances are good that he will cast the mystery voice as a mystery figure. Such figures are stock material. And, besides, they really do resemble that voice, materialized.

Now add other characteristics. Each tends to reinforce the mystery figure image. Each new characteristic further biases the figure's development in a given direction—in this case toward weird omnipotence. Thus, the knowing laugher becomes an accomplished lurker, a disguise master, a brilliant deducer, the head of a secret organization.

The process grows self-defining.

The Shadow possesses great wealth—he exercises a dual identity—exerts magnetic personal power—is feared by the underworld—aids the police with no thought of credit.

All these are conventional enough attributes—although seldom have so many been heaped upon a single individual.

But it is not simply borrowing an image from Dickens, a trait from Frank Packard, a trick from Nick Carter. Development of an integrated series character does not depend upon such intellectual shoplifting.

It does depend upon using materials that are personally meaningful to the author, so that the figure fires to life in his imagination. That figure dramatically expressed the wishes and beliefs of the author. It speaks directly to the wishes and beliefs of the reader.

"Writers and readers...are products of the same social and mental conditions: and the thoughts of one will be commonly of the same order and kind as the thoughts of the other. Even in the form which a writer gives to his thoughts, there will be the same compelling pressure from the world about him; he will unconsciously comply with what he feels to be the needs of his his readers; he will write so as best to be read."[53]

Prior to The Shadow, many mystery and justice figures filled public pages. There had appeared powerful deducers, secret organizers, and a few heroes who possessed blazing eyes.

None of these figures can be mistaken for The Shadow.

He is unique. And by his measure, Gibson's achievement is impressive. Using conventional materials, he fused a character of vigor and originality. He brought to life a figure of extraordinary power whose personal force was as concentrated as a river directed through a keyhole.

The strength of this character is even more remarkable when gauged by the stories featuring him. These were exciting emphemerals through which simplicities, called characters, experienced a lot of violence and complicated adventure. The narrative thrusts bravely along, showering forth its fights, its chases, its tricks and terrible traps and rescues.

Yet how cleverly it is all done. How cunningly is it paced, the scenes contrasted, the atmosphere built, the misdirection inserted. How deftly the complicated events are threaded into the larger story.

Under all this activity, clear statements are made, to those who will listen, about the individual and his community, and the world surrounding them. A pulp magazine is an odd place to hunt out moral positions. But you would hunt hard to find more conservative attitudes than are contained in these accounts of the extra-legal activities of a lethal unknown.

Thus, you are responsible to your community. You are obligated to support—even at considerable personal effort—the high requirements of justice. You are responsible for others, not only yourself. You tolerate no wrongs—and you celebrate excellent men.

Responsibility, effort, dedication, social integrity. No matter how gaudily the melodrama goes on, it is erected on solidly sober steel. The stories rise from a moral base. It existed all the time, concealed by clumps of exploded shells.

In their intricate simplicity, many of these stories reach the heights of minor works of art. Not all the gun smoke in the world can conceal that. The stories hold no high aspirations. Still for all their violence and all the limitations of their nature, they succeed energy and crisp audacity.

CHAPTER 4—THE MARK OF THE SHADOW

Up in North-east Ohio is a home with an admirable basement room. This, softly air conditioned and lighted, is bright with paint and the circling shelves, all around the room, glow with the bright spines of pulp magazines, precisely stacked.

Many difficult runs have found refuge here. FIGHT STORIES, NEW MYSTERY ADVENTURES, TERROR. A nice set of SCIENCE WONDER STORIES, white type on blue spine, and if you look closely, you may notice that rare single issue of SPICY ZEPPELIN STORIES. And a set of GOLDEN FLEECE, and one of G-MEN.

On the left side of the room, on shelves you can reach, the SHADOW MAGAZINES are stored. The early issues have white spines, delicately accented with red or blue touches. They wait quietly for your attention and admiration.

How beautiful they are. For years they have been collected, only the finest issues saved. The covers are unchipped and the spines whole and the paper, still fair, has avoided time's stain.

So much occured while these issues accrued, one by one, from April 1931 to early 1949. From Depression, Prohibition, Hoover, through economic disintegration, the rise of the dictatorships in Europe, to the big bands, war, the death of Roosevelt, the opening of the atomic age, the United Nations, the beginning of the Cold War and price escalations and television as an indoor sport.

The world destroyed and reborn again. A changed world rising on the bloody cinders of the old one; but the same sun, as far as anybody could tell, rising each day. Men's collars changed. So did their automobiles. So did feminine decoration, styles in book type, the cost of train and theatre tickets. Comic books became widely available, as did, paperbacked novels with strong sexual themes. A generation of funnymen moved from the stage to radio to the moving pictures and television. The von Braun team, captured in Germany, fired V-2's under the Army's eye in New Mexico; the pulp magazine age waned. And every year men and women graduated, became parents, smelled cool morning air, washed their hair, made the car do one year longer, wondered what next year promised—who would lead the country—who would lead the National League and the Big Ten and whatever happened to the nickle hot dog?

Through it all, the issues of THE SHADOW MAGAZINE, appeared as methodically as a turning wheel.

There, in that Ohio room, lie stacked witnesses to all that history, month by month.

Around The Shadows are stacked other series, which enlivened their day and faded:

The scarlet-backed SPIDERS. The yellow-spined PHANTOM DETECTIVE, THE WHISPERER (first and second series), THE SECRET SIX, DOC SAVAGE, TEN DETECTIVE ACES, SECRET AGENT X, G-8, AND HIS BATTLE ACES, OPERATOR 5, THE AVENGER...

On these painted shelves, the rich old spines offer wonder. Month after month, excitement, bloodshed, the heroic ideal, for only 10¢.

Once THE SHADOW DETECTIVE MONTHLY had shown the way, new magazines grew dense at the news stands and thrust their vivid titles forward, bold and assertive.

The Phantom Detective, the first issue of his magazine dated February 1933, was a wealthy young war veteran, grown bored with peace's inaction, who discovered that he had a flair for solving crimes. Able to disguise himself so cleverly that he could resemble any man, he warred with fists and .45 upon those master criminal fiends that the Law could not touch.

The Spider, first dated October 1933, was a wealthy young millionaire, who donned black cape, slouch hat, funny wig, grease paint, and became the deadly foe of the underworld, shooting down with his .45's those master criminals and their deadly hordes who ravaged the city and scared the girls. The Spider was aided by a small group of dedicated friends and was wanted by the police for multiple murders.

The Whisperer, who first appeared October 1936, was a disguised police commissioner moving through the underworld with deadly gun to accelerate the cause of justice, since the Law worked so slowly. In the second series of Whisperer novels (beginning October 1940), he trades gray clothing for black, and a hissing voice for a chuckle that expresses many things meaningfully.

Secret Agent X, a fine young war veteran with funding from an obscure Washington, D.C., budget, appeared February 1934. He was constantly in disguise, his true face never seen. He battled immense conspiracies of crime by boring from within, wearing every man's face. He didn't kill but those opposing him died anyway.

And those many others: The Green Lama, created because The Shadow was so popular and the Munsey Company wished to merchandise a competitor. The Black Bat, whose secret was that he was not, after all, blind, and with the help of friends became the hooded, caped Bat, who could see in the dark and shot as

necessary, and preyed on those criminals who... The Ghost was a
magician got up as a walking dead man who, aided by a few
friends and the Police Commissioner, battled some small-bore
fiends for the usual reasons. Moon Man, a wanted criminal
preying on criminals, in reality a policeman disguised by a
helmet of one-way glass. The Crimson Mask, The Park Avenue
Hunt Club, The Man in The Silver Mask...

Not all these derived from The Shadow, but all were influenced
by his success and the power of the world that unfolded through
his series. From 1932 on, The Shadow's shadow touched a
substantial number of the pages written during the next decade.

THE SHADOW MAGAZINE served as a lens which focused
popular themes and ideas from the preceding twenty years upon
the prose emerging in the 1930's pulp magazines. The extraordinary
growth of single-character magazines, and the increased
emphasis on series characters, derived directly from The
Shadow's success. It would likely have happened without him,
since the time was ripe for a strong lead character to represent the
popular heart in popular pages. But as things turned out, The
Shadow was accidentally first and, because of that, the image he
projected was influential. Also those influences which played
upon The Shadow were directly transmitted to those characters
following.

Nothing is so influential as success.

Thus many of those elements that passed through The Shadow
lens flamed through other series a year or so down the line. To
what extent The Shadow example influenced subsequent series,
and the extent that the on-going literary convention played a
part, is not easily untangled. Perhaps it cannot be untangled. The
images available to Walter Gibson were also available to R.T.M.
Scott and Norvell Page, Lester Dent and Paul Chadwick and
Norman Daniels and Jack D'Arcy and all the rest. It depended on
what they read and what they watched and what their individual
editors wanted—for they, too, had read and watched and listened,
in the night, for the public pulse.

Still, it is historical record that, for years after The Shadow's
appearance, pulp heroes strongly favored certain familiar
characteristics:

—A wealthy social lounger, once a war hero, employs a secret
identity to battle crime.

—This individual, an accomplished master of disguise, is aided
by a small group of friends. One of these is a beautiful girl; one or
more is an ethnic type.

—This individual also has a close friendship with one or more
high police officials, who speak very freely to him about private
police matters.

—In battling crime, the hero operates from a secret office, frequently with attached laboratory facilities. There he maintains records concerning criminals, disguises, armament.

—He has available to him a variety of machines: automobiles, airplanes, and boats, which he demolishes with a commendable single-mindedness.

—He is gifted in languages, speaking most standard modern languages, plus many dialects. His mind contrives to be both analytical and deductive. He excells in ju-juitsu, judo, and bar-room fighting. Has also a detailed knowledge of civil engineering, chemistry, physics, and criminology, and he has major gifts in analysis of personal dynamics, magic manipulations, and the deciphering of codes.

—Physically, this individual is rather tall and spare, but extremely strong. He is abstemious by choice, emotionally reserved, careful about women, and withholds emotional commitment from even his closest male friends. He customarily performs athletic feats that trained men can not duplicate.

—He shows little interest in fine arts or philosophy or economic theory. His personal preferences seem concentrated upon technical materials. Only rarely does he show an interest in music. He seems unaware of the social ambiguities through which he moves, nor does he appear to have any interest in those powerful forces then shaking society or the historical currents which shaped his world.

—His life is dedicated to battling crime, using a secret identity intended to fill the underworld with fear.

—Most usually, he fights cirminal organizations: gangsters hired to serve an unknown master; or armies of psychopathic killers, often oddly got up after the example of the Klu Klux Klan, who serve an insane genius.

—These engagements between the hero and the enemy are extended gun-fights in which numbers are killed. Sooner or later, the criminal leader is also killed; he is almost never taken alive.

—The gangster element is strongly emphasized, although paramilitary organizations are sometimes shown. Later in the 1930's, the size and ferocity of these groups is sharply cut back.

—The hero encounters frequent science-fictional devices being used by criminals.

—Numerous adventures involve Chinese, a deadly lot who spread, beneath the city, networks of booby-trapped tunnels and gloriously appointed headquarters concealed in the midst of slums.

—Ninety-one percent of the stories occur in and around New York City.

We know these abilities, these characteristics, these qualities admirable and otherwise. We know them well. In how many stories have these traits glittered down through the years:

—Nick Carter, disguised, trapped, faces one hundred Black Hand killers.

—Blue Jean Billy, in swimming suit and pistol, holds up the rich villain's luxurious yacht.

—The Crimson Clown, masked and in his scarlet costume, holds a roomfull of people at bay, his gas pistol steady, his cold laughter menacing.

—The flat menacing laughter of The Spider, a dreaded hunched figure, lanky hair hanging from beneath the slouch hat, that ruthless gash of a mouth

—uttering weird hissed words interrupted as The Whisperer whirled and lurid blue flame jetted

—from the .45's as The Phantom Detective desperately blazed at the snarling wave of killers who

—struck but blows did not seem to land on the elusive bronze figure. Fingers like steel tongs gripped the killer's neck and...

—The Marquis Trevor lowered the limp figure to the grass and with an impatient gesture signaled the others to hurry.

—in an instant, The Night Wind had slammed the door in their face. He darted up the stairs with his astonishing agility and, in another moment, darted off

—away from the mansion, tugging from his head the black hood which bore the symbol of The Thunderbolt

—the hood of the Green Lama

—the cowl of The Black Bat

—the weird shadow glided across the wall and from the gloom stepped a tall figure in a black cloak. Beneath the down-turned hat brim burned two flaming eyes. A whisper of chill mockery trembled in the room. The jetting muzzles of giant automatics froze crooks to their chairs.

Stiff-lipped, they mouthed:

"The Shadow!"

Not every weird radio voice had the good sense to become a national celebrity. Ralston had been correct. The public was ready for single-character publications, once again.

Of course, it isn't too clear just why a black-cloaked mystery, somehow associated with broadcasting, filled this need. But why does a mother-to-be want mangoes?

Still, it was more than good sense and good luck.

The radio voice contributed a few traits. The public domain contributed many conventional images. But The Shadow was more than the sum of these. Gibson fused the disparate elements into a superhuman figure, a living folk myth. The Shadow did not leap up complete from those first pages. Rather, he was shaped

slowly, one story, one set of characteristics at a time, as Gibson's
private vision slowly sharpened. Until at last, the figure of The
Shadow became that rarity, a new personality, prickly with life.
The figure is not entirely seamless. But it is coherent and makes
an eerie sense.

From the first novel, the figure lived, for it had enormous
vitality. Silent as thought, omnious as death, The Shadow
performed his self-appointed mission. He slipped through dank
alleys, hovered within mansions, listened in rooms where deadly
men planned horror. He was not entirely infallibile. Where is the
drama if your hero is infallible? But he was consistently
successful. And he radiated ability.

Some find his personality as uninviting as a steel mattress.
Undeniably, he was over-mysterious, violent, cold, intolerably
secretive and melodramatic, and domineering, and arrogant.
These characteristics gradually faded over the years. But even at
their height, they couldn't disguise his raw personal power.

The Shadow radiated personal force. You could rely upon him.
You recognized that, if he sought anything with passion, it was
the truth. He went hotly after the truth. And in getting it, he
probed what so many readers felt were the real causes of the
time's social woes—insofar as those causes could be explained
as master crooks, plotting gangsters, false lawyers, and narrow-
eyed bankers. Just as today, the 1930's found it easy to ascribe all
social woes to the plotting of a few special groups.

After the fine heat of those first novels, The Shadow firmed to a
pragmatic individual, practical and direct, ruthless as a surgeon
is ruthless. He could not cure all society's ills, but he could
eliminate certain problems.

This he did, twice a month.

For years, he dominated his field. His influence went
powerfully among the other magazines and left them green with
his urge for justice and his delight in adventurous ways. Other
heroes adopted his disguise techniques, numbers of
individualistic agents, friends in high places, and cavalier ways
with the heavy automatic. Few of them possessed The Shadow's
personal force, and none moved against a background as complex
as that provided by Gibson.

The Shadow has come down to us as a part of that heroic
tradition embossed by the 'Thirties. He has crossed that dim line
between fiction and folk lore, and his influence has gone off in
unexpected directions that no one anticipated.

His figure got into Jack Kerouac's imagination and stimulated
that prancing fantasy, Dr. Sax. The Shadow's voice echoed
mockingly from radio across the generations and returned to
mock again from long-playing records and cassettes. He has

appeared briefly on comic book racks and as the subject for a coloring book. His features look out from a dime store needlepoint kit. By this time, his image is inextricably mixed with that of the mystery figure. One or the other or both still appear on mystery collection covers or loom unexpectedly in ads for art materials, or is glimpsed, darting and bounding, through moving pictures striving for atmosphere.

The Shadow still generates his own personal force. He speaks to our time as once he spoke to the 1930's.

In a time eager for excellence, The Shadow embodied excellence.

In a time of confusion, he was coldly able and unshaken.

When the weeks were edged in black, when gangsters were invulnerable, when public officials were privately foul and public institutions glowed with corruption, The Shadow, untarnished, stood for intelligence and decency and merit, and justice equal and measured.

With effort, we might yet meet those standards demanded by his formidable presence. He is the embodiment, in black, of those high abstracts that are our final defense against the barbarians.

end

FOOTNOTES

1. A major figure in Street & Smith's gallery of money-makers, Nick Carter never really was retired. He lingered about the premises, a formidable ghost. Over the decades, he was repeatedly revived and updated. In times of stress, Street & Smith automatically turned to Nick, as to a talisman.

2. So stated in "Headquarters Chat," DETECTIVE STORY MAGAZINE, August 9, 1930, pps. 139-140. "It seems incredible, indeed, that the spoken voice alone—the actors' faces, forms, and gestures unseen—could hold millions of persons spellbound...as was the case last Thursday night./ 'But just wait till we really get into our full stride,' they told us after last night's performance'.... However these actors say that they not only can and will do better work next Thursday night but that during the half hour that is allocated to them on succeeding Thursday nights from now on, the show will constantly improve./ Again they keep secret from us what story will be chosen to dramatize and voice-act for you..."

3. Walter B. Gibson, "My Years With The Shadow," pages VII-XIX, contained in the Dover publication *The Crime Oracle and The Teeth of the Dragon, Two Adventures of The Shadow* (1975). In this essay, Gibson provides a wealth of information about the initial writing of The Shadow novels. Further information may also be found in *The Shadow's Scrapbook* (1979) in another long article, "Introducing The Shadow."

4. Matters were not quite as smooth as this. Gibson wrote six chapters, brought these in for approval—which was given, together with a request that he add Chinese elements to the story. That would allow use of some old THRILL BOOK (October 1, 1919) cover plates, saving the cost of new artwork.

5. Will Murray, "The *Duende* Shadow Index," contained in *The Duende History of The Shadow Magazine* (1979). Researched and compiled from Street and Smith records, this index is the indispensable document in understanding the publication sequencing of the Shadow novels. It clarifies numerous bibliographic problems.

6. An ad in the April 11, 1931, DETECTIVE STORY

MAGAZINE, tells us that The Shadow broadcasted "In a cloak with his face completely masked."

7. Lester Dent contributed one manuscript in 1932. Gibson revised this in 1938. The revision is not included in his 282 total.

8. Extracted from letter, John Nanovic to Will Murray, October 10, 1975; quoted in part in *Duende*, Winter 1976-1977, Vol. 1, No. 2, p. 48.

9. Duncan later appears in "The Red Menace" (November 1931) and "Atoms of Death" (July 15, 1935). He never makes agent. Probably too much like Vincent.

10. The Jimmie Dale stories, by Frank Packard, first appeared in the July 1914 PEOPLE'S MAGAZINE (a Street & Smith publication). They were wildly popular and were a major step in the transition from dime novel fiction to pulp magazine fiction.

11. The real Cranston's appearances, widely spread, include "The Black Falcon" (February 1, 1934): "Atoms of Death" (July 15, 1935); "The Spy Ring" (April 1, 1940); "Crime Over Miami" (November 1, 1940); "The Hydra" (December 1, 1942); and "The Money Master" (Dec 15, 1942.) He is an off-stage presence in a few others.

12. Extract from a taped interview of Walter Gibson by Will Murray, July 10, 1976.

13. Maxwell Grant (Walter Gibson), "The Shadow," from *The Great Detectives,*(1978), edited by Otto Penzler, pps. 213-214.

14. Apparently, The Shadow flails away with both automatics at full cock. Under those conditions, the .45's of that period have been known to fire inadvertently. Around 1938, the automatic's internal mechanism was beefed up to prevent such a regrettable incident. The Shadow's weapons were apparently modified earlier.

15. These powders seem to have been available in magic stores during the 1920's. Their use was banned following a severe accident during a demonstration for a customer.

16. Edgar Wallace, *The Terrible People,* Chapter 31., p. 137, Hodder, 1926.

17. Fred J. Cook, *Mafia,* (1973). Chapter 5 of this book ends with an account of this slaughter, which established the Syndicate as a functioning organization.

18. There was a real Arnaud, a wealthy businessman as widely traveled as Cranston. This is the first and last time that the real Arnaud is mentioned.

19. Walter Gibson, "The Shadow Speaks (An Exchange Between Nick Carr and Walter Gibson)", PULP, Vol. 1, No. 5, Winter 1973.

20. Gibson ran into trouble on this novel from too many characters and diffuse plot elements. At Nanovic's request, Gibson pared these down and rewrote a chunk of the novel. With the next story, he began preparing a synopsis of the action. This became ever more elaborate, growing to be a summary of the novel before writing started. This preliminary work, plus a pre-writing conference with Nanovic and Ralston, continued through most of the series. Reference Walter Gibson, "A Million Words A Year for Ten Straight Years," WRITER'S DIGEST, March 1941.

21. The contract ran from March 1932 to March 1933. The usual multiplicity of reasons exist for the twice-a-month schedule and contract: The bulk of Shadow sales occured during the first two weeks of sale; thus, twice-a-month would almost double profits. It was also prudent to assure that Gibson could handle the immense fiction production required; if he could not, a back-up writer could be used.

22. The phases are mentioned in Gibson's "Introduction" to *The Shadow, Crime Over Casco & The Mother Goose Murders*, p. lx.

23. Will Murray, from "The Men Who Cast The Shadow," *The Duende History of The Shadow Magazine*. This superb study considers the people, the governing editorial policies and relationships, and the narrative evolution which shaped the magazine. This work is lucid and definitive and its importance to an informed study of the magazine and the character can scarcely be overstated.

24. According the "The Shadow's Shadow," Vincent's identity and address are known to Farwell. For some reason—perhaps because Gibson forgot to arrange it—Harry does not change hotels. The crooks follow him, identify his contacts, and soon all sorts of Shadow agents are identified. Same thing happens in "Crime, Insured" (July 1, 1937), when most of the agents are scooped up because of similar carelessness.

25. Gibson and Carr, *op. cit.*

26. In the first chapter of "The Grove of Doom," all stops are out and the scene builds paragraph on paragraph, projecting images of gloom, thickness, choking evil. Throughout the novel, the atmosphere is an essential ingredient of the story. When the novel was reprinted in *The Weird Adventures of The Shadow*, and in the associated Tempo Paperback, the editor mutilated the effect by slashing about 40% of the prose, leaving hard-action bones—interesting but not quite what Gibson had intended.

27. This discussion is based upon details presented in "The

Duende Shadow Index" contained in the *History of the Shadow Magazine.*

28. Weston returned twelve novels later in "The Dark Death," written during the last of April 1934. This was not published until February 15, 1935, giving an exaggerated impression of Barth's term of service. Later Barth serves as Deputy Commissioner when Weston is on vacation.

29. Street & Smith also offered hardback editions of "The Living Shadow," "Eyes of The Shadow," and "The Shadow Laughs," for 25¢ each. These books came available in late 1934 as part of the ultimately six-volume Ideal Library. The first three adventures of Doc Savage were also published. More books about each character would have been printed. However, cost of publishing these books in the S&S printing shop was more than was received for the books. As John Nanovic remarked at the 1976 Pulpcon the books could have been printed more cheaply elsewhere. But S&S was intensely proud of their printing establishment and so the Ideal Library was dropped, although its volumes were selling briskly, a victim of organizational pride.

30. Theodore Tinsley remarked: "As far as I was concerned, the 'characters' were not people at all but were what Ezra Pound called 'Personae,' actually Masks," (Extract from letter to Will Murray, dated December 6, 1977.)

31. Theodore Tinsley to Will Murray, letter dated May 11, 1978. Street & Smith hesitated to interrupt Gibson's extraordinary fiction production. Apparently Tinsley was brought into the series not only as a back-up writer, but to try out a few changes—a more hard-boiled tone, more physical violence, and a strong increase in sexual elements. All these things, the Popular Publications single-character magazines were exploiting with loud success.

32. Theodore Tinsley to Will Murray, letter dated December 6, 1977.

33. Mrs. T.A. Tinsley to Robert Sampson. letter dated June 16, 1979. She remarks: "Norvell Page and Ted were close friends. As a matter of fact Ted and Norvell were friends before I went to New York around 1930. I met Norvell through one of the literary agents and afterwards met Ted since the three of them were friends. I feel quite certain that neither influenced the other's work in any way. Strong violent melodrama was the order of the day when they were writing and both were professional enough to write to please their editors."

34. A more detailed discussion of the Tinsley-Shadow characteristics may be found in "The Vulnerable Shadow," by Robert Sampson, included in *The Duende History of The Shadow Magazine.*

35. Theodore Tinsley to Will Murray, letter dated March 18, 1978.
36. Those who sought for information in back issues might possibly have found it. An editorial note in "The Pulse of a Nation" (April 1, 1937) indicates that, for 15¢ each or two for 25¢, you could still secure back issues as remote as "The Silent Seven" (February 1932, issue #7) or "Gray Fist" (February 15, 1934, issue #48). The availability of fresh new ideas in unsold/unread condition films these eyes with smarting tears, alas. Two for a quarter. How that scalds!
37. He so impressed the Xincas that they pried out one of their idol's fire opal eyes and presented it to him. The limp is entirely unnecessary and discloses The Shadow's predilection for excessive romantic trappings. Even as himself, he must use some element of disguise. Tricks lie within tricks; each deception conceals a deeper deception. The man Allard vanishes behind the glittering sleight-of-hand.
38. Here is another minor mystery. Four times in the series, a pair of dissimilar novels share the same title. The others are "Wizard of Crime" (February 15, 1943; and August 15, 1939); "The Shadow Meets The Mask," (August 15, 1941; and October 1944); and two so close they might as well be identical: "The Jade Dragon" (April 15, 1942) and "Jade Dragon" (August 1948).
39. For a more detailed discussion of Elliott's Shadow concepts, refer to "The Third Cranston," by Robert Sampson, in *The Duende History of The Shadow Magazine* (1979).
40. Walter Gibson, *The Shadow Scrapbook*, "The Shadow's Evolution as Portrayed in the Covers of The Magazine," p. 33. Canadian issues of these early Shadow magazines seem to have omitted the initial Table of Contents drawing (of Blackwell) and used the two small cuts of that blue-faced fellow laughing. Canadian issues were dated 10 months after the equivalent US issue of this period.
41. It is believed that this offer was slaved to the publication of THE SHADOW in Canada, the same plates being used.
42. Gibson had proposed that this glorious horror be used for the cover of the Shadow Christmas issue. This caused much hesitation, since S&S was given to sugar-paste covers featuring Christmas trees and merry Santas and bad men touched by the season. However, by a miracle, they ran the skeleton—and sold out the issue before it cooled from the press.
43. "Grace Note," by Robert Sampson (Xenophile #17, September 1975), discusses the series.
44. How Mr. Scott could have endorsed such a collection of bombs is scarcely understandable. My own personal listing, agreed

to by all reasonable people, is The Shadow's Shadow, The Black Hush, Gray Fist, The Crime Master, The Third Shadow, The Golden Masks, The Salamanders, The Strange Disappearance of Joe Cardona, Crime Insured, and The Wizard of Crime (8/15/39). (That's the list this week; next week it will be different.)

45. The Whisperer is considered in a fine essay by Will Murray, "The Many Faces of The Whisperer," in *Pulp* 7, Spring 1975.

46. "The Shadow Strikes" (1937); "International Crime" (1938); "The Shadow" (1940, a 15-chapter serial); "The Shadow Returns" (1946); "Behind the Mask" (1946); "The Missing Lady" (1946); and "Invisible Avenger" or "Bourbon Street Shadows" (1958). The Shadow serial is supposed to be the best of the lot. The stories and character cry out for a treatment such as was given to *The Godfather* but it is not likely that we shall see such on this planet.

47. The same thing happened in the March 1944 DOC SAVAGE, which announced Lester Dent as the author on the first page of the novel. The Table of Contents showed Kenneth Robeson.

48. This passage, extracted from the October 7, 1849, letter, has been widely quoted, although in small pieces. The complete letter is available in *The Nonesuch Dickens: The Letters of Charles Dickens, Vol. II (1847—1857)*, pps. 178—179 (1938). Partial quotations may be found in *Charles Dickens' Uncollected Writings from Household Words*, "Introduction," edited by Harry Stone, p. 12 (1968). And in Edgar Johnson's *Charles Dickens, His Tragedy and Triumph*, Vol. Two, Part Seven, Chapter 7, 701 (1952). And, finally, in Jim Harmon's *The Great Radio Heroes*, Chapter III, pps. 48-49 (1967).

49. F. Scott Fitzgerald, *The Basil and Josephine Stories*, edited by Jackson R. Bryer and John Kuehl, Scribners (1973). The "Introduction" gives the dates of the setting and the age of the hero, Basil Duke Lee, a barely fictionalized version of Fitzgerald, himself.

50. Bill Blackbeard, "Foreshadowings, "*Xenophile* #17, p. 59 (1975).

51. Dick Myers, "The Case of the Elusive Author," Part II, *Bronze Shadows*, Issue No. 10 1967. At this date, Myers assumed that Gibson had extracted the Shadow figure from the Wall Street story in FAME AND FORTUNE. When interviewed on this subject at the 1976 Pulpcon, both Gibson and Nanovic stated flatly that they had neither heard of "The Shadow of Wall Street" nor read FAME AND FORTUNE MAGAZINE.

52. Louisa May Alcott, *Plots and Counterplots*, edited by

Madeleine Stern, Popular Library, New York, 1978, p. 139.
53. John Richard Green, "Introduction," *Essays of Joseph Addison*, The Roger de Coverley Club, London and New York, undated.

BIBLIOGRAPHY

Addison, Joseph

Essays of Joseph Addison, "Introduction" by John Richard Green, Roger de Coverley Club, London and New York, undated. *Selections from Addison and Steele* (Edited by Will D. Howe), Charles Scribner's Sons, 1921

Alcott, Louisa May

Plots and Counterplots (Edited by Madeleine Stern), Popular Library, 1978

Blackbeard, Bill

"Foreshadowings," (Part I), *Xenophile* #17, 1975

Bulwer-Lytton, Edward

"The Haunters and The Haunted or The House and The Brain," *Great Tales of Terror and the Supernatural* (Edited by Herbert H. Wise and Phyllis Fraser), Random House, 1944, 2nd edition

Carr, Wooda Nicholas and McGregor, Herman S.

"Contemplating Seven of the Pulp Heroes," Bronze Shadows #12, October 1967

Cook, Fred J

Mafia, Paperback Library, 1973

Cook, Fred S.

"A Full-Length 'Shadow' Novel As Told To," *Bronze Shadows* #3, February 1966

Cox, J. Randolph

"That Mysterious Aide to the Forces of Law and Order," *The*

	Armchair Detective, Vol. 1, #4, July 1971
Dickens, Charles	*The Nonesuch Dickens: "The Letters of Charles Dickens"* (Volume II, 1847-1857), (Edited by Walter Dexter), The Nonesuch Press, Bloomsbury, England, 1938.
....	*A Christmas Carol,* Columbia University Press, 1956
....	*Uncollected Writings from 'Household Words',* (Edited and with "Introduction" by Harry Stone), Indiana University Press, 1968
Dunning, John	*Tune In Yesterday, The Ultimate Encyclopedia of Old-Time Radio, 1925-1976,* Prentice-Hall, 1976
Eisgruber, Frank	"Crime Under Cover" PULP, Vol. 1, #4, Spring 1972
....	*Gangland's Doom, The Shadow of the Pulps,* Weinberg, 1974 "Only The Shadow Knows," PULP Vol. 1 #3, Summer 1971
Fitzgerald, F. Scott	*The Basil and Josephine Stories,* (Edited and with "Introduction" by Jackson R. Bryer and John Kuehl), Scribner's, 1973
Gibson, Walter	*Interview,* 1975 Comic Art Convention Awards Luncheon, published in *1976 Comic Art Convention,* July 2-6, 1976, (Phil Seuling: editor)
....	*Interview,* taped, with Will Murray, Akron Pulpcon, July 10, 1976

....

"Introductions to the following volumes, all Crime Club, Doubleday and Co., Inc.:
—"The Mask of Mephisto" & "Murder by Magic" (1975)
—"A Quarter of Eight" & "The Freak Show Murders" (1978)
—"Crime Over Casco" & "The Mother Goose Murders" (1979)
—"Me And My Shadow," *The Weird Adventures of The Shadow*, Grosset & Dunlop, 1966

—"A Million Words a Year For Ten Straight Years," WRITER'S DIGEST, March 1941

—"My Years With The Shadow," *The Crime Oracle & The Teeth of The Dragon, Two Adventures of The Shadow,* Dover Publications, 1975

—"Out of The Shadows— Walter Gibson." *Duende* #, Winter 76-77

—"The Shadow", *The Great Detectives* (Edited by Otto Penzler), Little, Brown & Co 1978

—"The Shadow Speaks, An Exchange between Nick Carr and Walter Gibson," *Pulp*, Vol. 1, #5, Winter 1973

—*The Shadow Scrapbook,* with "Preface" by Chris Steinbrunner, and essays by Anthony Tollin, Harcourt Brace Janovich, 1979

Gladney, Graves

"Graves Gladney Speaks," *Duende,* Vol. 1, #1, 1975

Goulart, Ron

Cheap Thrills, Chapter IV: "A.K.A. The Shadow," Arlington House, 1972

Greene, Hugh

The American Rivals of Sherlock Holmes, Pantheon Books, 1976

Gruber, Frank

The Pulp Jungle, Sherbourne Press, Inc., 1967

Harmon, Jim

The Great Radio Heroes, Chapter III: "Who Knows What Evil Lurks," Ace, 1967

Johnson, Edgar

Charles Dickens, His Tragedy and Triumph, Vol. 2, Part Seven, Chapter 7, Simon & Schuster, 1952

Kerouac, Jack

Dr. Sax, Ballentine Books, 2nd printing, 1977

Murray, Will

The Duende History of The Shadow Magazne, 1980, including "The Duende Shadow Index" and "The Men Who Cast The Shadow"

....

"The Many Faces of The Whisperer", *Pulp* #7, Spring 1975

....

"The Other Shadow", *Xenophile* #10, January 1975

Myers, Dick

"The Case of the Elusive Author", *Bronze Shadows,* Part I: March 1967 (*Bronze Shadows* #9) Part II: June 1967 (*Bronze Shadows* #10)

Nanovic, John

"I Never Called Him Bill," *The Crime Oracle and The Teeth of the Dragon,* Dover Publications, 1975, Letter, partially

quoted, *Duende*, Vol. 1, #2,
Winter 1976-1977

New, Clarence Herbert

"Further Adventures of a
Diplomatic Free Lance, No. 1—
WHEN THE FOX STOLE
THE BAIT," BLUE BOOK,
April 1911

NICK CARTER LIBRARY #17, November 28, 1891

Packard, Frank

*The Adventures of Jimmie
Dale*, A.L. Burt Co., 1917

Penzler, Otto

Editor: *The Great Detectives*,
Little, Brown and Co., 1978

Poe, E.A.

*The Collected Works of Edgar
Allen Poe, Vol. II, Tales and
Sketches 1831-1842*, (Edited:
Thomas Ollive Mabbott,) The
Belknap Press of Harvard
University Press, 1978

Reynolds, Quinten

The Fiction Factory, Random
House, 1955

Sampson, Robert

"From The Blackness Spurted
Jabs From Huge Automatics,"
unpublished

—"Grace Note," *Xenophile* #17,
Sept. 1975

—"Just A Little Matter of
Doom," *Xenophile* #4, June
1974

—"The Third Cranston,"
contained in *The Duende
History of The Shadow
Magazine*

—"*The Vulnerable Shadow*,"
Pulp #5, 1970, and *The Duende
History of The Shadow
Magazine*

Tinsley, Mary (Mrs. T.A)   Letter to Robert Sampson, June 16, 1979

Tinsley, Theodore A.   Letters to Will Murray:
—December 6, 1977
—March 18, 1978
—May 11, 1978

Wallace, Edgar   *The Terrible People*, Hodder & Stoughton, 1926

Wolf, George   *"The Shadow Speaks,"* Bronze Shadows #14, March 1968

APPENDIXES

APPENDIX A. Variations in The Shadow Magazine Format

Issues Dated to	from	Magazine Size	No. Pages	Cost
Apr 31-6/1/38		6-¾ x 9-¾*	128**	10¢
6/15/38-11/15/39		as above	130	
2/15/39-3/1/39		6-¾ x 9-½		
3/15/39-11/15/39		6-⅝ x 9-¼	(Note: First trimmed edges: 11/1/39	
12/1/39-1/1/40		as above	114	
1/15/40-3/1/43		6-⅝ x 9-⅛		
4/43-5/43		as above	162	15¢
6/43		6-½ x 9-½	146	
10/43-1/47		as above	130	
12/43		5-⅜ x 7-⅞		
1/44-2/45		5-½ x 7-⅝		
3/45 x 7/46		5-⅝ x 7-⅝		
8/46-11/46		5-½ x 7-⅝		
1/47		5-⅝ x 7-¾		
2-3/47-8-9-48		5-⅞ x 7-¾	162	25¢
Fall 48-Sum 49		6-¾ x 9-¾*	130	(NOTE: un-trimmed)

*Add ¼" for cover overlap. While some dimensions are given to the nearest ⅛th, frequent variations occured of +1/16. It is suspected that dimensions will slightly vary even within issues of a given date.
** Page numbers include the front cover (pages 1 and 2) which, by convention, were always included in the page count. The back cover has not been included in the page count given here.

APPENDIX B. THE SHADOW IN REPRINT AND OTHERWISE

As Books:

1934   *The Living Shadow,* Street & Smith Ideal Library. (Reprint of April 1931 magazine novel. No dust jacket. Yellow binding. On cover, color picture of Shadow's reproduced from cover of 8/1/33 "The Black Hush.")

1935   *The Eyes of The Shadow,* Street & Smith Ideal Library. (Reprint of July 1931 magazine novel. No dust jacket. Yellow binding. On cover, reproduction of an eye, apparently from cover of 6/32 "Double Z.")

1935   *The Shadow Laughs!,* Street & Smith Ideal Library. (Reprint of October 1931 magazine novel. No dust jacket. Dark blue binding. On cover, color picture of a portion of the original magazine cover.) 1966 *Weird Adventures of The Shadow,* Grosset & Dunlap, #1095. (Mauve dust jacket, with cartoon of The Shadow on front and back. Binding is mauve and identical with dust jacket. Purple endpapers with reproductions from magazine illustrations. Contains 2-page Introduction by Walter Gibson. Reprints "Grove of Doom" (9/1/33); "Voodoo Death" (6/44); and "Murder By Moonlight" (12/43). All novels are abridged, ("Grove of Doom" severely so.)

NOTE The Ideal Library volumes measured 5 x 7-½ inches and were 1-½ inches thick. The paper was rank pulp. Selling for 25¢ each, the volumes remained in print throughout the 1930's.

1975   *The Crime Oracle and The Teeth of The Dragon, Two Adventures of The Shadow, Dover Publications, Inc., 6-½ x 9-¼ quality* paperback; the cover reproduces the cover of "The Crime Oracle." Contains two long essays by 1) Walter Gibson, "My Years with The Shadow," And 2) John L. Nanovic, "I Never Called Him Bill." Contains "The Crime Oracle" (June 1, 1936) and "The Teeth of The Dragon" (November 15, 1937), reproduced with the original illustrations.

1975   *The Shadow, The Mask of Mephisto and Murder By Magic,* The Crime Club, Doubleday & Company, Inc. with Introduction by Walter B. Gibson, 8-½ x 5-¾, with dust jacket. Reprints "The Mask of Mephisto" (July 1945) and "Murder By Magic" (August 1945).

1978   *The Shadow, A Quarter of Eight & The Freak Show Murders,* The Crime Club, Doubleday & Company, Inc., with Introduction by Walter B. Gibson, 8-½ x 5-¾, with dust jacket. Reprints "A Quarter of Eight" (October 1945) and "The Freak show Murders" (May 1944).

1979   *The Shadow, Crime Over Casco & The Mother Goose Murders,* The Crime Club, Doubleday & Company, Inc. with Introduction by Walter B. Gibson, 8-½ x 5-¾, with dust jacket. Reprints "Crime Over Casco" (April 1946) and "Mother Goose Murders" (March 1946).

As Better Little Books:

1940   *The Shadow and The Living Death,* #1430, Whitman Publishing Company. Illustrated by Erwin L. Hess

1941   *The Shadow and the Master of Evil,* #1443, Whitman Publishing Company. Illustrated by Erwin L. Hess

1942   *The Shadow and The Ghost Makers,*#1495. Front cover illustration by Burroughs. Interior illustrations by Erwin L. Darwin.

NOTE Both *Master of Evil* and *Ghost Makers* have a flip movie in in upper right corner of book.

As Magazines:

NOTE Three SHADOW ANNUALS were published. These were 25¢ pulp magazines, bedsheet size, measuring 9-½ x 11 inches. Each reprinted three Shadow novels, as indicated:

1942   Deep red cover. The illustration is redrawn from the cover of 1/1/39 "Silver Skull" novel. Contains "The Living Shadow" (April-June 1931); "The Black Hush" (8/1/33); and "The Ghost Makers" (10/15/32).

1943   Cover is textured blue, simulating a padded cover, in the center of which is inserted, a small square picture of Cranston. Contains "The Voodoo Master" (3/1/36); "Hidden Death" (9/32); and "The Gray Ghost" (5/1/36).

1947   Light blue cover with gigantic Shadow shown towering over Small fringe of buildings; the drawing is inept. Contains "Toll of Death" (3/45); "No Time For Murder" (12/44); and "Murder By Magic" (8/45).

As Paperbacks

1941   *"The Shadow and The Voice of Murder,"* bantam Books, 4-¼ x 6 inches, blue and gold cover containing spot drawing of a chicken head—apparently the publisher's totem. This is a reprint of the 2/15/40 "Voice of Death" without internal illustrations. Another issue of this paperback is known to have been released with an illustrated

cover; this has not been
examined. A picture of this issue
is shown on the front cover of *The
Shadow Scrapbook.*
1963/Sept *"The Return of The Shadow,"* By
Walter Gibson. Belmont Books

NOTE The following paperbacks, published by Belmont Books,
are signed Maxwell Grant and written by Dennis Lynds.

1964/Oct	The Shadow Strikes
1965/Jan	Shadow Beware
/Apr	Cry Shadow
/Oct	The Shadow's Revenge
1966/May	Mark of The Shadow
/Sept	Shadow, Go Mad
/Nov	Night of the Shadow
1967/Mar	Destination Moon
1969	The Grove of Doom, Tempo. (NOTE This is a paperback edition of the abridged "Grove" which appeared in *The Weird Adventures of The Shadow*)

NOTE The following paperbacks, published by Bantam Books
Inc., are signed Maxwell Grant (Walter Gibson)

1969/June	The Living Shadow (4/31)
/Aug	The Eyes of The Shadow (7/31)
/Oct	The Shadow Laughs (10/31)
/Dec	The Death Tower (1/32)
1970/Aug	The Ghost Makers (10/15/32)
/Oct	Hidden Death (9/32)
1970/Dec	Gangdom's Doom (12/31)

NOTE: The following paperbacks were published by Pyramid
Books. All are signed Maxwell Grant)

1974/Oct	The Living Shadow (4-6/1931)
/Oct	The Black Master (3/32)
/Dec	(The) Mobsmen On the Spot (4/32)
1975/Jan	Hands In the Dark (5/32)
/Feb	Double Z (6/32)
/Mar	The Crime Cult (7/32)
/Aug	The Red Menace (11/31)
/Sep	Mox (11/15/33)
/Oct	The Romanoff Jewels (12/1/32)
/Dec	The Silent Seven (2/32)
1976/Feb	Kings of Crime (12/15/32)
/Mar	Shadowed Millions (1/1/33)

1977/Jan	Green Eyes (10/1/32)
/May	The Creeping Death (1/15/33)
/June	Gray Fist (2/15/34)
/July	The Shadow's Shadow (2/1/33)

NOTE The following paperbacks were published by Jove Publications, Inc. All are signed Maxwell Grant.

1977/Sep	Fingers of Death (3/1/33)
/Oct	The Living Shadow (4-6/31)
/Oct	Murder Trail (3/15/33)
/Nov	The Romanoff Jewels (12/1/32)
/Nov	Zemba (12/1/35)
/Dec	Charg, Monster (7/1/34)
1978/Feb	The Wealth Seeker (1/15/34)
/Feb	Kings of Crime (12/15/32)
/Mar	The Silent Death (4/1/33)
/April	The Death Giver (5/15/33)
/April	Shadowed Millions (1/1/32)

In Short Stories:

| 1979 | "The Riddle of the Rangoon Ruby" in THE SHADOW SCRAPBOOK |
| 1979 | "Blackmail Bay" in THE DUENDE HISTORY OF THE SHADOW MAGAZINE |

APPENDIX C. THE SHADOW novels by issue dates. Numbers indicate the order in which novels were written (Adapted from *The Duende History of the Shadow Magazine*)

1931
1) Apr   THE LIVING SHADOW
2) Jul   EYES OF THE SHADOW
3) Oct   THE SHADOW LAUGHS
4) Nov   THE RED MENACE
5) Dec   GANGDOM'S DOOM

1932

6) Jan   THE DEATH TOWER
7) Feb   THE SILENT SEVEN
8) Mar   THE BLACK MASTER
9) Apr   MOBSMEN ON THE SPOT
10) May   HANDS IN THE DARK
11) June   DOUBLE Z
12) July   THE CRIME CULT
13) Aug   THE BLACKMAIL RING
14) Sept   HIDDEN DEATH
15) Oct 1 GREEN EYES
16) Oct 15 THE GHOST MAKERS
17) Nov 1 THE FIVE CHAMELEONS
18) Nov 15 DEAD MEN LIVE
20) Dec 1 THE ROMANOFF JEWELS
21) Dec 15 KINGS OF CRIME

1933

19) Jan 1 SHADOWED MILLIONS
22) Jan 15 THE CREEPING DEATH
23) Feb 1 THE SHADOW'S SHADOW
25) Feb 15 SIX MEN OF EVIL
27) Mar 1 FINGERS OF DEATH
28) Mar 15 MURDER TRAIL
31) Apr 1 THE SILENT DEATH
30) Apr 15 THE SHADOW'S JUSTICE
26) May 1 THE GOLDEN GROTTO
29) May 15 THE DEATH GIVER
35) Jun 1 THE RED BLOT
32) Jun 15 GHOST OF THE MANOR
34) Jul 1 THE LIVING JOSS
36) Jul 15 THE SILVER SCOURGE
33) Aug 1 THE BLACK HUSH
37) Aug 15 THE ISLE OF DOUBT

24) Sept 1 THE GROVE OF DOOM
39) Sept 15 MASTER OF DEATH
38) Oct 1   ROAD OF CRIME
40) Oct 15 THE DEATH TRIANGLE
41) Nov 1   THE KILLER
42) Nov 15 MOX
43) Dec 1   THE CRIME CLINIC
44) Dec 15 TREASURES OF DEATH

1934

49) Jan 1   THE EMBASSY MURDERS
46) Jan 15 THE WEALTH SEEKER
47) Feb 1   THE BLACK FALCON
45) Feb 15 GRAY FIST
51) Mar 1   THE CIRCLE OF DEATH
52) Mar 15 THE GREEN BOX
50) Apr 1   THE COBRA
61) Apr 15 CRIME CIRCUS
53) May 1   TOWER OF DEATH
54) May 15 DEATH CLEW
59) Jun 1   THE KEY
48) Jun 15 THE CRIME CRYPT
57) Jul 1   CHARG, MONSTER
58) Jul 15 CHAIN OF DEATH
56) Aug 1   THE CRIME MASTER
55) Aug 15 GYPSY VENGENCE
60) Sept 1 SPOILS OF THE SHADOW
62) Sept 15 THE GARAUCAN SWINDLE
63) Oct 1   MURDER MARSH
65) Oct 15 THE DEATH SLEEP
68) Nov 1   THE CHINESE DISCS
64) Nov 15 DOOM ON THE HILL
69) Dec 1   THE UNSEEN KILLER
72) Dec 15 CYRO

1935

66) Jan 1   THE FOUR SIGNETS
71) Jan 15 THE BLUE SPHINX
70) Feb 1   THE PLOT MASTER
73) Feb 15 THE DARK DEATH
75) Mar 1   CROOKS GO STRAIGHT
67) Mar 15 BELLS OF DOOM
79) Apr 1   LINGO
76) Apr 15 THE TRIPLE TRAIL
77) May 1   THE GOLDEN QUEST

78)   May 15 THE THIRD SKULL
81)   Jun 1 MURDER EVERY HOUR
83)   Jun 15 THE CONDOR
89)   Jul 1   THE FATE JOSS
80)   Jul 15 ATOMS OF DEATH
82)   Aug 1 THE MAN FROM SCOTLAND YARD
88)   Aug 15 THE CREEPER
95)   Sept 1 MARDI GRAS MYSTERY
96)   Sept 15 THE LONDON CRIMES
85)   Oct 1   THE RIBBON CLUES
84)   Oct 15 THE HOUSE THAT VANISHED
92)   Nov 1   THE CHINESE TAPESTRY
90)   Nov 15 THE PYTHON
98)   Dec 1   ZEMBA
87)   Dec 15 THE CASE OF CONGRESSMAN COYD

1936

91)   Jan 1   THE GHOST MURDERS
97)   Jan 15 CASTLE OF DOOM
86)   Feb 1   DEATH RIDES THE SKYWAY
101) Feb 15 NORTH WOODS MYSTERY
99)   Mar 1   THE VOODOO MASTER
93)   Mar 15 THE THIRD SHADOW
108) Apr 1   THE SALAMANDERS
109) Apr 15 THE MAN FROM SHANGHAI
106) May 1   THE GRAY GHOST
110) May 15 THE CITY OF DOOM
100) Jun 1   THE CRIME ORACLE
94)   Jun 15 MURDER TOWN
107) Jul 1   THE YELLOW DOOR
105) Jul 15 THE BROKEN NAPOLEANS
102) Aug 1   THE SLEDGE HAMMER CRIMES
74)   Aug 15 TERROR ISLAND
113) Sept 1 THE GOLDEN MASKS
114) Sept 15 JIBARO DEATH
112) Oct 1   CITY OF CRIME
116) Oct 15 DEATH BY PROXY
115) *Nov 1 PARTNERS OF PERIL
117) Nov 15 STRANGE DISAPPEARANCE OF JOE
             CARDONA
118) Dec 1   SEVEN DROPS OF BLOOD
119) Dec 15 INTIMIDATION INC.

*Tinsley

1937

121)	Jan 1	VENGENCE IS MINE
125)	*Jan 15	FOXHOUND
122)	Feb 1	LOOT OF DEATH
126)	Feb 15	QUETZAL
120)	Mar 1	DEATH TOKEN
123)	Mar 15	MURDER HOUSE
124)	Apr 1	THE WASHINGTON CRIMES
127)	Apr 15	THE MASKED HEADSMAN
131)	*May 1	CUP OF CONFUCIUS
128)	May 15	TREASURE TRAIL
129)	Jun 1	BROTHERS OF DOOM
132)	Jun 15	THE SHADOW'S RIVAL
133)	Jul 1	CRIME INSURED
103)	Jul 15	HOUSE OF SILENCE
134)	Aug 1	THE SHADOW UNMASKS
135)	Aug 15	THE YELLOW BAND
104)	Sept 1	BURIED EVIDENCE
111)	Sept 15	THE RADIUM MURDERS
137)	*Oct 1	THE POOLTEX TANGLE
130)	Oct 15	THE KEEPER'S GOLD
136)	Nov 1	DEATH TURRETS
138)	Nov 15	TEETH OF THE DRAGON
140)	Dec 1	THE SEALED BOX
139)	Dec 15	RACKET TOWN

1938

142)	Jan 1	THE CRYSTAL BUDDAH
141)	Jan 15	HILLS OF DEATH
144)	*Feb 1	THE FIFTH NAPOLEAN
145)	Feb 15	THE MURDER MASTER
150)	Mar 1	THE GOLDEN PAGODA
147)	Mar 15	FACE OF DOOM
149)	*Apr 1	THE CRIMSON PHOENIX
152)	Apr 15	SERPENTS OF SIVA
151)	May 1	CARDS OF DEATH
159)	May 15	THE HAND
156)	Jun 1	VOODOO TRAIL
143)	Jun 15	THE RACKETS KING
160)	Jul 1	MURDER FOR SALE
161)	**Jul 15	THE GOLDEN VULTURE

*Tinsley
**Dent/Gibson

146) Aug 1 DEATH JEWELS
148) Aug 15 THE GREEN HOODS
157) *Sept 1 THE GOLDEN DOG MURDERS
153) Sept 15 CRIME OVER BOSTON
154) Oct 1   THE DEAD WHO LIVED
155) Oct 15 VANISHED TREASURE
158) Nov 1   THE VOICE
162) Nov 15 CHICAGO CRIME
163) Dec 1   SHADOW OVER ALCATRAZ
164) *Dec 15 DOUBLE DEATH

1939

169) Jan 1   SILVER SKULL
167) Jan 15 CRIME RIDES THE SEA
168) Feb 1   REALM OF DOOM
171) Feb 15 THE LONE TIGER
166) *Mar 1 RIVER OF DEATH
172) Mar 15 THE VINDICATOR
165) Apr 1   DEATH SHIP
175) Apr 15 BATTLE OF GREED
173) *May 1 DEATH'S HARLEQUIN
174) May 15 THE THREE BROTHERS
170) Jun 1   SMUGGLERS OF DEATH
180) Jun 15 CITY OF SHADOWS
176) *Jul 1 NOOSE OF DEATH
178) Jul 15 DEATH FROM NOWHERE
179) Aug 1   ISLE OF GOLD
183) Aug 15 THE WIZARD OF CRIME
181) Sept 1 THE CRIME RAY
182) Sept 15 THE GOLDEN MASTER
177) Oct 1   CASTLE OF CRIME
184) Oct 15 THE MASKED LADY
188) Nov 1   SHIPS OF DOOM
187) Nov 15 CITY OF GHOSTS
189) Dec 1   SHIWAN KHAN RETURNS
190) Dec 15 HOUSE OF SHADOWS

1940

193) Jan 1   DEATH'S PREMIUM
194) Jan 15 THE HOODED CIRCLE
197) Feb 1   THE GETAWAY RING
199) Feb 15 VOICE OF DEATH
196) Mar 1 INVINCIBLE SHIWAN KHAN
201) Mar 15 THE VEILED PROPHET
*Tinsley

202) Apr 1   THE SPY RING
186) *Apr 15 THE PRINCE OF EVIL
203) May 1   DEATH IN THE STARS
200) May 15 MASTERS OF DEATH
185) Jun 1   SCENT OF DEATH
204) Jun 15 "Q"
191) *Jul 1 MURDER GENIUS
205) Jul 15 GEMS OF DOOM
206) Aug 1   CRIME AT SEVEN OAKS
207) Aug 15 THE FIFTH FACE
209) Sep 1   CRIME COUNTRY
192) *Sep 15 THE MAN WHO DIED TWICE
210) Oct 1   THE WASP
208) *Oct 15 CITY OF FEAR
211) Nov 1   CRIME OVER MIAMI
195) *Nov 15 THE DEVIL'S PAYMASTER
213) Dec 1   XITLI, GOD OF FIRE
216) Dec 15 SHADOW, HAWK, AND SKULL

NOTE 198) SATAN'S SIGNATURE by Tinsley (written Sept. 1939) was not accepted as a Shadow novel. Later rewritten, it appeared in CLUES (11/41) as "THE PHANTOM KILLER," the Shadow having been deleted.

1941

214) Jan 1   FORGOTTEN GOLD
215) Jan 15 THE GREEN TERROR
219) Feb 1   THE WASP RETURNS
218) Feb 15 THE CHINESE PRIMROSE
220) Mar 1   MANSION OF CRIME
217) *Mar 15 THE WHITE COLUMN
221) Apr 1   THE TIME MASTER
222) Apr 15 THE HOUSE ON THE LEDGE
223) May 1   LEAGUE OF DEATH
212) *May 15 MASTER OF FLAME
224) Jun 1   CRIME UNDER COVER
225) Jun 15 THE THUNDER KING
226) Jul 1   THE STAR OF DELHI:
227) Jul 15 THE BLUR
229) *Aug 1 THE CRIMSON DEATH
230) Aug 15 THE SHADOW MEETS THE MASK
231) *Sep 1 GEMS OF JEOPARDY

*Tinsley

228) Sep 15 THE DEVIL MASTER
234) Oct 1   GARDEN OF DEATH
232) Oct 15 DICTATOR OF CRIME
236) Nov 1 THE BLACKMAIL KING
239) Nov 15 TEMPLE OF CRIME
238) Dec 1   MURDER MANSION
235) Dec 15 CRIME'S STRONGHOLD

1942

233) Jan 1   ALIBI TRAIL
240) Jan 15 THE BOOK OF DEATH
237) Feb 1   DEATH DIAMONDS
242) *Feb 15 BLUE FACE
241) Mar 1   VENGENCE BAY
243) Mar 15 FORMULA FOR CRIME
244) Apr 1   ROOM OF DOOM
245) Apr 15 THE JADE DRAGON
246) May 1 THE NORTHDALE MYSTERY
247) *May 15 DEATH'S BRIGHT FINGER
248) Jun 1   TWINS OF CRIME
249) Jun 15 THE DEVIL'S FEUD
252) Jul 1   FIVE IVORY BOXES
251) Jul 15 DEATH ABOUT TOWN
253) Aug 1 LEGACY OF DEATH
254) Aug 15 JUDGE LAWLESS
256) Sept 1 THE VAMPIRE MURDERS
257) *Sept 15 SYNDICATE OF SIN
259) *Oct 1 THE DEVIL'S PARTNER
260) Oct 15 CLUE FOR CLUE
250) Nov 1 TRAIL OF VENGENCE
255) Nov 15 THE MURDERING GHOST
261) Dec 1   THE HYDRA
262) Dec 15 THE MONEY MASTER

1943

258) Jan 1   THE MUSEUM MURDERS
263) Jan 15 DEATH'S MASQUERADE
265) Feb 1   THE DEVIL MONSTERS
266) Feb 15 WIZARD OF CRIME
268) Mar   THE BLACK DRAGON
267) *Apr   YOUNG MEN OF DEATH
269) May   THE ROBOT MASTER
270) Jun   MURDER LAKE

*Tinsley

271)	*Jul	THE GOLDEN DOOM
272)	Aug	MESSENGER OF DEATH
273)	Sept	HOUSE OF GHOSTS
264)	Oct	KING OF THE BLACK MARKET
274)	Nov	THE MUGGERS
275)	Dec	MURDER BY MOONLIGHT

1944

276)	Jan	THE CRYSTAL SKULL
277)	Feb	SYNDICATE OF DEATH
278)	Mar	THE TOLL OF DEATH
279)	Apr	CRIME CARAVAN
280)	May	THE FREAK SHOW MURDERS
281)	Jun	VOODOO DEATH
282)	Jul	TOWN OF HATE
283)	Aug	DEATH IN THE CRYSTAL
284)	Sept	THE CHEST OF CHU CHEN
285)	Oct	THE SHADOW MEETS THE MASK
286)	Nov	FOUNTAIN OF DEATH
287)	Dec	NO TIME FOR MURDER

1945

288)	Jan	GUARDIAN OF DEATH
289)	Feb	MERRY MRS. MACBETH
290)	Mar	FIVE KEYS TO CRIME
291)	Apr	DEATH HAS GRAY EYES
292)	May	TEAR-DROPS OF BUDDAH
293)	Jun	THREE STAMPS OF DEATH
294)	Jul	THE MASK OF MEPHISTO
295)	Aug	MURDER BY MAGIC
296)	Sept	TIAWAN JOSS
297)	Oct	A QUARTER OF EIGHT
298)	Nov	THE WHITE SKULLS
299)	Dec	THE STARS PROMISE DEATH

1946

300)	Jan	THE BANSHEE MURDERS
301)	Feb	CRIME OUT OF MIND
302)	Mar	MOTHER GOOSE MURDERS
303)	Apr	CRIME OVER CASCO
304)	May	THE CURSE OF THOTH
305)	Jun	ALIBI TRAIL

*Tinsley

306) Jul   MALMORDO
307) **Aug THE BLACKEST MAIL
308) **Sept HAPPY DEATH DAY
309) **Oct THE SEVEN DEADLY ARTS
310) **Nov NO SAFETY IN NUMBERS
312) **Dec DEATH ON ICE

1947

311) **Jan DEATH STALKS THE UN
313) **Feb-Mar MURDER IN WHITE
314) **Apr-MayROOM 1313
315) **Jun-Jul MODEL MURDER
316) **Aug-Sep SVENGALI KILL
317) **Oct-Nov JABBERWOCKY THRUST
318) **Dec-Jan TEN GLASS EYES

1948

319) **Feb-Mar THE TELEVISION MURDERS
320) **Apr-MayMURDER ON MAIN STREET
321) **Jun-Jul REIGN OF TERROR
322) Aug-Sept JADE DRAGON
323) Fall   DEAD MAN'S CHEST

1949

324) Winter MAGIGALS MYSTERY
325) Spring THE BLACK CIRCLE
326) Summer WHISPERING EYES

**Elliott

APPENDIX D. THE SHADOW MAGAZINE: A PICTORIAL HISTORY

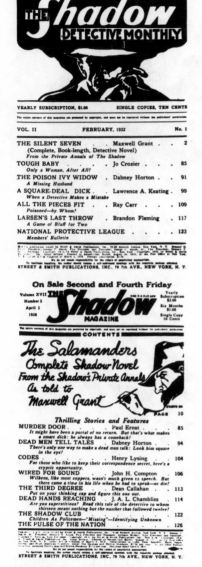

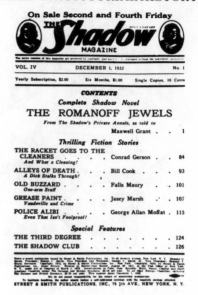

SHADOW TITLE PAGES ACROSS THE YEARS: **February 1932**: The sinister individual is Frank Blackwell, DETECTIVE STORY MAGAZINE editor; **December 1, 1932**: The two circular illustrations celebrate the hooded mystery figure, whose face also appeared on the lower-right cover edge from October 1931 through March 1932; **April 1, 1936**: The classic SHADOW title page, handwritten by the master, himself; **June-July 1948**: Page decorations by Cartier in his best UNKNOWN style.

Complete
In This Issue

From the Private Annals
of The Shadow

Complete
in this
issue

as told to
**Maxwell
Grant**

INTERIOR ART
FIRST PAGE ART FROM 1932. **Upper Illustration** (from DOUBLE Z, June
1932), Rutledge Mann fails to kill himself; the rendering of The Shadow is without
character. **Lower Illustration** (from THE ROMANOFF JEWELS, December 1,
1932). The drawing is by Tom Lovell who did not, during this perios, conceal The
Shadow's face.

SHA—1   *Illustration for "The Silent Seven"*

Slowly, each step steady, he found his footing in the furnace. The Shadow was using the process of the Oriental fire walkers, who tread bare footed through beds of flame.

SHAD 4A

The master criminal, like his lieutenant, was dead. The Shadow and Amakar had gained a simultaneous triumph!

Upper Left: Early issues contained only one illustration, as this from THE SILENT SEVEN (February 1932). **Upper Right**: The novels use sleighs, escapes, devices drawn from professional stage magic; here, a fire-walking sequence from THE SALAMANDERS (April 1, 1936). **Bottom**: Thomas Lovell's brilliantly accomplished drawings raised Shadow interiors to heights unexcelled in the pulps. Actions spread across two pages during the mid-1930's, as from THE CASTLE OF DOOM (January 15, 1936).

Framed against the glow of the passage were enemies, perhaps the strangest that The Shadow had ever encountered. Grotesque foemen stood to block The Shadow's path

A Complete Book-length Novel from the
Private Annals of The Shadow.

Vanished Treasure

Ghostly footfalls trod the old Beld mansion,
and bloodshed and murder followed in their
wake! But only The Shadow knew the secret
of the buried, bloody treasure!

CHAPTER I.
MIDNIGHT VISITORS.

As told to
Maxwell Grant

Top: Lovell's double art pages characteristically balanced The Shadow against an artistic grouping of killers on the opposite page. From THE SALAMANDERS (April 1, 1936). **Bottom**: Ed Cartier, whose work phased into the magazine during 1936, was a virtuoso of the action drawing; this example from VANISHED TREASURE (October 15, 1938).

FOUR CARTIER SINGLES: **Upper Left**: *Smugglers of Death*, June 1, 1939; the exquisite Cartier girl in the usual mess. **Upper Right**: *Wizard of Crime*, August 15, 1939: Lamont Cranston and friend from a fresh new angle. **Lower Left**: *Masters of Death*, May 15, 1940: The Shadow meets bizarre peril once more—and note the "huge .45". **Lower Right**: *Jade Dragon*, September 1948. The last Shadow novel illustrated by Cartier in a style frigid as glacier's blood.

Earl Mayan's Shadow wore a modified cloak and blasted fiercely into masses of realistically dying crooks, as in the **Upper** illustration from "Q" (June 15, 1940) **Bottom Left**: Detail from Myan's double-page spread, MANSION OF CRIME (March 1, 1941). **Bottom Right**: Paul Orban, THE STAR OF DELHI (July 1, 1941).

SHADOW COVER ART

THE BLACK MASTER, March 1932 (George Rozen): The Shadow's familiar face is exposed for the first time, mighty nose and all. In lower right, the blue-faced mystery figure makes its final cover appearance.

THE BLACKMAIL RING, August 1932 (G. Rozen): This is the first of Rozen's many symbolic hand covers—crime in the clutch of Justice.

THE SILENT DEATH, April 1, 1933 (G. Rozen): Science-fictional devices frequently appear in the novels; the weird tube shown provides a three-lobe background upon which The Shadow's figure is superimposed; Rozen frequently employed this technique of composition.

THE DEATH GIVER, May 15, 1933 (G. Rozen): The freize of background faces sets off The shadow, who is busy with symbolic action. Only rarely, during this cover period, does The Shadow hold a gun.

THE GROVE OF DOOM, September 1, 1933 (G. Rozen): The Shadow trapped—if not for long. The composition is static, yet successfully suggests suspense, danger, action.

GYPSY VENGENCE, August 15, 1934 (G. Rozen): The two figures stand against a richly detailed background, again in three parts.

THE HOSE THAT VANISHED, October 15, 1935 (G. Rozen): During 1934 and 1935, covers more often featured symbolic composition, clenched hands, and portraits than scenes drawn from the novel.

CASTLE OF DOOM, January 15, 1936 (G. Rozen): Late 1935 and 1936 covers began picturing hand-to-hand struggles, as the cover style slowly evolved from the more static compositions of the past.

JIBARO DEATH, September 15, 1936 (G. Rozen): About once an issue, The Shadow got himself into a ghastly trap, then greased slickly out of it. Here it's about to happen again.

PARTNERS OF PERIL, November 1, 1936 (G. Rozen): The definitive Shadow portrait. The novel is Theodore Tinsley's first Shadow.

TREASURE TRAIL, May 15, 1937 (G. Rozen): About three years before The Shadow comic book, pictorial sequences appeard on Shadow covers—this one and on THE SHADOW UNMASKS. The upper center illustration, "DYNAMITE FILE," is for a short story in this issue.

THE FIFTH NAPOLEON, February 1, 1938 (G. Rozen): The 1938 covers are superb, The Shadow menacing or menaced, bullets sailing about. For some reason, his automatics were shown as .38's, always cocked.

THE GOLDEN PAGODA, March 1, 1938 (G. Rozen): A beautifully designed still life, but full of vitality and excitement. The automatic remains uncocked.

VANISHED TREASURE, October 15, 1938 (G. Rozen): The final scene of every Shadow novel, presented here in an image of concentrated power.

THE VOICE, November 1, 1938 (G. Rozen): Hard action while the bullets fly—and almost a scene from the novel.

THE VINDICATOR, March 15, 1939 (G. Rozen): This was the final Rozen cover painting until 1941. With the next issue, Graves Gladney took over the cover work.

CASTLE OF CRIME, October 1, 1939 (Graves Gladney): In this sharply defined painting, The Shadow's face is thinner, the nose less massive. Beneath the cloak lies a neat, double-breasted suit.

SHIWAN KHAN RETURNS, December 1, 1939 (G. Gladney): Intense action peaking in a back alley and rendered with almost photographic clarity.

THE SCENT OF DEATH, June 1, 1940 (G. Gladney): A cover of unusual brilliance, selected as the best pulp magazine cover of 1940.

THE CHINESE PRIMROSE, February 15, 1941 (G. Gladney): The painting style is softer. Covers from this period incorporated up to four figures in action, often including a girl in peril and The Shadow swooping in from the rear.

THE CHEST OF CHU CHAN, September 1944 (Modest Stein): Stein's digest covers were pleasantly decorative, mildly impressionistic, and bland.

TEN GLASS EYES, December-January 1948, (H. Swenson): A composite cover, line drawing on half tone—and illustrating the Cornell Woolrich short story, rather than the Shadow novel.

JADE DRAGON, August-September 1948, (S.R. Powell): Pure comic book art and masses of type muddle the final digest cover.

DEAD MAN'S CHEST, Fall 1948 (George Rozen): The old-time Shadow returns, not a day older, on the first of four pulp-sized issues.